W9-CLN-721

WESTERN AND
SOUTHERN EUROPE

−Andorra−

The current legislation on trafficking in persons in Andorra covers all forms of trafficking indicated in the UN Trafficking in Persons Protocol. In 2017, Law 9/2017 was introduced which concerns the protection of victims of trafficking in persons.

There were no recorded cases of trafficking in persons during the reporting period.

Source: Police Department / Interpol/ Ministry of Social Affairs, Justice and Interior/ judicial authorities

−Austria−

The current legislation on trafficking in persons in Austria covers all forms of trafficking indicated in the UN Trafficking in Persons Protocol.

Investigations and suspects

The Austrian authorities use two different statistical sources. The first is the Police Crime Statistics, which is maintained by the Federal Police of Austria. The second is the Automation Court Procedure, which refers to the number of cases brought to the public prosecution offices.

Source: Police Crime Statistics and Automation Court Procedure.

Number of cases of trafficking in persons recorded, 2014 – September 2017

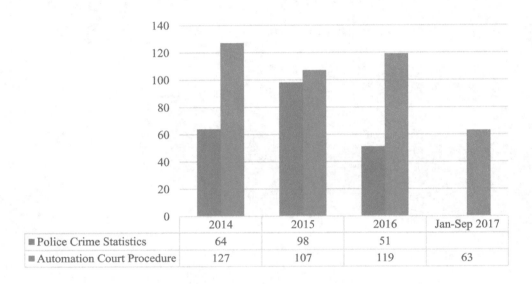

	2014	2015	2016	Jan-Sep 2017
■ Police Crime Statistics	64	98	51	
■ Automation Court Procedure	127	107	119	63

Source: Police Crime Statistics and Automation Court Procedure.

Number of persons brought into formal contact with the police and/or criminal justice system because they have been suspected of, arrested for or cautioned for trafficking in persons, by sex, 2014 – September 2017**

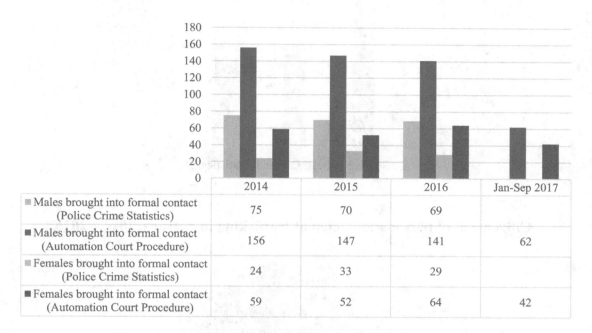

	2014	2015	2016	Jan-Sep 2017
▪ Males brought into formal contact (Police Crime Statistics)	75	70	69	
▪ Males brought into formal contact (Automation Court Procedure)	156	147	141	62
▪ Females brought into formal contact (Police Crime Statistics)	24	33	29	
▪ Females brought into formal contact (Automation Court Procedure)	59	52	64	42

Source: Source: Police Crime Statistics and Automation Court Procedure.

**Note: Formal contact with the police and/or criminal justice system may include persons suspected, arrested, or cautioned at the national level.

Number of persons prosecuted for trafficking in persons, by sex, 2014 – September 2017

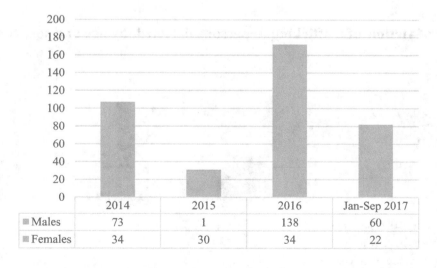

	2014	2015	2016	Jan-Sep 2017
▪ Males	73	1	138	60
▪ Females	34	30	34	22

Source: Automation Court Procedure.

Number of persons convicted of trafficking in persons, 2014 – 2016

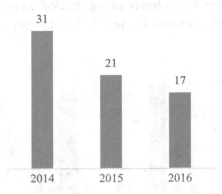

Source: Judicial Criminal Statistics.

Citizenship of persons convicted of trafficking in persons, 2014 – 2016

Source: Judicial Crime Statistic

Victims

Number of victims of trafficking in persons detected, by age and sex, 2014 – 2016

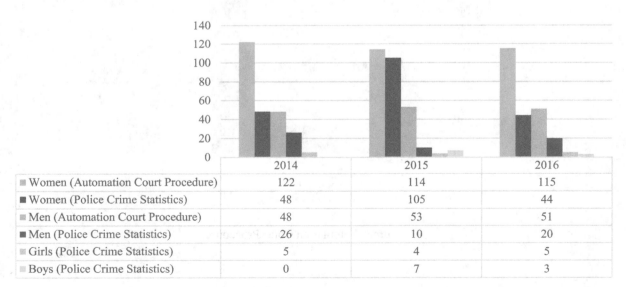

	2014	2015	2016
▪ Women (Automation Court Procedure)	122	114	115
▪ Women (Police Crime Statistics)	48	105	44
▪ Men (Automation Court Procedure)	48	53	51
▪ Men (Police Crime Statistics)	26	10	20
▪ Girls (Police Crime Statistics)	5	4	5
▪ Boys (Police Crime Statistics)	0	7	3

Source: Police Crime Statistics and Automation Court Procedure.

Citizenships of persons identified as victims of trafficking in persons by state authorities**, 2014 – September 2017

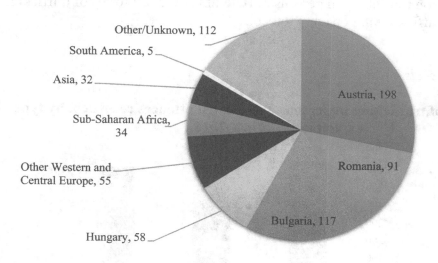

Other/Unknown, 112
South America, 5
Asia, 32
Sub-Saharan Africa, 34
Other Western and Central Europe, 55
Hungary, 58
Bulgaria, 117
Romania, 91
Austria, 198

Source: Police Crime Statistics.

Three Austrian victims were domestically trafficked in 2016.

Source: Police Crime Statistics.

−Belgium−

The current legislation on trafficking in persons in Belgium covers all forms of trafficking indicated in the UN Trafficking in Persons Protocol.

Investigations and suspects

Number of cases of trafficking in persons and related offences recorded, by type of exploitation, 2014 – 2016

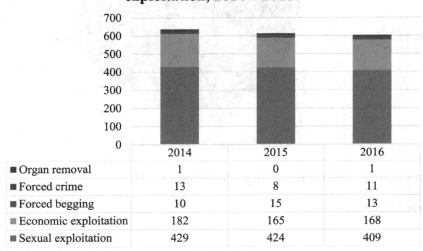

	2014	2015	2016
■ Organ removal	1	0	1
■ Forced crime	13	8	11
■ Forced begging	10	15	13
■ Economic exploitation	182	165	168
■ Sexual exploitation	429	424	409

Source: Integrated Data of the Police of Belgium.

Number of persons brought into formal contact with the police and/or criminal justice system because they have been suspected of, arrested for or cautioned for trafficking in persons and related offences, by sex**, 2014 – 2016

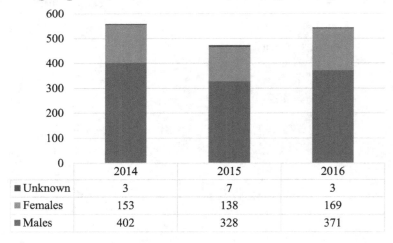

	2014	2015	2016
■ Unknown	3	7	3
■ Females	153	138	169
■ Males	402	328	371

Source: Integrated Data of the Police of Belgium.

**Note: Formal contact with the police and/or criminal justice system may include persons suspected, arrested, or cautioned at the national level.

Number of persons brought into formal contact with the police and/or criminal justice system because they have been suspected of, arrested for or cautioned for trafficking in persons and related offences, by form of exploitation, 2014 – 2016

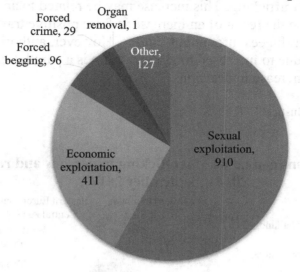

Source: Integrated Data of the Police of Belgium.

Additional information

During this period, the majority of those suspected of, arrested for or cautioned for trafficking in persons in all categories were men. However, in the category of organ removal, the one individual was female. In 2014, 389 persons were prosecuted for the crime of trafficking in persons while in 2015, 461 were prosecuted.

Source: Integrated Data of the Police of Belgium and Data Bank of the College of Attorneys General – Crown Prosecution Analysts.

Number of persons convicted of trafficking in persons and related offences, by sex, 2014 – September 2017

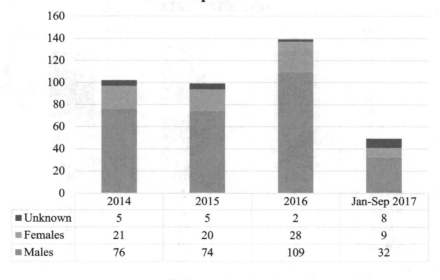

	2014	2015	2016	Jan-Sep 2017
■ Unknown	5	5	2	8
■ Females	21	20	28	9
■ Males	76	74	109	32

Source: Federal Public Service Justice.

The Federal Public Service Justice of Belgium notes that in 2016, there is a significant increase in convictions for trafficking. This increase may be related to an actual increase in decisions, but it may also be the result of an increase in false positive trafficking cases due to the increased migration of refugees throughout Europe. However, authorities note that despite the impact on convictions due to increased migration, there is a parallel increase in trafficking which also has caused an increase in decisions.

Source: Federal Public Service Justice.

Citizenships of persons convicted of trafficking in persons and related offences, 2014 – September 2017

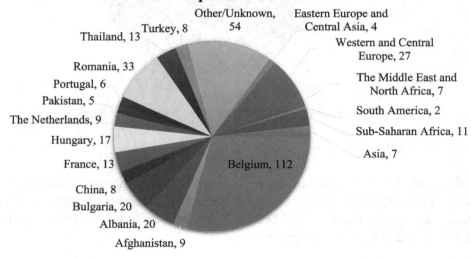

Source: Federal Public Service Justice.

Victims

Number of victims of trafficking in persons and related offences detected, by age and sex, 2014 – 2016

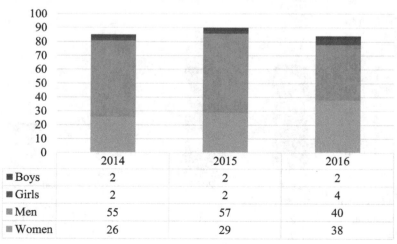

	2014	2015	2016
■ Boys	2	2	2
■ Girls	2	2	4
■ Men	55	57	40
■ Women	26	29	38

Source: Foreign Office.

Number of victims of trafficking in persons and related offences detected, by form of exploitation, 2014 – August 2017

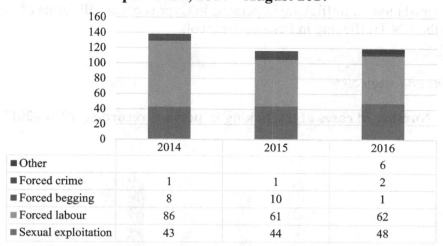

	2014	2015	2016
■ Other			6
■ Forced crime	1	1	2
■ Forced begging	8	10	1
■ Forced labour	86	61	62
■ Sexual exploitation	43	44	48

Source: Foreign Office.

Citizenships of persons identified as victims of trafficking in persons and related offences by state authorities, 2014 – 2016

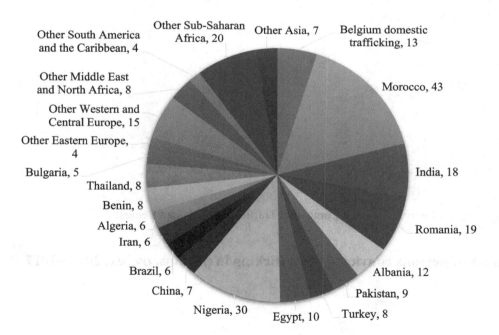

Source: Foreign Office.

The current legislation on trafficking in persons in Cyprus covers all forms of trafficking indicated in the UN Trafficking in Persons Protocol.

Investigations and suspects

Number of cases of trafficking in persons recorded, 2014 –2017

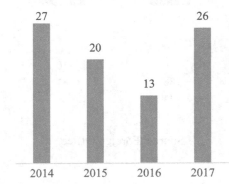

Source: Office of Combating Trafficking in Human Beings.

Number of persons prosecuted for trafficking in persons, by sex, 2014 – September 2017

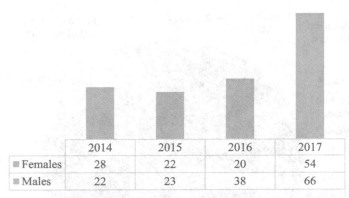

	2014	2015	2016	2017
■ Females	28	22	20	54
■ Males	22	23	38	66

Source: Office of Combating Trafficking in Human Beings.

Number of persons convicted of trafficking in persons, by sex, 2014 –2017

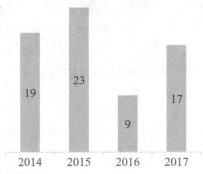

Source: Office of Combating Trafficking in Human Beings.

Citizenships of persons convicted of trafficking in persons, 2014 –2017

Source: Office of Combating Trafficking in Human Beings.

Victims

Number of victims of trafficking in persons detected, by age and sex, 2014 –2017

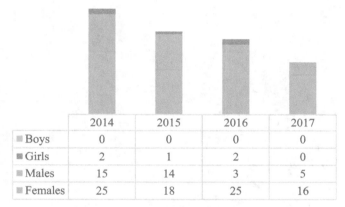

	2014	2015	2016	2017
▪ Boys	0	0	0	0
▪ Girls	2	1	2	0
▪ Males	15	14	3	5
▪ Females	25	18	25	16

Source: Office of Combating Trafficking in Human Beings.

Number of victims of trafficking in persons detected, by form of exploitation, 2014 –2017

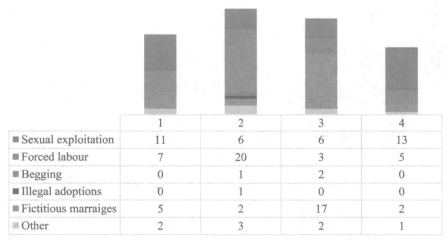

	1	2	3	4
▪ Sexual exploitation	11	6	6	13
▪ Forced labour	7	20	3	5
▪ Begging	0	1	2	0
▪ Illegal adoptions	0	1	0	0
▪ Fictitious marraiges	5	2	17	2
▪ Other	2	3	2	1

Source: Office of Combating Trafficking in Human Beings.

Citizenships of persons identified as victims of trafficking in persons by state authorities, 2014 –2017

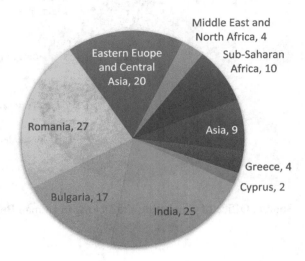

Source: Office of Combating Trafficking in Human Beings.

−Denmark−

The current legislation on trafficking in persons in Denmark covers all forms of trafficking indicated in the UN Trafficking in Persons Protocol.

Investigations and suspects

Number of cases of trafficking in persons reported to police, 2014 − September 2017**

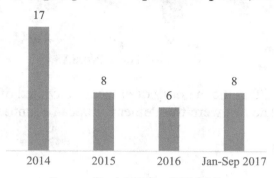

Source: Danish Police POLSAS.

**The system which the Danish Police uses, POLSAS, is dynamic and continuously updated. Consequently, data is subject to certain inconsistencies.

Number of persons brought into formal contact with the police and/or criminal justice system because they have been suspected of, arrested for or cautioned for trafficking in persons **, 2014 − September 2017

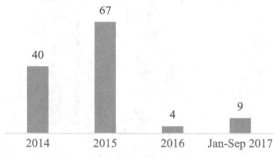

Source: Danish Police POLSAS.

**Note: Formal contact with the police and/or criminal justice system may include persons suspected, arrested, or cautioned at the national level.

Number of persons prosecuted for trafficking in persons, 2014 − September 2017

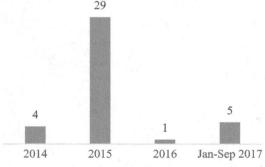

Source: Danish Police POLSAS.

Number of persons convicted of trafficking in persons, 2014 – September 2017

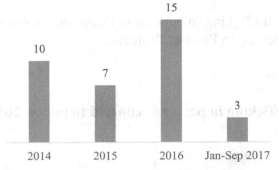

Source: Danish Police POLSAS.

The Danish Police reported that the majority of citizens convicted of trafficking in persons were Romanian citizens. The rest were from other European countries, Asia, and others.

Source: Danish Police POLSAS

Victims

Number of victims of trafficking detected, by age and sex, 2014 – September 2017

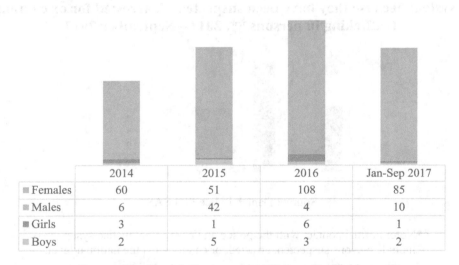

	2014	2015	2016	Jan-Sep 2017
■ Females	60	51	108	85
■ Males	6	42	4	10
■ Girls	3	1	6	1
■ Boys	2	5	3	2

Source: The Danish Centre against Human Trafficking.

Number of victims of trafficking detected, by form of exploitation, 2014 – September 2017

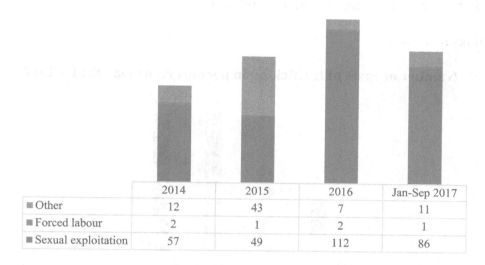

	2014	2015	2016	Jan-Sep 2017
▪ Other	12	43	7	11
▪ Forced labour	2	1	2	1
▪ Sexual exploitation	57	49	112	86

Source: The Danish Centre against Human Trafficking.

Citizenships of persons identified as victims of trafficking in persons by state authorities, 2014 – September 2017

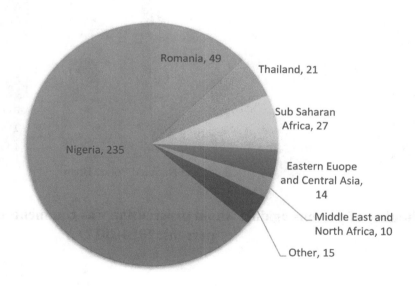

Source: The Danish Centre against Human Trafficking.

—Finland—

The current legislation on trafficking in persons in Finland covers all forms of trafficking indicated in the UN Trafficking in Persons Protocol.

Investigations and suspects

Number of cases of trafficking in persons recorded, 2014 – 2017

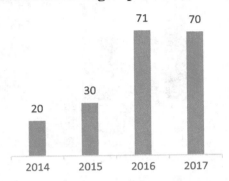

Source: The National Police Board.

Number of persons brought into formal contact with the police and/or criminal justice system because they have been suspected of trafficking in persons, by sex, 2014 – 2017

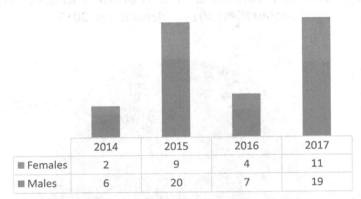

	2014	2015	2016	2017
■ Females	2	9	4	11
■ Males	6	20	7	19

Source: The National Police Board.

Number of persons against whom prosecution was commenced for trafficking in persons, 2014-2017

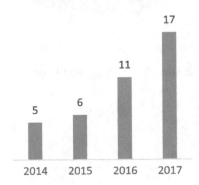

Source: Ministry of Justice; data from case management system Sakari.

Number of persons convicted of trafficking in persons in the first instance, 2015-2017

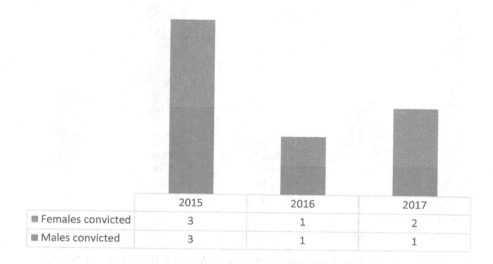

	2015	2016	2017
■ Females convicted	3	1	2
■ Males convicted	3	1	1

Source: BOXI-system, The Office of the Prosecutor General.

Victims

Number of victims of trafficking in persons detected, by form of exploitation, 2014 – September 2017

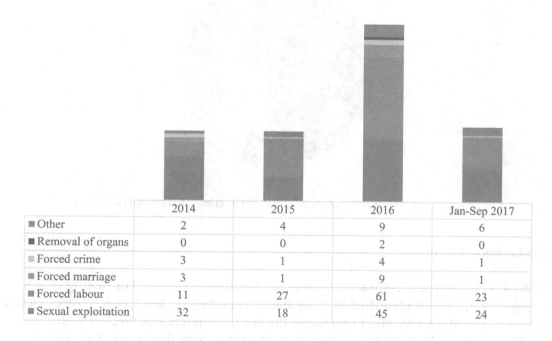

	2014	2015	2016	Jan-Sep 2017
■ Other	2	4	9	6
■ Removal of organs	0	0	2	0
■ Forced crime	3	1	4	1
■ Forced marriage	3	1	9	1
■ Forced labour	11	27	61	23
■ Sexual exploitation	32	18	45	24

Source: The National Assistance System for Victims of Human Trafficking.

Number of victims of trafficking in persons detected, by age and sex, 2014 – September 2017

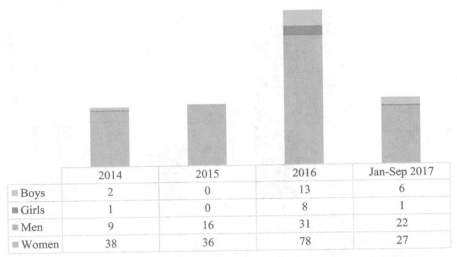

	2014	2015	2016	Jan-Sep 2017
▪ Boys	2	0	13	6
▪ Girls	1	0	8	1
▪ Men	9	16	31	22
▪ Women	38	36	78	27

Source: The National Assistance System for Victims of Human Trafficking.

Citizenships of persons identified as victims of trafficking in persons by state authorities, 2014 – June 2017

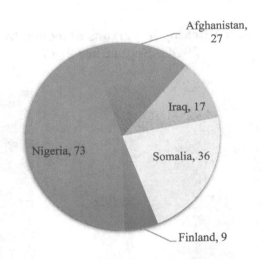

Source: The National Assistance System for Victims of Human Trafficking.

Additional information

After 2014, The National Assistance System for Victims of Human Trafficking stopped recording citizenships of identified victims that amount to less than five to protect victim privacy. As such, the above chart represents the accurate number of victims with certain citizenships from the largest groups. Additional victims came from other Sub-Saharan African countries, Asia, North Africa and the Middle East, and other Western European countries.

Source: The National Assistance System for Victims of Human Trafficking.

−France−

The current legislation on trafficking in persons in France covers all forms of trafficking indicated in the UN Trafficking in Persons Protocol.

Investigations and suspects

Number of cases of trafficking in persons and related offences recorded, 2015 – 2017

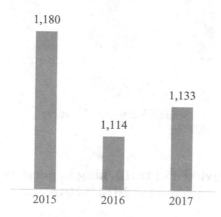

Source: Ministry of the Interior.

Number of persons brought into formal contact with the police and/or criminal justice system because they have been suspected of, arrested for or cautioned for trafficking in persons, by sex**, 2016 – 2017

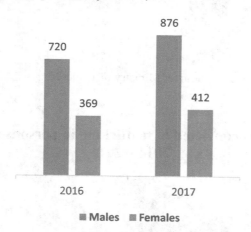

■ Males ■ Females

Source: Ministry of the Interior.

**Note: Formal contact with the police and/or criminal justice system may include persons suspected, arrested, or cautioned at the national level.

Number of persons prosecuted for trafficking in persons and related offences, by sex, 2014 – 2017

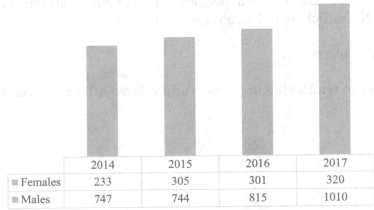

	2014	2015	2016	2017
▪ Females	233	305	301	320
▪ Males	747	744	815	1010

Source: Ministry of Justice.

Number of persons convicted of trafficking in persons and related offences, by sex, 2014 – 2016

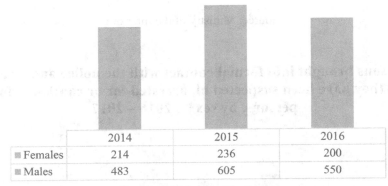

	2014	2015	2016
▪ Females	214	236	200
▪ Males	483	605	550

Source: Ministry of Justice.

Citizenships of persons convicted of trafficking in persons and related offences, 2014 – 2016

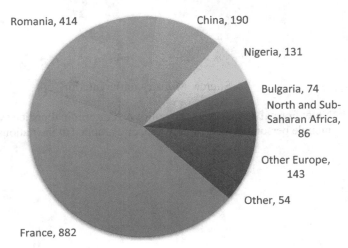

Romania, 414
China, 190
Nigeria, 131
Bulgaria, 74
North and Sub-Saharan Africa, 86
Other Europe, 143
Other, 54
France, 882

Source: Ministry of Justice.

Victims

Number of victims of trafficking in persons and related offences detected, by age and sex**, 2015 – 2016

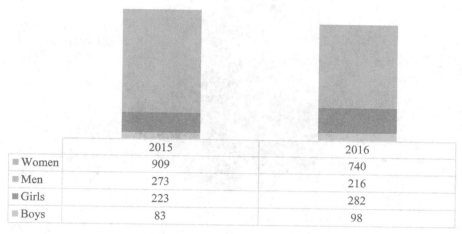

	2015	2016
■ Women	909	740
■ Men	273	216
■ Girls	223	282
■ Boys	83	98

Source: Ministry of the Interior.

**The age and/or sex of 28 victims in the indicated period is unknown.
Some victims may be placed in two or more categories of trafficking.

Number of victims of trafficking in persons and related offences detected, by form of exploitation, 2016 – 2017

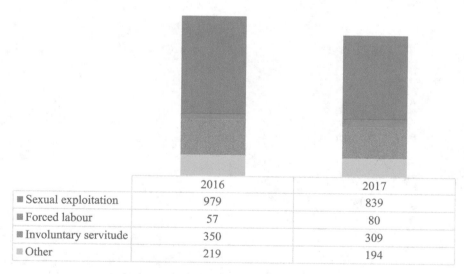

	2016	2017
■ Sexual exploitation	979	839
■ Forced labour	57	80
■ Involuntary servitude	350	309
■ Other	219	194

Source: Ministry of the Interior.

Citizenships of persons identified as victims of trafficking in persons and related offences by state authorities, 2016 – 2017

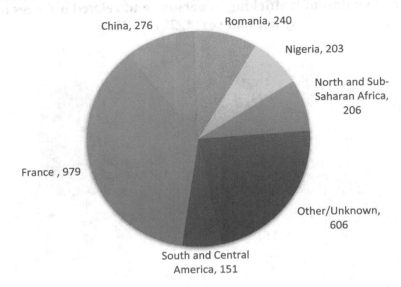

China, 276

Romania, 240

Nigeria, 203

North and Sub-Saharan Africa, 206

France , 979

Other/Unknown, 606

South and Central America, 151

Source: Ministry of the Interior.

–Germany–

The current legislation on trafficking in persons in Germany covers all forms of trafficking indicated in the UN Trafficking in Persons Protocol.

Investigations and suspects

Number of cases of trafficking in persons recorded, 2014 – 2016

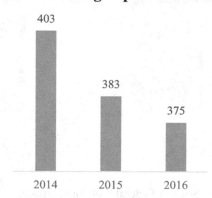

Source: Ministry of the Interior.

Number of persons brought into formal contact with the police and/or criminal justice system because they have been suspected of, arrested for or cautioned for trafficking in persons, by sex**, 2014 – 2016

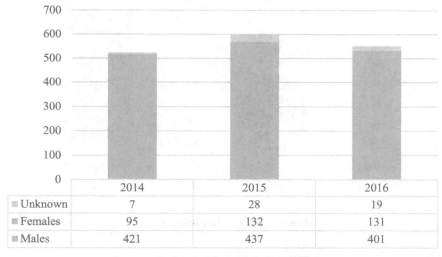

	2014	2015	2016
Unknown	7	28	19
Females	95	132	131
Males	421	437	401

Source: Federal Criminal Police Office.

**Note: Formal contact with the police and/or criminal justice system may include persons suspected, arrested, or cautioned at the national level.

Number of persons prosecuted for trafficking in persons, by sex, 2014 – 2015

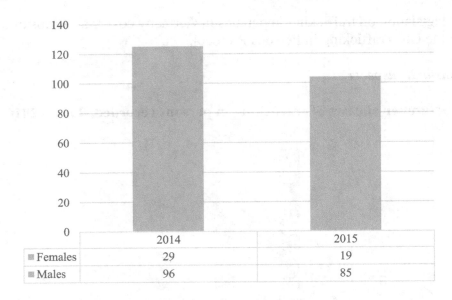

	2014	2015
▪ Females	29	19
▪ Males	96	85

Source: Federal Statistical Office.

Number of persons convicted of trafficking in persons, by sex, 2014 – 2015

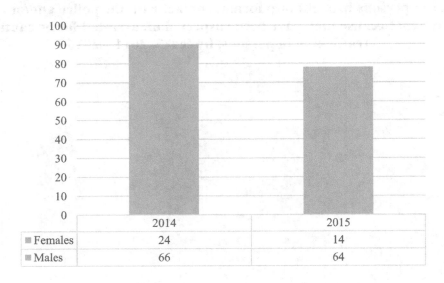

	2014	2015
▪ Females	24	14
▪ Males	66	64

Source: Federal Statistical Office.

Citizenships of persons convicted of trafficking in persons 2014 – 2015

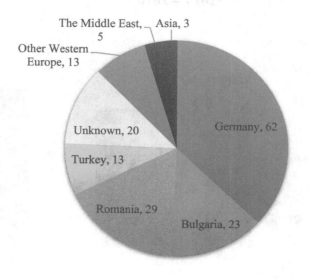

Source: Federal Statistical Office.

Victims

Number of victims of trafficking in persons detected, by age and sex, 2014 – 2016

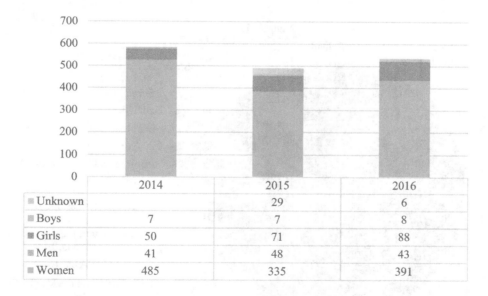

	2014	2015	2016
▪ Unknown		29	6
▪ Boys	7	7	8
▪ Girls	50	71	88
▪ Men	41	48	43
▪ Women	485	335	391

Source: Federal Criminal Office.

Number of victims of trafficking in persons detected, by form of exploitation, 2014 – 2016

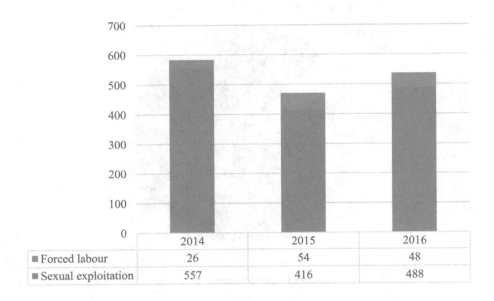

	2014	2015	2016
■ Forced labour	26	54	48
■ Sexual exploitation	557	416	488

Source: Federal Criminal Police Office.

Citizenships of persons identified as victims of trafficking in persons by state authorities, 2014 – 2016

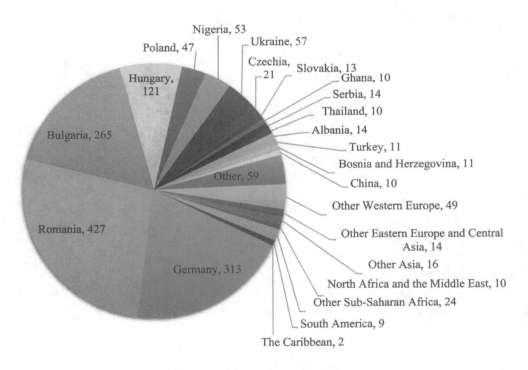

Source: Federal Criminal Police Office.

The current legislation on trafficking in persons in Greece covers all forms of trafficking indicated in the UN Trafficking in Persons Protocol.

Investigations and suspects

Number of cases of trafficking in persons recorded, 2014 –2017

Source: Office of the National Rapporteur on Human Trafficking.

Number of persons brought into formal contact with the police and/or criminal justice system because they have been suspected of, arrested for or cautioned for trafficking in persons, by sex**, 2014 – March 2017

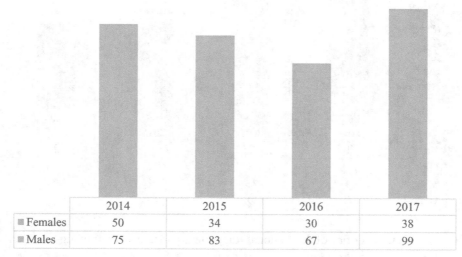

	2014	2015	2016	2017
▪ Females	50	34	30	38
▪ Males	75	83	67	99

Source: Office of the National Rapporteur on Human Trafficking.

**Note: Formal contact with the police and/or criminal justice system may include persons suspected, arrested, or cautioned at the national level.

Number of persons prosecuted for trafficking in persons, 2014 – 2017

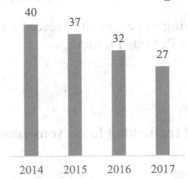

Source: Office of the National Rapporteur on Human Trafficking.

Of the persons prosecuted for trafficking in persons, 13 were convicted in 2014, 15 in 2015, and eight in 2016.

Source: Office of the National Rapporteur on Human Trafficking.

Victims

Number of victims of trafficking in persons detected, by age and sex, 2014 –2017

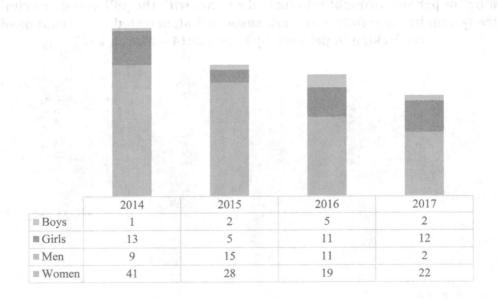

	2014	2015	2016	2017
Boys	1	2	5	2
Girls	13	5	11	12
Men	9	15	11	2
Women	41	28	19	22

Source: Office of the National Rapporteur on Human Trafficking.

Number of victims of trafficking in persons detected, by form of exploitation, 2014 –2017

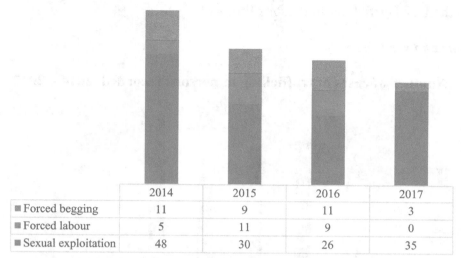

	2014	2015	2016	2017
▪ Forced begging	11	9	11	3
▪ Forced labour	5	11	9	0
▪ Sexual exploitation	48	30	26	35

Source: Office of the National Rapporteur on Human Trafficking.

Citizenships of persons identified as victims of trafficking in persons by State authorities, 2014-2017

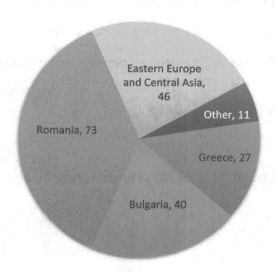

Source: Office of the National Rapporteur on Human Trafficking.

The current legislation on trafficking in persons in Ireland covers all forms of trafficking indicated in the UN Trafficking in Persons Protocol.

Investigations and suspects

Number of cases of trafficking in persons recorded, 2014 – 2017

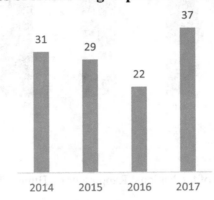

Source: Anti-Human Trafficking Unit, Department of Justice and Equality.

According to national authorities, 14 men were prosecuted for trafficking in persons in 2015, 17 men in 2015, and 20 in 2016. Two women were prosecuted for the crime in 2015. Of those prosecuted, 11 men were convicted in 2014, twelve men in 2015, and seven men in 2016. During the indicated period, no women were convicted of trafficking in persons.

Source: Anti-Human Trafficking Unit, Department of Justice and Equality.

National authorities reported that the majority of persons convicted of trafficking in persons between 2014 and 2016 were Irish nationals.

Source: Anti-Human Trafficking Unit, Department of Justice and Equality.

Victims

Number of victims of trafficking in persons detected, by age and sex, 2014 – 2017

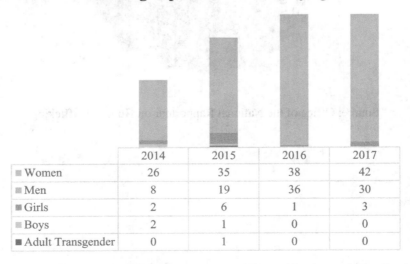

	2014	2015	2016	2017
▪ Women	26	35	38	42
▪ Men	8	19	36	30
▪ Girls	2	6	1	3
▪ Boys	2	1	0	0
▪ Adult Transgender	0	1	0	0

Source: Anti-Human Trafficking Unit, Department of Justice and Equality.

Number of victims of trafficking in persons detected, by form of exploitation, 2014 – 2017

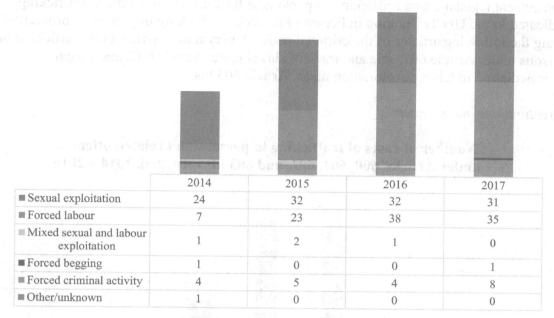

	2014	2015	2016	2017
■ Sexual exploitation	24	32	32	31
■ Forced labour	7	23	38	35
■ Mixed sexual and labour exploitation	1	2	1	0
■ Forced begging	1	0	0	1
■ Forced criminal activity	4	5	4	8
■ Other/unknown	1	0	0	0

Source: Anti-Human Trafficking Unit, Department of Justice and Equality.

Citizenships of persons identified as victims of trafficking in persons by state authorities, 2014 – 2016

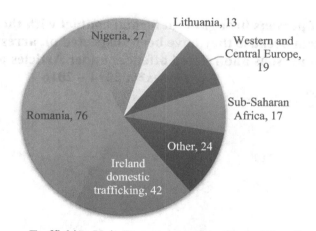

Source: Anti-Human Trafficking Unit, Department of Justice and Equality.

Additional information

Until 2017, offences related to child sexual exploitation and/or child pornography were included in Ireland's human trafficking statistics. Henceforth, these are no longer being classified as victims of human trafficking. This explains the discrepancy between previously reported victim figures and the above, which have been corrected to remove victims of child sexual exploitation and pornography.

Source: Anti-Human Trafficking Unit, Department of Justice and Equality.

–Italy–

The current legislation on trafficking in persons in Italy covers all forms of trafficking indicated in the UN Trafficking in Persons Protocol. Trafficking in persons is prosecuted using the following articles of the criminal code: slavery under Article 600, trafficking in persons under Article 601, sale and trade of slaves under Article 602, and illegal intermediation in labour exploitation under Article 603 bis.

Investigations and suspects

**Number of cases of trafficking in persons and related offences
under Articles 600, 601, 602, and 603 bis recorded, 2014 – 2016**

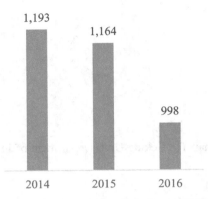

Source: Ministry of the Interior – Department of Public Security, Police Coordination and Planning Office, International Relations Service, and Multilateral Business Division.

Number of persons brought into formal contact with the police and/or criminal justice system because they have been suspected of, arrested for or cautioned for trafficking in persons and related offences under Articles 600, 601, 602, and 603 bis, by sex, 2014 – 2016**

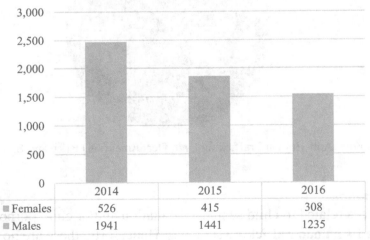

	2014	2015	2016
Females	526	415	308
Males	1941	1441	1235

Source: Ministry of the Interior – Department of Public Security, Police Coordination and Planning Office, International Relations Service, and Multilateral Business Division.

**Note: Formal contact with the police and/or criminal justice system may include persons suspected, arrested, or cautioned at the national level.

Victims

Number of victims of trafficking in persons and related offences under Articles 600, 601, 602, and 603 bis detected, by age and sex, 2014 – 2016

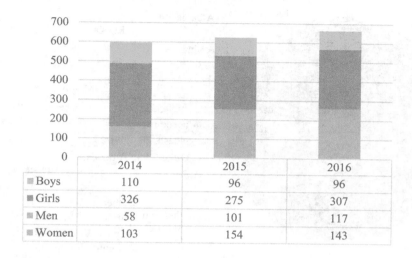

	2014	2015	2016
■ Boys	110	96	96
■ Girls	326	275	307
■ Men	58	101	117
■ Women	103	154	143

Source: Ministry of the Interior – Department of Public Security, Police Coordination and Planning Office, International Relations Service, and Multilateral Business Division.

Number of victims of trafficking in persons and related offences under Articles 600, 601, 602, and 603 bis detected, by form of exploitation, 2014 – 2016

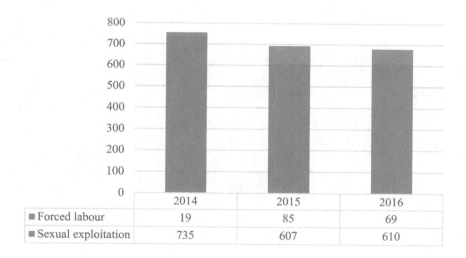

	2014	2015	2016
■ Forced labour	19	85	69
■ Sexual exploitation	735	607	610

Source: Ministry of the Interior – Department of Public Security, Police Coordination and Planning Office, International Relations Service, and Multilateral Business Division.

Citizenships of persons identified as victims of trafficking in persons and related offences under Articles 600, 601, 602, and 603 bis by state authorities, 2014 – 2016

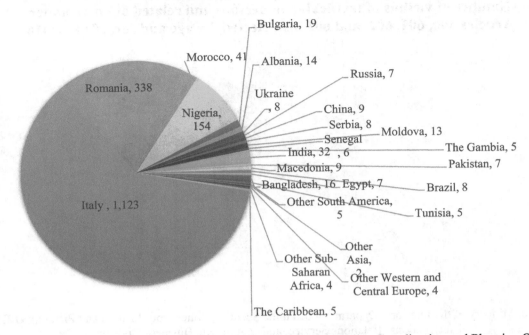

Source: Ministry of the Interior – Department of Public Security, Police Coordination and Planning Office, International Relations Service, and Multilateral Business Division.

−Malta−

The current legislation on trafficking in persons in Malta covers all forms of trafficking indicated in the UN Trafficking in Persons Protocol.

Investigations and suspects

Between 2014 and 2016, national authorities in Malta recorded seven cases of trafficking in persons. During this period, 12 males were prosecuted for the crime, but none were convicted.

Source: Ministry for Home Affairs and National Security.

Victims

Number of victims of trafficking in persons detected, by age and sex, 2014 – 2016

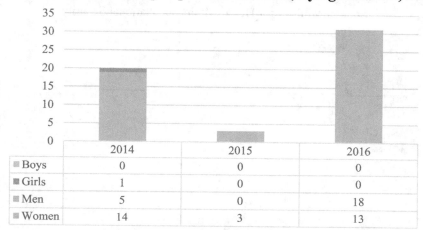

	2014	2015	2016
▪ Boys	0	0	0
▪ Girls	1	0	0
▪ Men	5	0	18
▪ Women	14	3	13

Source: Ministry for Home Affairs and National Security.

Number of victims of trafficking in persons detected, by form of exploitation, 2014 – 2016

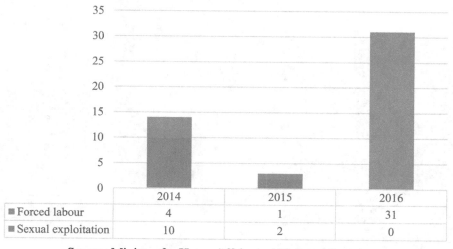

	2014	2015	2016
▪ Forced labour	4	1	31
▪ Sexual exploitation	10	2	0

Source: Ministry for Home Affairs and National Security.

Citizenships of persons identified as victims of trafficking in persons by state authorities, 2014 – 2016

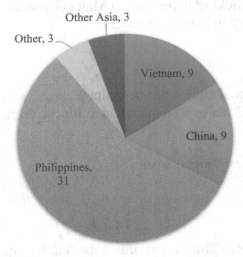

Source: Ministry for Home Affairs and National Security.

The current legislation on trafficking in persons in Norway covers all forms of trafficking indicated in the UN Trafficking in Persons Protocol.

Investigations and suspects

Number of cases of trafficking in persons recorded, 2014 – 2016

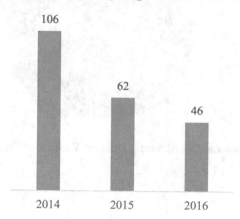

Source: STRASAK, The Norwegian Police Register for Criminal Cases.

Number of persons convicted of trafficking in persons, by sex, 2014 – 2016

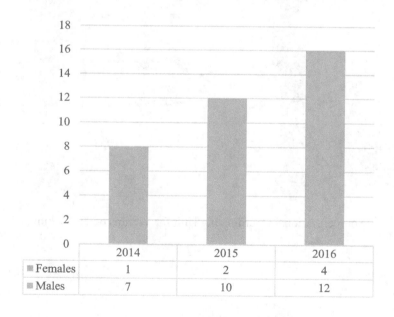

	2014	2015	2016
■ Females	1	2	4
■ Males	7	10	12

Source: National Coordinating Unit for Victims of Trafficking.

Citizenships of persons convicted of trafficking in persons, 2014 – 2016

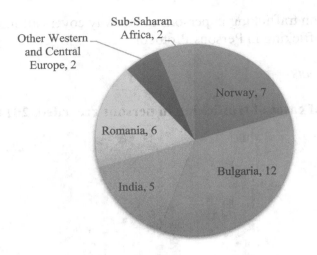

Source: National Coordinating Unit for Victims of Trafficking.

Victims

Number of victims of trafficking in persons detected, by age and sex, 2014 – 2016

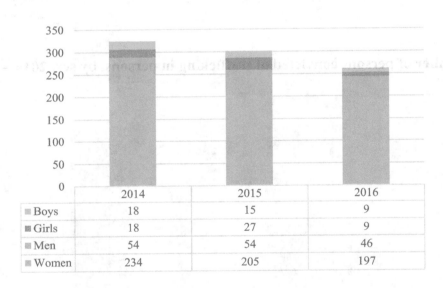

	2014	2015	2016
■ Boys	18	15	9
■ Girls	18	27	9
■ Men	54	54	46
■ Women	234	205	197

Source: National Coordinating Unit for Victims of Trafficking.

Number of victims of trafficking in persons detected, by form of exploitation, 2014 – 2016

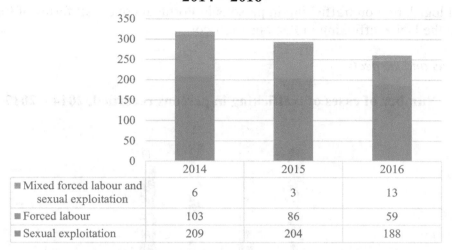

	2014	2015	2016
■ Mixed forced labour and sexual exploitation	6	3	13
■ Forced labour	103	86	59
■ Sexual exploitation	209	204	188

Source: National Coordinating Unit for Victims of Trafficking.

Citizenships of persons identified as victims of trafficking in persons by state authorities, 2014 – 2016

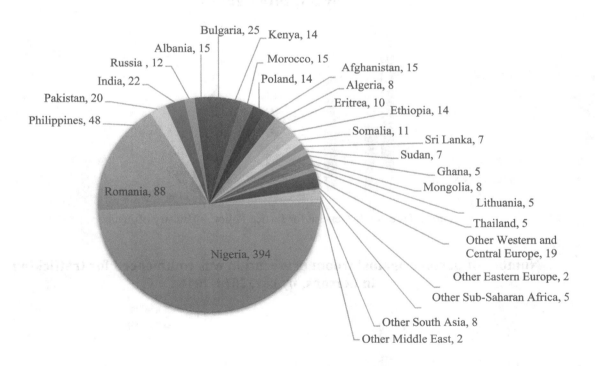

Source: National Coordinating Unit for Victims of Trafficking.

−Portugal−

The current legislation on trafficking in persons in Portugal covers all forms of trafficking indicated in the UN Trafficking in Persons Protocol.

Investigations and suspects

Number of cases of trafficking in persons recorded, 2014 – 2017

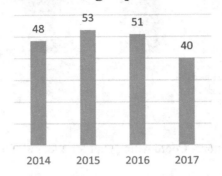

Source: Directorate General for Justice Policy – Ministry of Justice.

Number of persons brought into formal contact with the police and/or criminal justice system because they have been suspected of trafficking in persons, by sex, 2014 – 2017

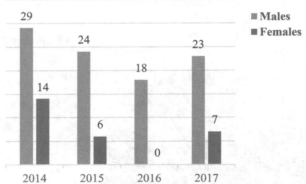

Source: Directorate General for Justice Policy – Ministry of Justice.

Number of persons against whom prosecution was commenced for trafficking in persons, by sex, 2014-2016

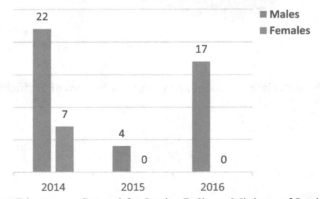

Source: Directorate General for Justice Policy – Ministry of Justice.

Additional information

Of those suspected of trafficking in persons in 2014, 29 were males and 14 were females. In 2015, 24 males and six females were suspected.

Source: Directorate General for Justice Policy – Ministry of Justice.

In 2014, 31 persons were prosecuted for trafficking and in 2015, six were prosecuted. In 2014, 22 persons were convicted of the crime.

Source: Directorate General for Justice Policy – Ministry of Justice.

National authorities in Portugal reported that the majority of persons convicted of trafficking in persons in 2014 were Portuguese and Romanian nationals.

Source: Directorate General for Justice Policy – Ministry of Justice.

Victims

Number of victims of trafficking in persons detected, by age, 2014 – 2016

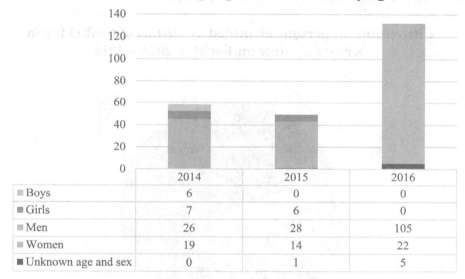

	2014	2015	2016
▪ Boys	6	0	0
▪ Girls	7	6	0
▪ Men	26	28	105
▪ Women	19	14	22
▪ Unknown age and sex	0	1	5

Source: Observatory on Trafficking in Human Beings, Ministry of Internal Administration.

Additional information

In 2014, of the adult victims identified, 26 were males and 19 were females. Of the child victims identified, six were males and seven were females. In 2015, 28 adult males and 14 adult females were identified as victims of trafficking in persons. In 2016, 105 adult males and 22 adult females were identified as victims.

Source: Observatory on Trafficking in Human Beings, Ministry of Internal Administration.

Number of victims of trafficking in persons detected, by form of exploitation, 2014 – 2016

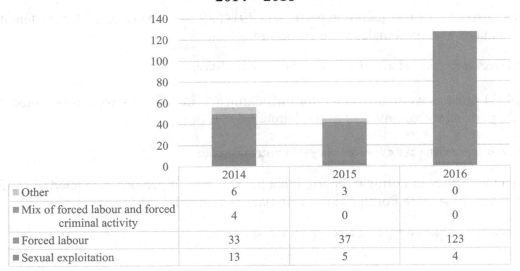

	2014	2015	2016
■ Other	6	3	0
■ Mix of forced labour and forced criminal activity	4	0	0
■ Forced labour	33	37	123
■ Sexual exploitation	13	5	4

Source: Observatory on Trafficking in Human Beings, Ministry of Internal Administration

Citizenships of persons identified as victims of trafficking in persons by state authorities, 2014 – 2016

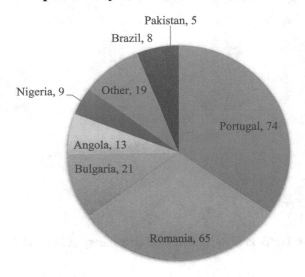

Source: Observatory on Trafficking in Human Beings, Ministry of Internal Administration.

Identified victims of trafficking, by type of trafficking, 2014 – July 2017

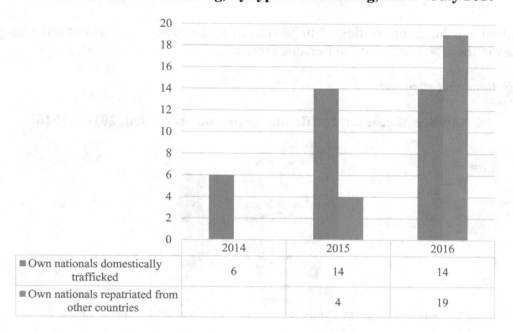

	2014	2015	2016
■ Own nationals domestically trafficked	6	14	14
■ Own nationals repatriated from other countries		4	19

Source: Observatory on Trafficking in Human Beings, Ministry of Internal Administration.

The current legislation on trafficking in persons in Spain covers all forms of trafficking indicated in the UN Trafficking in Persons Protocol.

Investigations and suspects

Number of cases of trafficking in persons recorded, 2014 – 2016

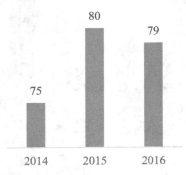

Source: Intelligence Centre for Counter-Terrorism and Organized Crime.

Number of persons brought into formal contact with the police and/or criminal justice system because they have been arrested for trafficking in persons, by sex, 2014 –2016

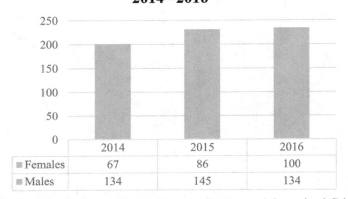

	2014	2015	2016
Females	67	86	100
Males	134	145	134

Source: Intelligence Centre for Counter-Terrorism and Organized Crime.

Number of persons prosecuted for trafficking in persons, by sex, 2014 – 2016

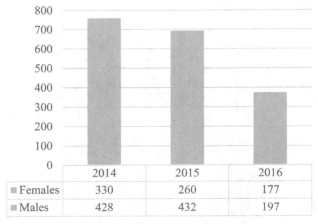

	2014	2015	2016
Females	330	260	177
Males	428	432	197

Source: Delegate Prosecutors of Aliens,
Immigration Unit of the State Attorney General's Office.

Number of persons convicted of trafficking in persons, by sex, 2014 – 2016

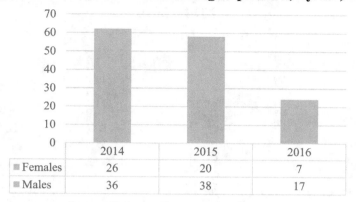

	2014	2015	2016
▪ Females	26	20	7
▪ Males	36	38	17

Source: Delegate Prosecutors of Aliens,
Immigration Unit of the State Attorney General's Office.

Citizenships of persons convicted of trafficking in persons, 2014 – 2016

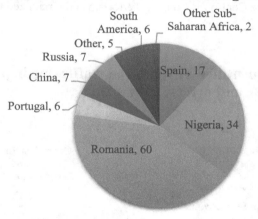

Source: Delegate Prosecutors of Aliens,
Immigration Unit of the State Attorney General's Office.

Victims

Number of victims of trafficking in persons detected, by age and sex, 2014 – 2016

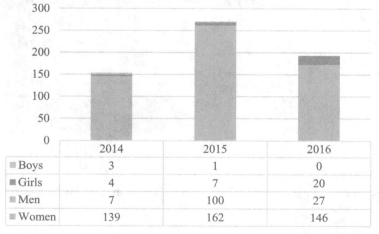

	2014	2015	2016
▪ Boys	3	1	0
▪ Girls	4	7	20
▪ Men	7	100	27
▪ Women	139	162	146

Source: Intelligence Centre for Counter-Terrorism and Organized Crime.

Number of victims of trafficking in persons detected, by form of exploitation, 2014 – 2016

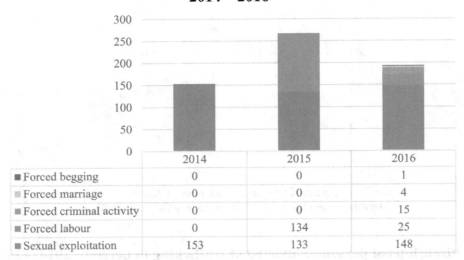

	2014	2015	2016
■ Forced begging	0	0	1
■ Forced marriage	0	0	4
■ Forced criminal activity	0	0	15
■ Forced labour	0	134	25
■ Sexual exploitation	153	133	148

Source: Intelligence Centre for Counter-Terrorism and Organized Crime.

Citizenships of persons identified as victims of trafficking in persons by state authorities, 2014 – 2016

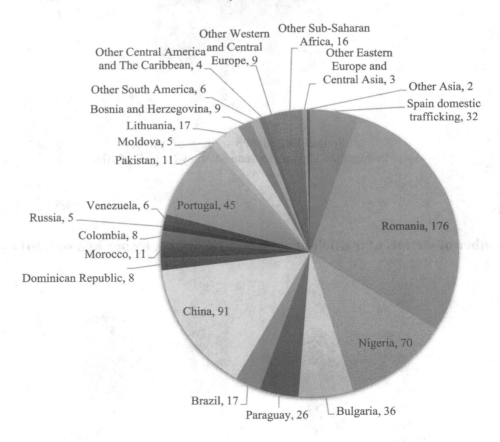

Source: Intelligence Centre for Counter-Terrorism and Organized Crime.

The current legislation on trafficking in persons in Sweden covers all forms of trafficking indicated in the UN Trafficking in Persons Protocol.

Investigations and suspects

Number of cases of trafficking in persons recorded, 2014 – 2016

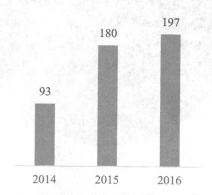

Source: Swedish National Rapporteur.

Four persons were prosecuted for trafficking in persons in 2014, two in 2015, and eight in 2016. Of those prosecuted, three were convicted in 2014, two in 2015 and six in 2016.

Source: Swedish National Rapporteur.

The majority of persons convicted of trafficking in persons between 2014 and 2016 were nationals of Bulgaria.

Source: Swedish National Rapporteur.

Victims

Number of cases of trafficking in persons detected, by form of exploitation, 2014 – 2016

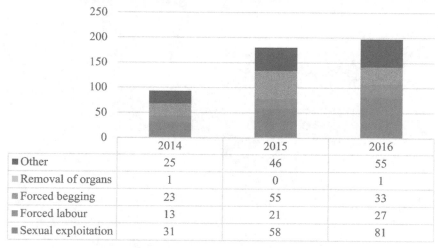

	2014	2015	2016
■ Other	25	46	55
■ Removal of organs	1	0	1
■ Forced begging	23	55	33
■ Forced labour	13	21	27
■ Sexual exploitation	31	58	81

Source: Swedish Rapporteur.

Number of temporary residence permits issued for victims of trafficking in persons, by citizenship, 2014 - 2016

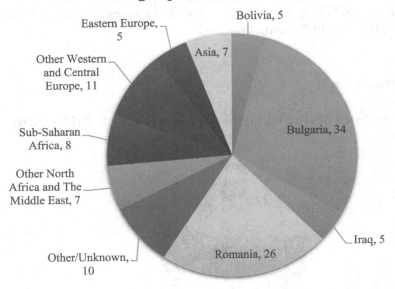

Source: Swedish Migration Board.

The current legislation on trafficking in persons in Switzerland covers all forms of trafficking indicated in the UN Trafficking in Persons Protocol.

Investigations and suspects

Number of cases of trafficking in persons recorded, 2014 – 2016

Source: Police Crime Statistics.

Number of persons brought into formal contact with the police and/or criminal justice system because they have been suspected of, arrested for or cautioned for trafficking in persons, by sex**, 2014 – 2016

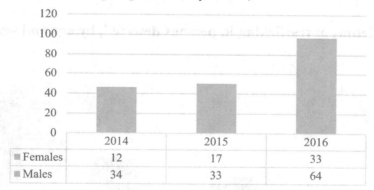

	2014	2015	2016
Females	12	17	33
Males	34	33	64

Source: Police Crime Statistics.

**Note: Formal contact with the police and/or criminal justice system may include persons suspected, arrested, or cautioned at the national level.

Number of persons convicted of trafficking in persons, by sex, 2014 – 2016

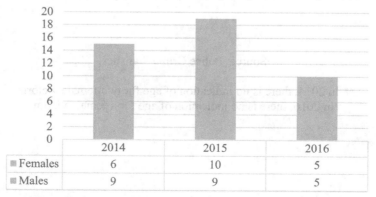

	2014	2015	2016
Females	6	10	5
Males	9	9	5

Source: Statistics of Criminal Convictions (SUS), Statistics of Criminal Convictions of Juveniles (JUSUS).

Citizenships of persons convicted of trafficking in persons, 2014 – 2016

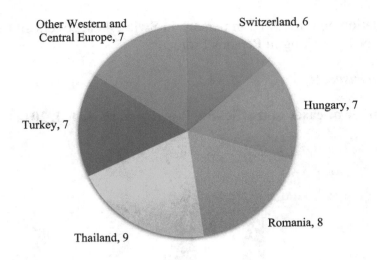

Source: Statistics of Criminal Convictions (SUS), Statistics of Criminal Convictions of Juveniles (JUSUS).

Victims

Number of victims of trafficking in persons detected, by age and sex, 2014 – 2016

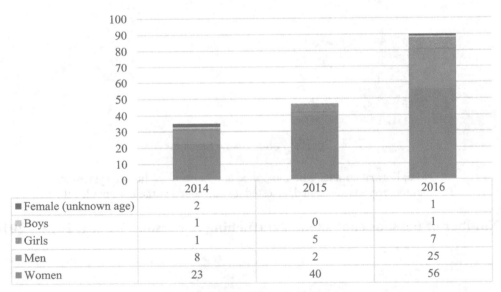

	2014	2015	2016
■ Female (unknown age)	2		1
■ Boys	1	0	1
■ Girls	1	5	7
■ Men	8	2	25
■ Women	23	40	56

Source: Police Crime Statistics.

** In 2014, there is no indication of age for two female victories.
In 2016, there is no indication of age for a female victim.

Citizenships of persons identified as victims of trafficking in persons by state authorities, 2014 – 2016

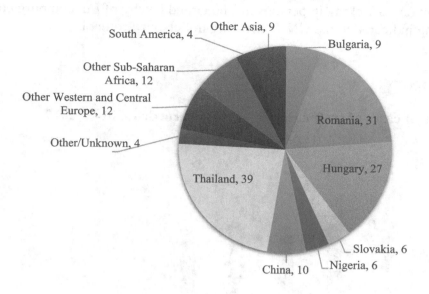

Source: Police Crime Statistics.

All identified Swiss victims of trafficking in persons were trafficked domestically.

Source: Police Crime Statistics.

–The Grand Duchy of Luxembourg –

The current legislation on trafficking in persons in The Grand Duchy of Luxembourg covers all forms of trafficking indicated in the UN Trafficking in Persons Protocol.

Investigations and suspects

Number of cases of trafficking in persons recorded, 2014 – 2017

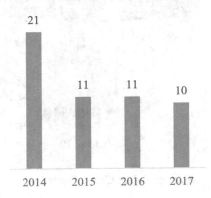

Source: Police Grand-Ducale.

Number of persons brought into formal contact with the police and/or criminal justice system because they have been suspected of, arrested for or cautioned for trafficking in persons, by sex**, 2014 – 2017

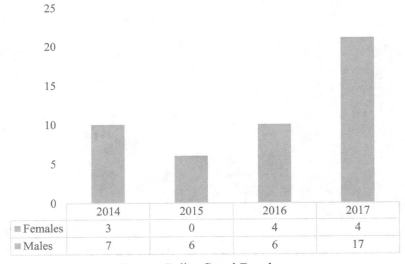

	2014	2015	2016	2017
■ Females	3	0	4	4
■ Males	7	6	6	17

Source: Police Grand-Ducale.

**Note: Formal contact with the police and/or criminal justice system may include persons suspected, arrested, or cautioned at the national level.

Number of persons prosecuted for trafficking in persons, by sex, 2014 – 2017

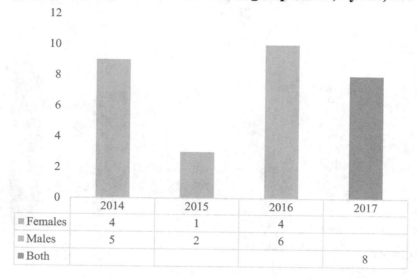

	2014	2015	2016	2017
■ Females	4	1	4	
■ Males	5	2	6	
■ Both				8

Source: Parquet de Luxembourg.

In the reporting period between 2014 and 2017, 14 persons from West European countries were convicted of trafficking in persons, along with 7 from East European countries, and 5 from other countries.

Source: Ministry of Justice.

Victims

Number of victims of trafficking in persons detected, by age and sex, 2014 – 2017

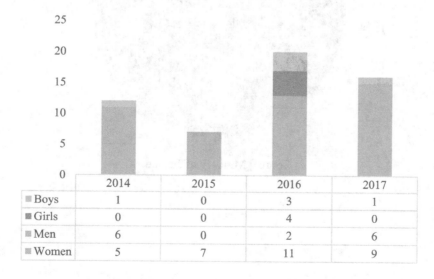

	2014	2015	2016	2017
■ Boys	1	0	3	1
■ Girls	0	0	4	0
■ Men	6	0	2	6
■ Women	5	7	11	9

Source: Police Grand-Ducale

Note: Statistics reflect presumed and identified victims.

Number of victims of trafficking in persons detected, by form of exploitation, 2014 – 2017

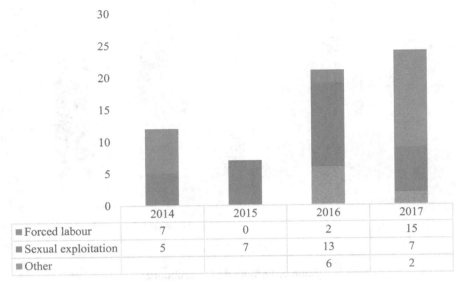

	2014	2015	2016	2017
■ Forced labour	7	0	2	15
■ Sexual exploitation	5	7	13	7
■ Other			6	2

Source: Ministry of Justice

Citizenships of persons identified as victims of trafficking in persons by state authorities, 2014 – 2017

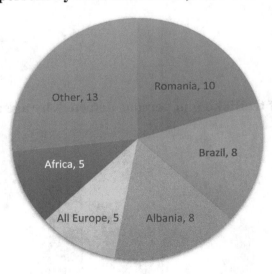

Source: Ministry of Justice

−Principality of Liechtenstein−

The current legislation on trafficking in persons in the Principality of Liechtenstein covers all forms of trafficking indicated in the UN Trafficking in Persons Protocol.

No cases were detected during in the reporting period.

Source: The Permanent Mission of the Principality of Lichtenstein to the United Nations.

The current legislation on trafficking in persons in The Netherlands covers all forms of trafficking indicated in the UN Trafficking in Persons Protocol.

Investigations and suspects

Number of persons brought into formal contact with the police and/or criminal justice system because they have been suspected of, arrested for or cautioned for trafficking in persons, by sex**, 2014 – 2015

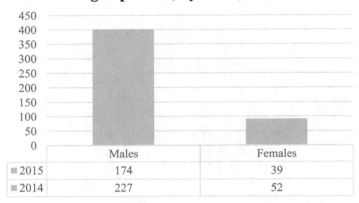

	Males	Females
2015	174	39
2014	227	52

Source: Public Prosecution Service.

**Note: Formal contact with the police and/or criminal justice system may include persons suspected, arrested, or cautioned at the national level. This number does not include those who have made contact with the police.

In 2014, 193 persons were prosecuted for trafficking in persons, and in 2015, 184 were prosecuted. Of those prosecuted, 129 were convicted in 2014 and 124 were convicted in 2015.

Source: Public Prosecution Service

Victims

Number of victims of trafficking in persons detected, by age and sex, 2014 – 2016

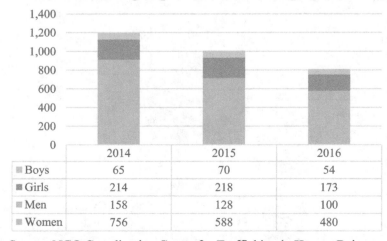

	2014	2015	2016
Boys	65	70	54
Girls	214	218	173
Men	158	128	100
Women	756	588	480

Source: NGO Coordination Centre for Trafficking in Human Beings.

Number of victims of trafficking in persons detected, by form of exploitation, 2014 – 2016

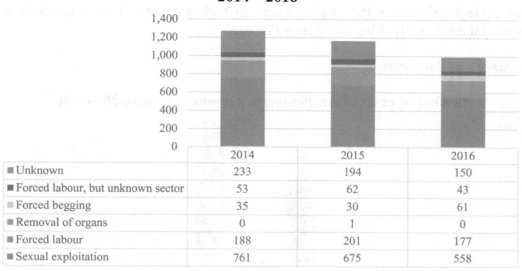

	2014	2015	2016
■ Unknown	233	194	150
■ Forced labour, but unknown sector	53	62	43
■ Forced begging	35	30	61
■ Removal of organs	0	1	0
■ Forced labour	188	201	177
■ Sexual exploitation	761	675	558

Source: NGO Coordination Centre for Trafficking in Human Beings.

Citizenships of persons identified as victims of trafficking in persons by state authorities, 2014 – 2016

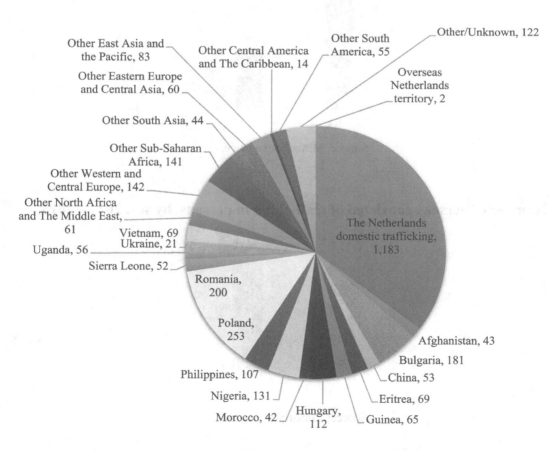

Source: NGO Coordination Centre for Trafficking in Human Beings.

<h1 style="text-align:center">−Turkey−</h1>

The current legislation on trafficking in persons in Turkey covers all forms of trafficking indicated in the UN Trafficking in Persons Protocol.

Investigations and suspects

Number of cases of trafficking in persons recorded, 2014 – 2015

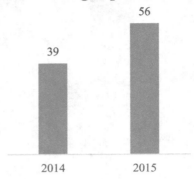

Source: Ministry of Justice.

Number of persons prosecuted for trafficking in persons, by sex, 2014 – 2015

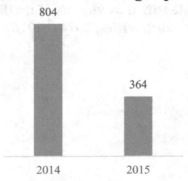

Source: Ministry of Justice.

Number of persons convicted of trafficking in persons, by sex, 2014 – 2015

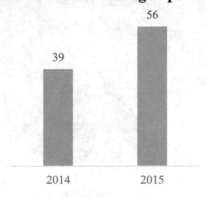

Source: Ministry of Justice.

Victims

Number of victims of trafficking in persons detected, by age and sex, 2014 – 2015

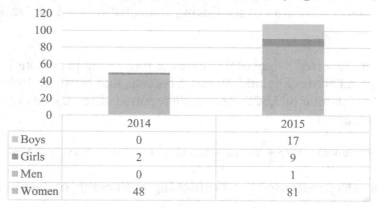

	2014	2015
■ Boys	0	17
■ Girls	2	9
■ Men	0	1
■ Women	48	81

Source: Ministry of the Interior.

Number of victims of trafficking in persons detected, by form of exploitation, 2014 – 2015

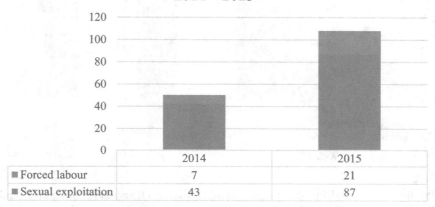

	2014	2015
■ Forced labour	7	21
■ Sexual exploitation	43	87

Source: Ministry of the Interior.

Citizenships of persons identified as victims of trafficking in persons by state authorities, 2014 – 2015

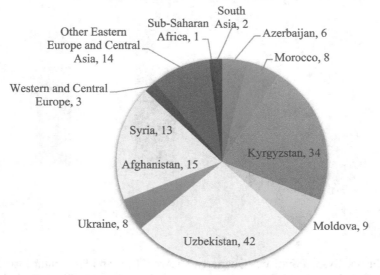

Source: Ministry of the Interior.

−The United Kingdom of Great Britain and Northern Ireland−

The current legislation on trafficking in persons in The United Kingdom of Great Britain and Northern Ireland covers all forms of trafficking indicated in the UN Trafficking in Persons Protocol.

The United Kingdom reported a total of 937 cases of trafficking in persons between April 2015 and March 2016 spread across England, Wales, Scotland, and Northern Ireland. Between April 2016 and March 2017, a total of 2,325 cases were reported. The majority of cases were located in England and Wales.

Source: The Office for National Statistics, Police Scotland, and the Police Service of Northern Ireland.

Number of persons prosecuted for Trafficking in Persons, by location, 2014 – 2016

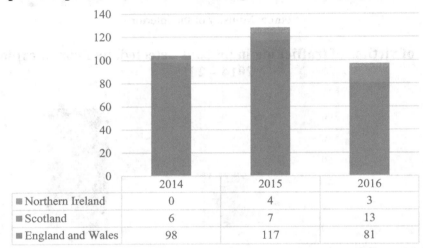

	2014	2015	2016
■ Northern Ireland	0	4	3
■ Scotland	6	7	13
■ England and Wales	98	117	81

Source: Published Criminal Justice System Statistics, Crown Office and Procurator Fiscal Service, Police Scotland, and the Public Prosecution Service/Police Service of Northern Ireland.

Number of persons convicted of Trafficking in Persons, by location, 2014 – 2016

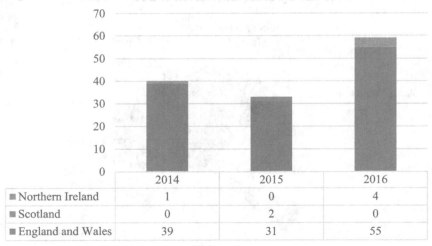

	2014	2015	2016
■ Northern Ireland	1	0	4
■ Scotland	0	2	0
■ England and Wales	39	31	55

Source: Criminal Justice System Statistics Quarterly, Crown Office and Procurator Fiscal Service, Police Scotland, and the Public Prosecution Service/Police Service of Northern Ireland.

Victims

Number of victims of Trafficking in Persons detected, by age and sex, 2014 – 2016

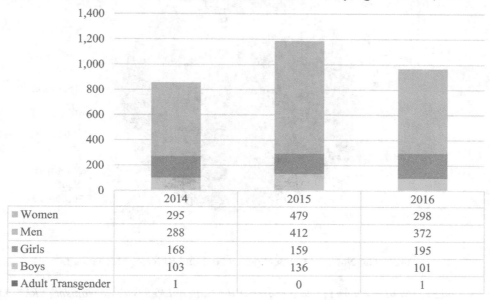

	2014	2015	2016
Women	295	479	298
Men	288	412	372
Girls	168	159	195
Boys	103	136	101
Adult Transgender	1	0	1

Source: The National Crime Agency National Referral Mechanism.

Number of victims of Trafficking in Persons detected, by form of exploitation, 2014 – 2016

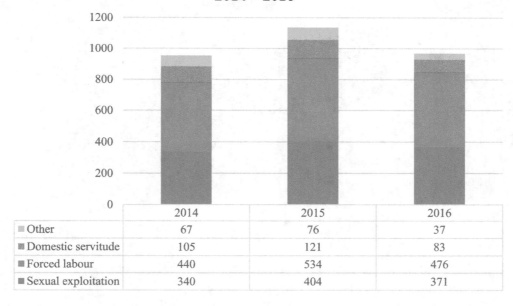

	2014	2015	2016
Other	67	76	37
Domestic servitude	105	121	83
Forced labour	440	534	476
Sexual exploitation	340	404	371

Source: The National Crime Agency National Referral Mechanism.

Citizenships of persons identified as victims of Trafficking in Persons, 2014 – 2016

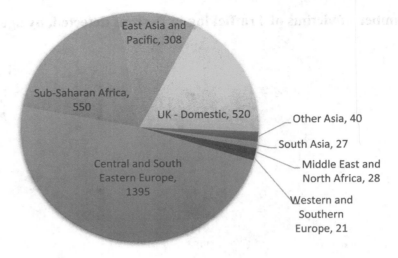

Source: The National Crime Agency National Referral Mechanism.

Disclaimer for Country Profile: Where the data source is the National Referral Mechanism (NRM), identified victims are counted in the year in which they were referred into the NRM (i.e. 31 December 2016), rather than the year in which a conclusive grounds decision was made on their victim status (i.e. 1 January 2017). As the decision-making process is continuous, the number of identified victims was correct as of 7 July 2017, but will rise as further decisions are made. Therefore all listed figures should be treated as a changeable snapshot in time, and do not represent the conclusive number of victims per year.

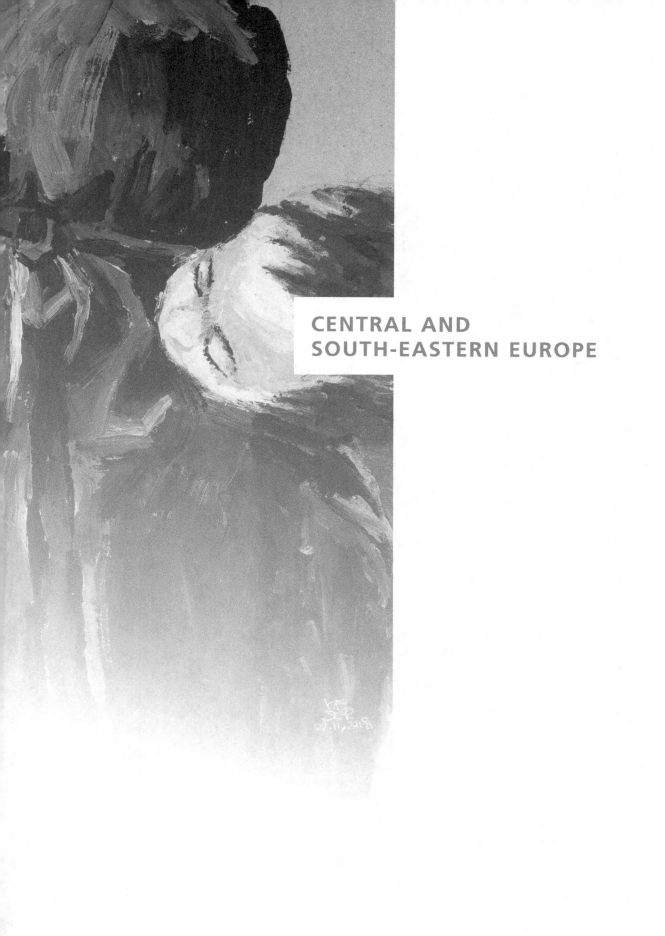

CENTRAL AND SOUTH-EASTERN EUROPE

–Bosnia and Herzegovina–

The current legislation on trafficking in persons in Bosnia and Herzegovina covers all forms of trafficking indicated in the UN Trafficking in Persons Protocol.

Investigations and suspects

Number of cases of trafficking in persons recorded, 2014 –2017

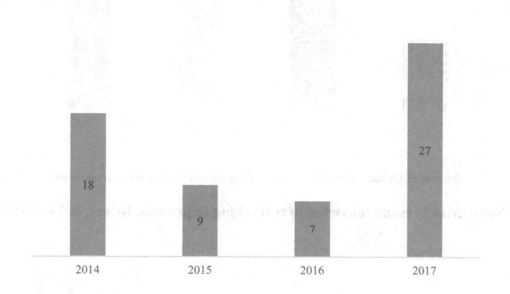

Source: High Judicial and Prosecutorial Council of Bosnia and Herzegovina.

Number of persons brought into formal contact with the police and/or criminal justice system because they have been suspected of, arrested for or cautioned for trafficking in persons, by sex**, 2014 –2017

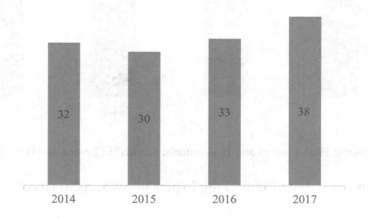

Source: High Judicial and Prosecutorial Council of Bosnia and Herzegovina.

**Note: Formal contact with the police and/or criminal justice system may include persons suspected, arrested, or cautioned at the national level.

Number of persons prosecuted for trafficking in persons, by sex, 2014 –2017

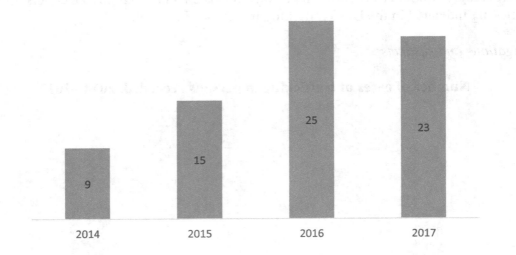

Source: High Judicial and Prosecutorial Council of Bosnia and Herzegovina.

Number of persons convicted of trafficking in persons, by sex, 2014 –2017

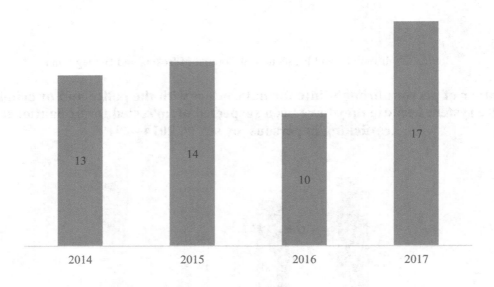

Source: High Judicial and Prosecutorial Council of Bosnia and Herzegovina.

All of the persons convicted of trafficking in persons were nationals of Bosnia and Herzegovina.

Source: Ministry of Security

Victims

Number of victims of trafficking in persons detected, by age and sex, 2014 –2017

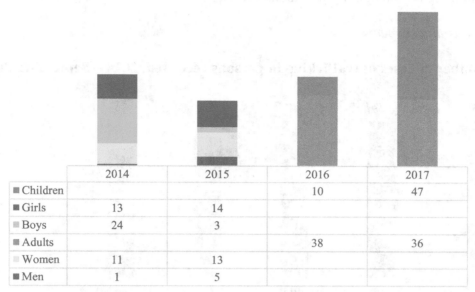

	2014	2015	2016	2017
■ Children			10	47
■ Girls	13	14		
■ Boys	24	3		
■ Adults			38	36
■ Women	11	13		
■ Men	1	5		

Source: Situation Reports on Trafficking in Human Beings in Bosnia and Herzegovina

Number of victims of trafficking in persons detected, by form of exploitation, 2014 – September 2017

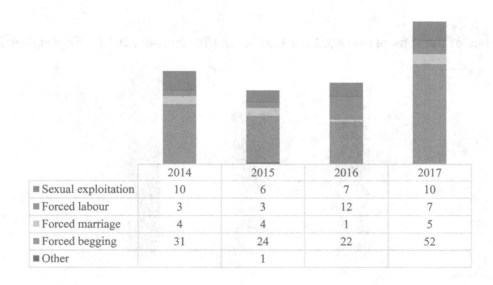

	2014	2015	2016	2017
■ Sexual exploitation	10	6	7	10
■ Forced labour	3	3	12	7
■ Forced marriage	4	4	1	5
■ Forced begging	31	24	22	52
■ Other		1		

Source: Situation Reports on Trafficking in Human Beings in Bosnia and Herzegovina.

All of the detected victims were nationals of Bosnia and Herzegovina and most were trafficked domestically. Three of the detected victims were trafficked internationally and repatriated from other countries in Central and Eastern Europe.

Source: Situation Reports on Trafficking in Human Beings in Bosnia and Herzegovina, Ministry of Security.

The current legislation on trafficking in persons in Bulgaria covers all forms of trafficking indicated in the UN Trafficking in Persons Protocol.

Investigations and suspects

Number of cases of trafficking in persons recorded, 2014 – September 2017

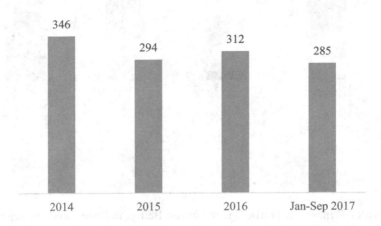

Source: Supreme Cassation Prosecution Office.

Number of persons prosecuted for trafficking in persons, 2014 – September 2017

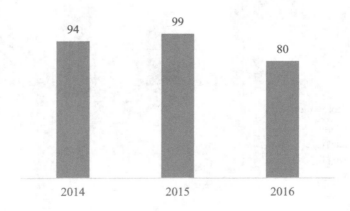

Source: Supreme Cassation Prosecution Office.

Number of persons convicted of trafficking in persons, 2014 – September 2017

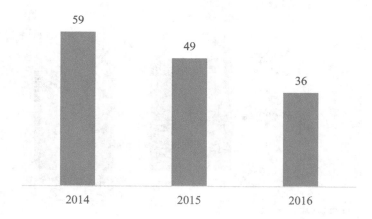

Source: Supreme Cassation Prosecution Office.

While this information is not explicitly provided by the Office of the Prosecutor, it should be noted that almost all the suspects or accused traffickers are Bulgarian nationals. Within the last four to five years there have not been more than four foreign citizens whom have been arrested for trafficking in Bulgaria.

Source: The Unified Database System for Crime Victims.

Victims

Number of victims of trafficking in persons detected, by age and sex**, 2014 – September 2017

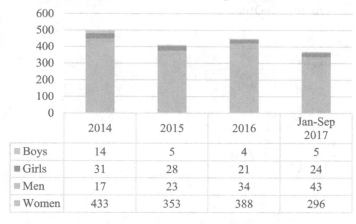

	2014	2015	2016	Jan-Sep 2017
Boys	14	5	4	5
Girls	31	28	21	24
Men	17	23	34	43
Women	433	353	388	296

Women Men Girls Boys

Source: Supreme Cassation Prosecution Office.

**Provided data are accumulated numbers of victims in criminal proceedings which may not be concluded within a given year.

Number of victims of trafficking in persons detected, by form of exploitation**, 2014 – September 2017

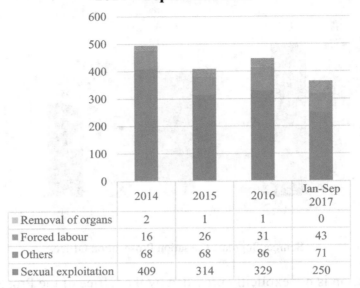

	2014	2015	2016	Jan-Sep 2017
Removal of organs	2	1	1	0
Forced labour	16	26	31	43
Others	68	68	86	71
Sexual exploitation	409	314	329	250

Source: Supreme Cassation Prosecution Office.

**Provided data are accumulated numbers of victims in criminal proceedings which may not be concluded within a given year.

All victims of trafficking in persons for the specified time period have been identified as Bulgarian nationals. However, according to the data of the Secretariat of the National Commission for Combatting Trafficking in Human Beings, investigations have been conducted where there are presumed trafficking cases and where the presumed victims were thought to be foreigners of EU countries or third country nationals.

Source: Supreme Cassation Prosecution Office.

−Croatia−

The current legislation on trafficking in persons in Croatia covers all forms of trafficking indicated in the UN Trafficking in Persons Protocol.

Investigations and suspects

Number of cases of trafficking in persons recorded, 2014 – September 2017

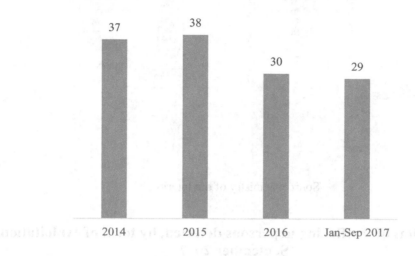

Source: Ministry of the Interior.

Number of persons brought into formal contact with the police and/or criminal justice system because they have been suspected of, arrested for or cautioned for trafficking in persons, by sex**, 2014 – September 2017

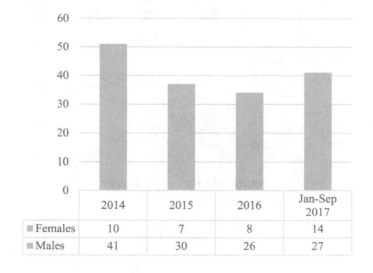

	2014	2015	2016	Jan-Sep 2017
Females	10	7	8	14
Males	41	30	26	27

Source: Ministry of the Interior.

**Note: Formal contact with the police and/or criminal justice system may include persons suspected, arrested, or cautioned at the national level.

Victims

Number of victims of trafficking in persons detected, by age and sex, 2014 – September 2017

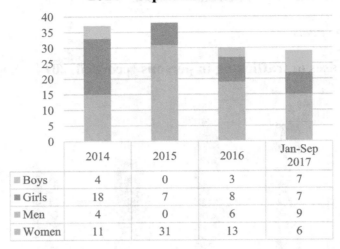

	2014	2015	2016	Jan-Sep 2017
▪ Boys	4	0	3	7
▪ Girls	18	7	8	7
▪ Men	4	0	6	9
▪ Women	11	31	13	6

Source: Ministry of the Interior.

Number of victims of trafficking in persons detected, by form of exploitation, 2014 – September 2017

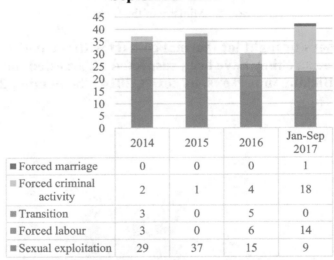

	2014	2015	2016	Jan-Sep 2017
▪ Forced marriage	0	0	0	1
▪ Forced criminal activity	2	1	4	18
▪ Transition	3	0	5	0
▪ Forced labour	3	0	6	14
▪ Sexual exploitation	29	37	15	9

Source: Ministry of the Interior.

Citizenships of persons identified as victims of trafficking in persons by state authorities, 2014 – September 2017

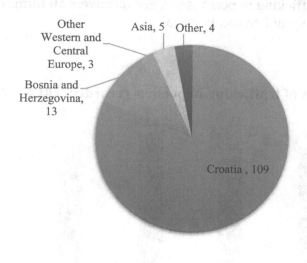

Source: Ministry of the Interior.

Identified Croatian victims of trafficking in persons who were trafficked internationally were repatriated from Bosnia and Herzegovina and the FYR of Macedonia.

Source: Ministry of the Interior.

– Czechia –

The current legislation on trafficking in persons in Czechia covers all forms of trafficking indicated in the UN Trafficking in Persons Protocol.

Investigations and suspects

Number of cases of trafficking in persons recorded, 2014 –2017**

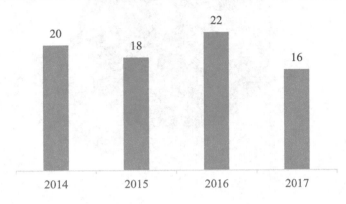

Source: Police of the Czech Republic.

**It is important to note that since 2016 there has been a change in the method of counting the number of prosecuted persons where all criminal acts committed by offenders are counted, including concurrent criminal acts. This change may influence the statistics and thus the statistics since the year 2016 are not fully comparable to previous periods.

Number of persons brought into formal contact with the police and/or criminal justice system because they have been suspected of, arrested for or cautioned for trafficking in persons, by sex**, 2014 –2017

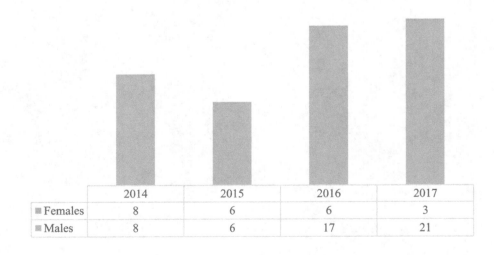

	2014	2015	2016	2017
■ Females	8	6	6	3
■ Males	8	6	17	21

Source: Police of the Czech Republic.

**Note: Formal contact with the police and/or criminal justice system may
include persons suspected, arrested, or cautioned at the national level.
The Police of the Czech Republic define this as the beginning of their investigation into a case.

Number of persons prosecuted for trafficking in persons, by sex, 2014 – 2017

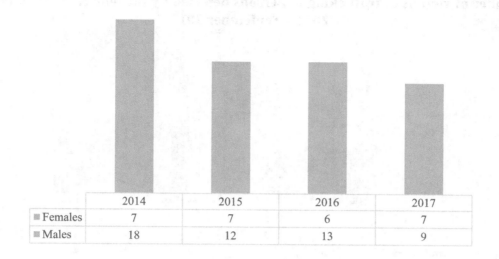

	2014	2015	2016	2017
▪ Females	7	7	6	7
▪ Males	18	12	13	9

Source: Prosecutor's Office Statistical Data Sheets.

Number of persons convicted of trafficking in persons, by sex, 2014 – 2017

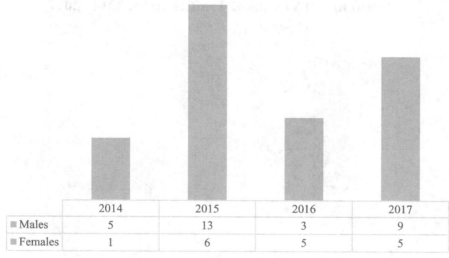

	2014	2015	2016	2017
▪ Males	5	13	3	9
▪ Females	1	6	5	5

Source: Prosecutor's Office Statistical Data Sheets.

The majority of those persons convicted of trafficking in persons were citizens of Czechia. A small number were from other European countries.

Source: Prosecutor's Office Statistical Data Sheets.

Victims

Number of victims of trafficking in persons detected by the police, by age and sex, 2014 – September 2017

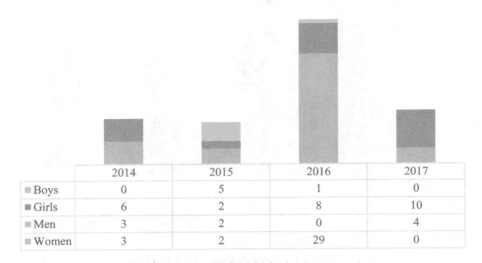

	2014	2015	2016	2017
■ Boys	0	5	1	0
■ Girls	6	2	8	10
■ Men	3	2	0	4
■ Women	3	2	29	0

Source: Police of the Czech Republic.

Number of victims of trafficking in persons detected by the Programme of Victims of Trafficking**, 2014 –2017

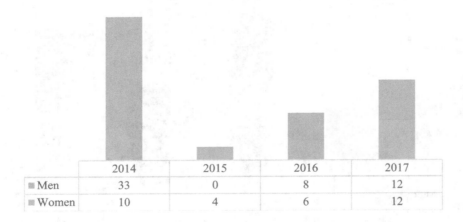

	2014	2015	2016	2017
■ Men	33	0	8	12
■ Women	10	4	6	12

Source: Programme of Support and Protection of Victims of Trafficking (Ministry of the Interior).

**The Programme of Support and Protection of Victims of Trafficking of the Ministry of the Interior refers to the victims who were interested in services within a specialized program designed for victims of trafficking in human beings over the age of eighteen.

Additional Information

In addition to the statistics provided by the Police of the Czech Republic and the Programme of Victims of Trafficking, the Ministry of Justice also maintained a record of persons identified as victims of trafficking in persons for 2014 – 2016. During this period, the Ministry of Justice reported a total of nine child victims and 14 adult victims, mostly females.

Source: Court Statistical Data Sheets.

Number of victims of trafficking in persons detected by the Programme of Victims of Trafficking, by form of exploitation, 2014 –2017

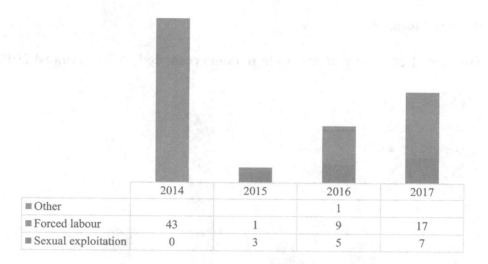

	2014	2015	2016	2017
■ Other			1	
■ Forced labour	43	1	9	17
■ Sexual exploitation	0	3	5	7

Source: Programme of the Support and Protection of Victims of Trafficking (Ministry of the Interior).

Additional Information

The Ministry of Justice recorded persons identified as victims of trafficking in persons for sexual exploitation purposes between 2014 and 2016. During this period, the Ministry of Justice recorded a total of 23 detected victims, nine of which were children.

Source: Court Statistical Data Sheets.

Citizenships of persons identified as victims of trafficking in persons by state authorities, 2014 –2017

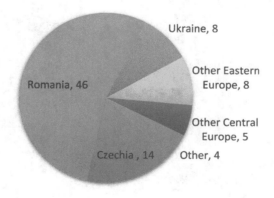

Source: Programme of the Support and Protection of Victims of Trafficking (Ministry of the Interior).

Four nationals of Czechia were repatriated from Western Europe between 2014 and 2016.

Source: Programme of the Support and Protection of Victims of Trafficking (Ministry of the Interior).

—Estonia—

The current legislation on trafficking in persons in Estonia covers all forms of trafficking indicated in the UN Trafficking in Persons Protocol.

Investigations and suspects

Number of cases of trafficking in persons recorded, 2014 – August 2017

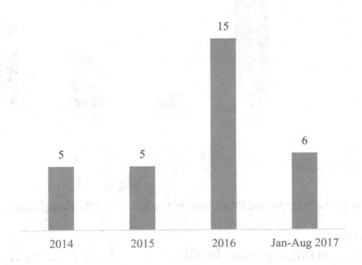

Source: Register of Criminal Proceedings.

Number of persons brought into formal contact with the police and/or criminal justice system because they have been suspected of, arrested for or cautioned for trafficking in persons, by sex**, 2014 – August 2017

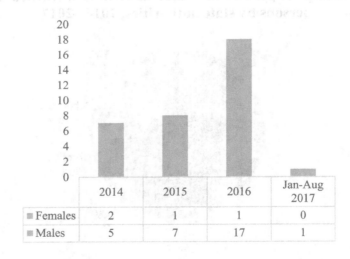

	2014	2015	2016	Jan-Aug 2017
Females	2	1	1	0
Males	5	7	17	1

Source: Police and Border Guard Board Procedural Information System.

**Note: Officials in Estonia define this statistic of persons suspected of trafficking in persons and data is taken from interrogation protocols.

Number of persons prosecuted for trafficking in persons, by sex, 2014 – August 2017

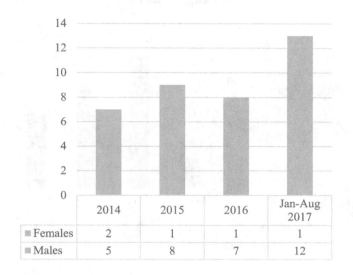

	2014	2015	2016	Jan-Aug 2017
Females	2	1	1	1
Males	5	8	7	12

Source: Register of Criminal Proceedings.

During the reporting period, more males than females were convicted of trafficking in persons. Two men were convicted in 2014, four men in 2015, 10 men and one woman in 2016, and one man in the first eight months of 2017. Of those convicted, 13 were citizens of Estonia while five were foreign.

Source: Information System of Courts.

Victims

Number of victims of trafficking in persons detected, by age and sex, 2014 – August 2017

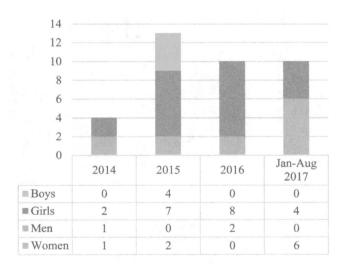

	2014	2015	2016	Jan-Aug 2017
Boys	0	4	0	0
Girls	2	7	8	4
Men	1	0	2	0
Women	1	2	0	6

Source: National Social Insurance Board.

Number of victims of trafficking in persons detected, by form of exploitation, 2014 – August 2017

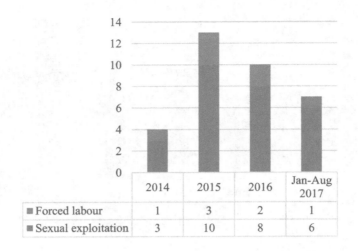

	2014	2015	2016	Jan-Aug 2017
■ Forced labour	1	3	2	1
■ Sexual exploitation	3	10	8	6

Source: National Social Insurance Board.

The majority of victims detected by national authorities were citizens of Estonia. Other victims came from Asia and other European countries. Of the Estonian citizens trafficked, most were trafficked domestically.

Source: National Social Insurance Board.

The current legislation on trafficking in persons in Hungary covers all forms of trafficking indicated in the UN Trafficking in Persons Protocol. In addition, authorities make use of a list other articles of the criminal code to prosecute offences related to trafficking in persons such as prostitution and child pornography.

Investigations and suspects

Number of cases of trafficking in persons and related offences recorded**, 2014 – 2016

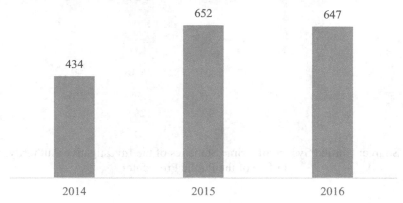

Source: Unified System of Crime Statistics of the Investigative Authority,
Office of the Public Prosecutor.

Number of persons brought into formal contact with the police and/or criminal justice system because they have been suspected of, arrested for or cautioned for trafficking in persons and related offences, by sex**, 2014 – October 2017

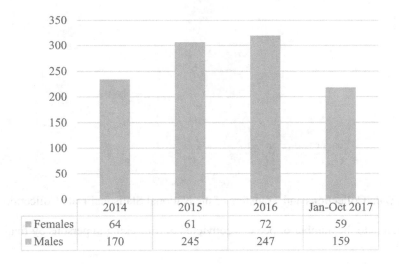

	2014	2015	2016	Jan-Oct 2017
Females	64	61	72	59
Males	170	245	247	159

Source: Unified System of Crime Statistics of the Investigative Authority,
Office of the Public Prosecutor.

**Note: Formal contact with the police and/or criminal justice system may
include persons suspected, arrested, or cautioned at the national level.

Number of persons prosecuted for trafficking in persons and related offences, by sex, 2014 – October 2017

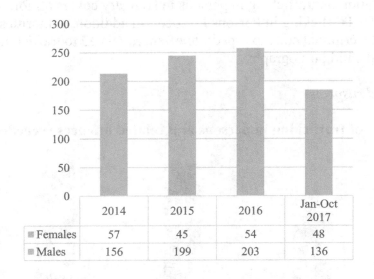

	2014	2015	2016	Jan-Oct 2017
■ Females	57	45	54	48
■ Males	156	199	203	136

Source: Unified System of Crime Statistics of the Investigative Authority, Office of the Public Prosecutor.

Number of persons convicted of trafficking in persons and related offences**, by sex, 2014 – March 2017

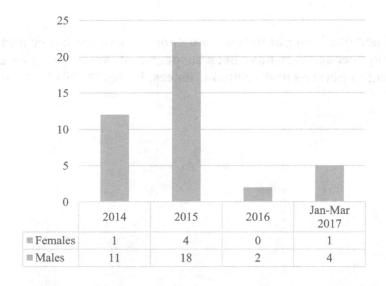

	2014	2015	2016	Jan-Mar 2017
■ Females	1	4	0	1
■ Males	11	18	2	4

Source: Data Collections and Transfers of the National Statistical Data Collection Program.

**This data refers to the number of persons convicted of trafficking in persons by final court decision.

National authorities in Hungary reported that all persons convicted of trafficking in persons and related offences were citizens of Hungary.

Source: Data Collections and Transfers of the National Statistical Data Collection Program.

Victims

Number of victims of trafficking in persons and related offences detected, by age and sex, 2014 – October 2017

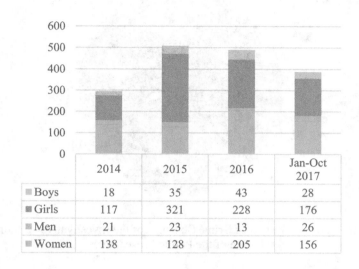

	2014	2015	2016	Jan-Oct 2017
■ Boys	18	35	43	28
■ Girls	117	321	228	176
■ Men	21	23	13	26
■ Women	138	128	205	156

Source: Unified System of Crime Statistics of the Investigative Authority, Office of the Public Prosecutor.

Number of victims of trafficking in persons and related offences detected, by form of exploitation, 2014 – October 2017

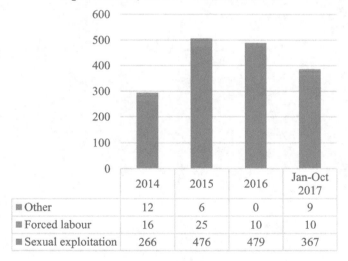

	2014	2015	2016	Jan-Oct 2017
■ Other	12	6	0	9
■ Forced labour	16	25	10	10
■ Sexual exploitation	266	476	479	367

Source: Unified System of Crime Statistics of the Investigative Authority, Office of the Public Prosecutor.

Citizenships of persons identified as victims of trafficking in persons and related offences by state authorities, 2014 – October 2017

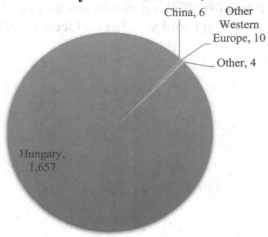

China, 6 Other Western Europe, 10

Other, 4

Hungary, 1,657

Source: Unified System of Crime Statistics of the Investigative Authority, Office of the Public Prosecutor.

The current legislation on trafficking in persons in Latvia covers all forms of trafficking indicated in the UN Trafficking in Persons Protocol. Latvia uses both a general human trafficking law and a law against "sending a person for sexual exploitation" to prosecute cases of trafficking in persons.

Investigations and suspects

Number of cases of trafficking in persons recorded**, 2014 –2017

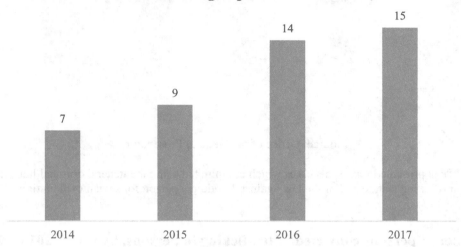

Source: State Police Anti-Trafficking Unit.

**Data presented represents cases which are initiated using the general criminal human trafficking statute and/or the law against "sending a person for sexual exploitation."

Number of persons brought into formal contact with the police and/or criminal justice system because they have been suspected of trafficking in persons, by sex**, 2014 – 2017

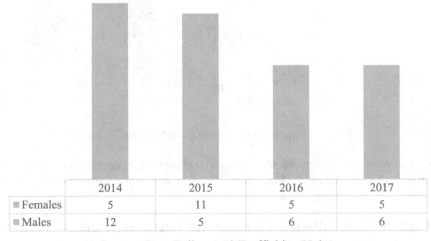

	2014	2015	2016	2017
■ Females	5	11	5	5
■ Males	12	5	6	6

Source: State Police Anti-Trafficking Unit.

**Data presented represents persons under a suspicion of general criminal human trafficking and/or "sending a person for sexual exploitation."

Number of persons prosecuted for trafficking in persons, by sex**, 2014 – 2017

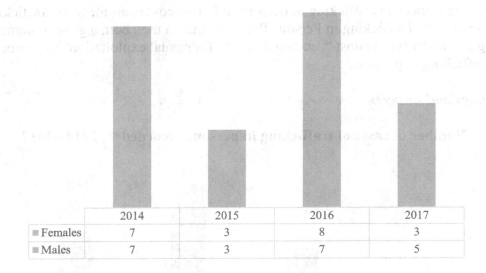

	2014	2015	2016	2017
■ Females	7	3	8	3
■ Males	7	3	7	5

Source: Office of the General Prosecutor.

**Data presented represents cases which are initiated using the general criminal human trafficking statute and/or the law against "sending a person for sexual exploitation."

Number of persons convicted of trafficking in persons, by sex**, 2014 – 2017

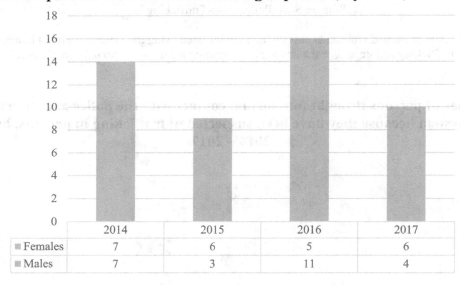

	2014	2015	2016	2017
■ Females	7	6	5	6
■ Males	7	3	11	4

Source: Court Information System.

**Data presented represents persons convicted under the general criminal human trafficking statute and/or the law against "sending a person for sexual exploitation."

Between 2014 and 2017, 43 citizens of Latvia were convicted of trafficking in persons. A smaller number came from other or unknown countries.

Source: Court Information System.

Number of victims of trafficking in persons detected, by age and sex, 2014 – 2017

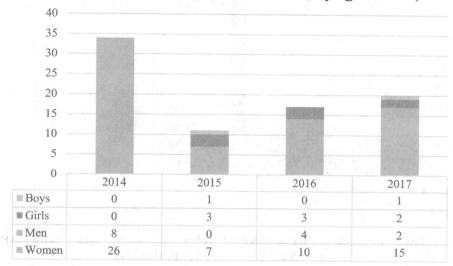

	2014	2015	2016	2017
■ Boys	0	1	0	1
■ Girls	0	3	3	2
■ Men	8	0	4	2
■ Women	26	7	10	15

Source: Ministry of Welfare,
mandated NGOs "Shelter "Safe House"" and "Centre MARTA",
and the State Police Anti-Trafficking Unit.

Number of victims of trafficking in persons detected, by form of exploitation, 2014 – 2017

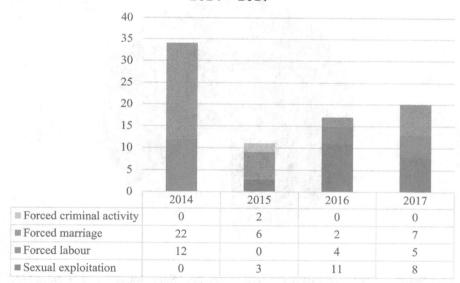

	2014	2015	2016	2017
■ Forced criminal activity	0	2	0	0
■ Forced marriage	22	6	2	7
■ Forced labour	12	0	4	5
■ Sexual exploitation	0	3	11	8

Source: Ministry of Welfare,
mandated NGOs "Shelter "Safe House"" and "Centre MARTA",
and the State Police Anti-Trafficking Unit.

National authorities reported that between 2014 and 2017, 79 victims were citizens of Latvia. Others were citizens of other Eastern European and Central Asian countries.

Source: Ministry of Welfare, mandated NGOs "Shelter "Safe House"" and "Centre MARTA", and the State Police Anti-Trafficking Unit.

Identified victims of trafficking, by type of trafficking, 2014 –2017

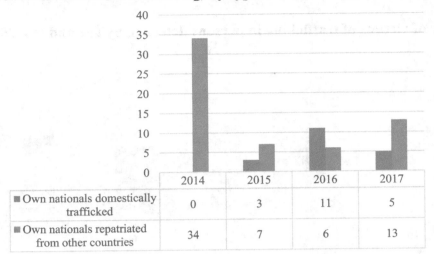

	2014	2015	2016	2017
■ Own nationals domestically trafficked	0	3	11	5
■ Own nationals repatriated from other countries	34	7	6	13

Source: Ministry of Welfare, mandated NGOs "Shelter "Safe House"" and "Centre MARTA",
and the State Police Anti-Trafficking Unit.

Countries from which identified victims were repatriated, 2014 – 2017

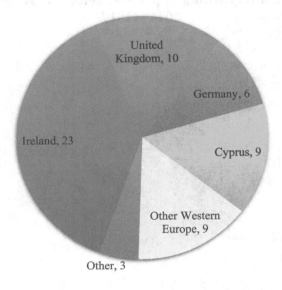

Source: Ministry of Welfare, mandated NGOs "Shelter "Safe House"" and "Centre MARTA",
and the State Police Anti-Trafficking Unit.

—Montenegro—

The current legislation on trafficking in persons in Montenegro covers all forms of trafficking indicated in the UN Trafficking in Persons Protocol.

Investigations and suspects

In 2014, national authorities in Montenegro recorded two cases of trafficking in persons. One male from Central Europe was prosecuted and convicted for the crime.

Source: National Office for the Fight Against Trafficking in Human Beings.

Victims

National authorities in Montenegro identified two presumed victims in 2014 (one female child and one female adult victim). Between January 2015 and May 2017, seven female child victims were identified. The majority of victims were trafficked for the purpose of forced marriages. A smaller number were trafficked for sexual exploitation or forced labour. The victims identified were citizens of Montenegro and Central European countries. The victims of Montenegrin citizenship were trafficked domestically.

Source: National Office for the Fight Against Trafficking in Human Beings.

−Poland−

The current legislation on trafficking in persons in Poland covers all forms of trafficking indicated in the UN Trafficking in Persons Protocol.

Investigations and suspects

Number of cases of trafficking in persons and related offences recorded, 2014 −2017

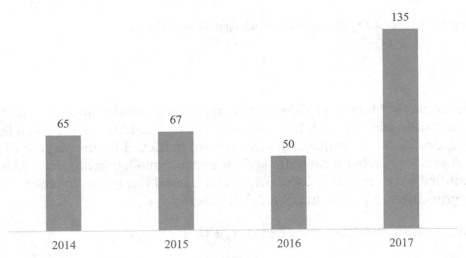

Source: Report on coordination of preliminary proceedings with a view to trafficking in persons 2014, 2015 and 2016, and data form the Office of the Prosecutor.

Number of persons brought into formal contact with the police and/or criminal justice system because they have been suspected of trafficking in persons and related offences, by sex, 2014 −2017

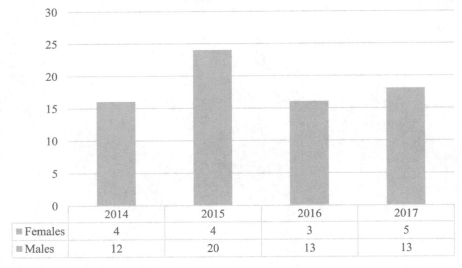

	2014	2015	2016	2017
▪ Females	4	4	3	5
▪ Males	12	20	13	13

Source: Combined data from the Police and Border Guard.

Number of persons prosecuted for trafficking in persons and related offences, 2014 –2017

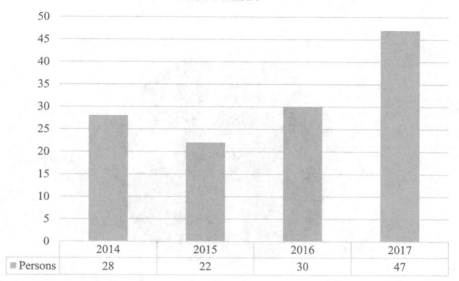

	2014	2015	2016	2017
■ Persons	28	22	30	47

Source: Report on coordination of preliminary proceedings with a view to trafficking in persons 2014, 2015 and 2016, and data form the Office of the Prosecutor.

Number of persons convicted of trafficking in persons and related offences, by sex, 2014 – 2016

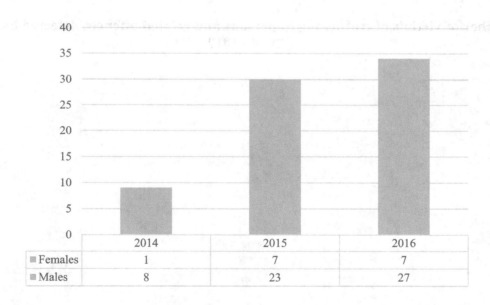

	2014	2015	2016
■ Females	1	7	7
■ Males	8	23	27

Source: Ministry of the Interior and Administration

Citizenships of persons convicted of trafficking in persons and related offences, 2014 – 2016

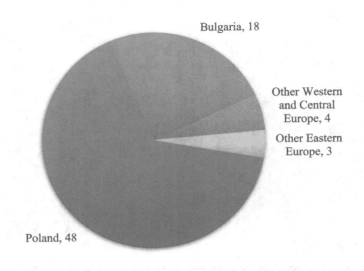

Source: Ministry of the Interior and Administration

Victims

Number of victims of trafficking in persons and related offences detected by age, 2014 –2017

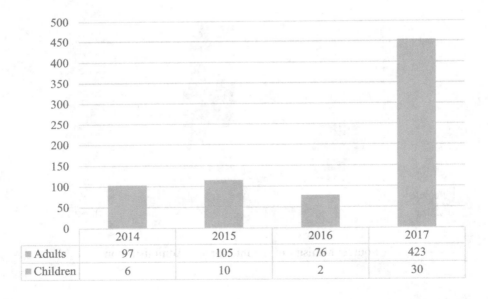

	2014	2015	2016	2017
Adults	97	105	76	423
Children	6	10	2	30

Source: Report on coordination of preliminary proceedings with a view to trafficking in persons 2014, 2015 and 2016, and data form the Office of the Prosecutor.

Number of victims of trafficking in persons and related offences detected, by form of exploitation, 2014 –2017

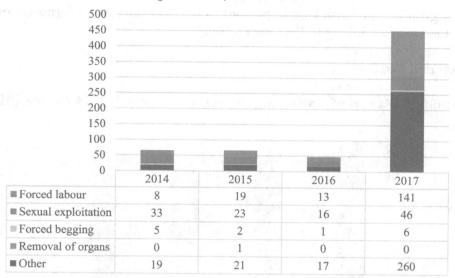

	2014	2015	2016	2017
■ Forced labour	8	19	13	141
■ Sexual exploitation	33	23	16	46
■ Forced begging	5	2	1	6
■ Removal of organs	0	1	0	0
■ Other	19	21	17	260

Source: Report on coordination of preliminary proceedings with a view to trafficking in persons 2014, 2015 and 2016, and data form the Office of the Prosecutor.

Citizenships of persons identified as victims of trafficking in persons and related offences by state authorities, 2014 –2017

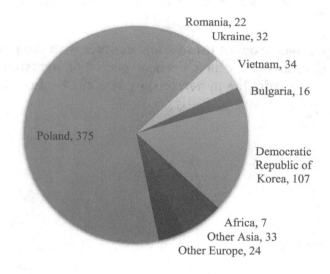

Source: Report on coordination of preliminary proceedings with a view to trafficking in persons 2014, 2015 and 2016, and data form the Office of the Prosecutor.

Additional information

The reporting authorities flag that the increased numbers of offences in 2017 can be attributed to an increase in the rate of prosecution and does not necessarily correlate to a larger scale of trafficking in persons in Poland

–Romania–

The current legislation on trafficking in persons in Romania covers all forms of trafficking indicated in the UN Trafficking in Persons Protocol.

Investigations and suspects

Number of cases of trafficking in persons recorded, 2014 – June 2017

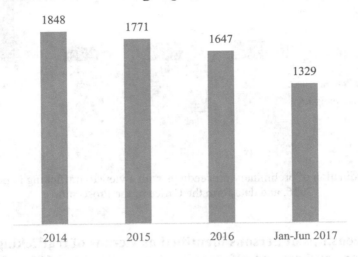

Source: Service for Combatting Organized Crime – DIICOT.

Number of persons brought into formal contact with the police and/or criminal justice system because they have been suspected of, arrested for or cautioned for trafficking in persons, by sex, 2014 – June 2017

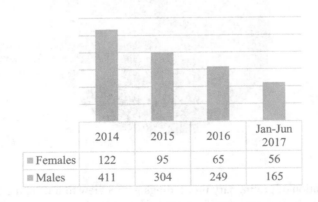

	2014	2015	2016	Jan-Jun 2017
▪ Females	122	95	65	56
▪ Males	411	304	249	165

Source: Service for Combatting Organized Crime – DIICOT.

Additional information
Of those persons in the above category, 279 were arrested in 2014, 232 in 2015, 186 in 2016, and 140 in the first six months of 2017.

Source: Service for Combatting Organized Crime – DIICOT.

Number of persons prosecuted for trafficking in persons, by sex, 2014 – June 2017

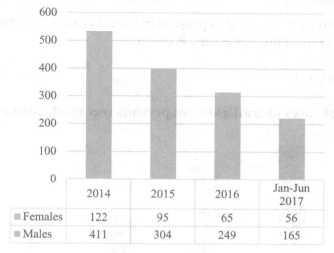

	2014	2015	2016	Jan-Jun 2017
▪ Females	122	95	65	56
▪ Males	411	304	249	165

Source: Service for Combatting Organized Crime – DIICOT.

National authorities reported that the majority of persons convicted of trafficking in persons between January 2014 and June 2017 were Romanian nationals. Other persons convicted were nationals of Turkey, Hungary, and Serbia.

Source: Service for Combatting Organized Crime – DIICOT.

Victims

Number of victims of trafficking in persons detected, by age and sex, 2014 – June 2017

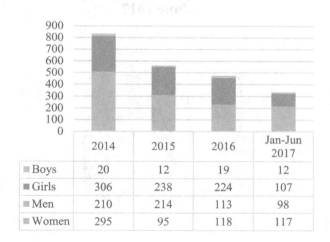

	2014	2015	2016	Jan-Jun 2017
▪ Boys	20	12	19	12
▪ Girls	306	238	224	107
▪ Men	210	214	113	98
▪ Women	295	95	118	117

Source: Service for Combatting Organized Crime – DIICOT.

National authorities reported that the majority of persons identified as victims of trafficking in persons between January 2014 and June 2017 were trafficked for sexual exploitation. A smaller number were trafficked for purposes of forced labour or begging.

Source: Service for Combatting Organized Crime – DIICOT.

The current legislation on trafficking in persons in Serbia covers all forms of trafficking indicated in the UN Trafficking in Persons Protocol.

Investigations and suspects

Number of cases of trafficking in persons recorded, 2014 – June 2017

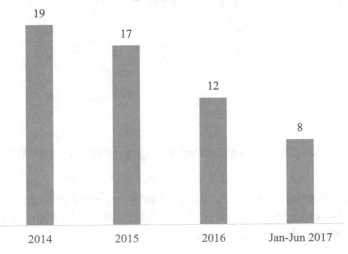

Source: Ministry of the Interior, General Police Directorate, and Border Police Directorate.

Number of persons brought into formal contact with the police and/or criminal justice system because they have been suspected of trafficking in persons, by sex**, 2014 – June 2017

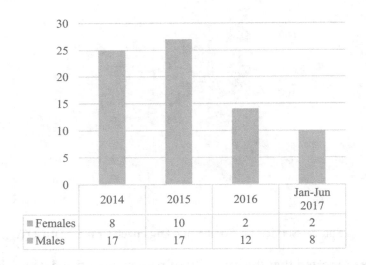

	2014	2015	2016	Jan-Jun 2017
■ Females	8	10	2	2
■ Males	17	17	12	8

Source: Ministry of the Interior, General Police Directorate, and Border Police Directorate.

National officials in Serbia reported that between January 2014 and June 2017, the majority of persons convicted of trafficking in persons were Serbian nationals.

Source: Ministry of the Interior, General Police Directorate, and Border Police Directorate.

Number of victims of trafficking in persons detected, by age and sex, 2014 – June 2017

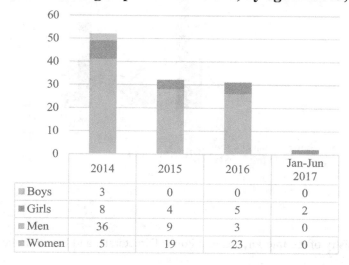

	2014	2015	2016	Jan-Jun 2017
Boys	3	0	0	0
Girls	8	4	5	2
Men	36	9	3	0
Women	5	19	23	0

Source: Ministry of the Interior, General Police Directorate, and Border Police Directorate.

Number of victims of trafficking in persons detected, by form of exploitation, 2014 – June 2017

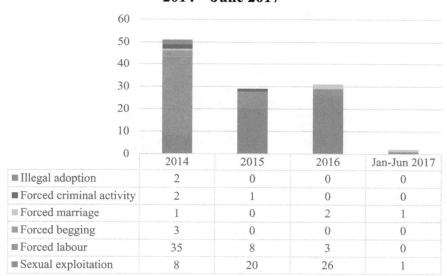

	2014	2015	2016	Jan-Jun 2017
Illegal adoption	2	0	0	0
Forced criminal activity	2	1	0	0
Forced marriage	1	0	2	1
Forced begging	3	0	0	0
Forced labour	35	8	3	0
Sexual exploitation	8	20	26	1

Source: Ministry of the Interior, General Police Directorate, and Border Police Directorate.
All identified victims of trafficking in persons in the indicated period were citizens of Serbia.

Source: Ministry of the Interior, General Police Directorate, and Border Police Directorate.

Identified victims of trafficking, by type of trafficking, 2014 – June 2017

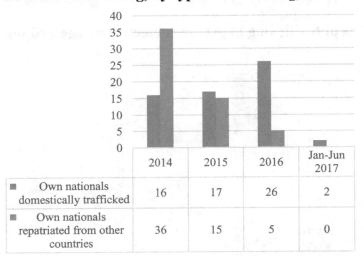

	2014	2015	2016	Jan-Jun 2017
■ Own nationals domestically trafficked	16	17	26	2
■ Own nationals repatriated from other countries	36	15	5	0

Source: Ministry of the Interior, General Police Directorate, and Border Police Directorate.

The current legislation on trafficking in persons in Slovakia covers all forms of trafficking indicated in the UN Trafficking in Persons Protocol.

Investigations and suspects

Number of cases of trafficking in persons recorded, 2014 −2017

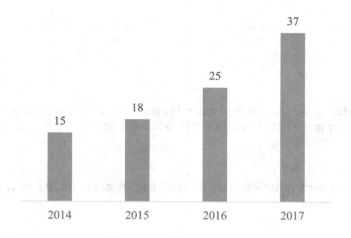

Source: Ministry of the Interior of the Slovak Republic.

Number of persons brought into formal contact with the police and/or criminal justice system because they have been suspected of trafficking in persons, by sex, 2014 −2017

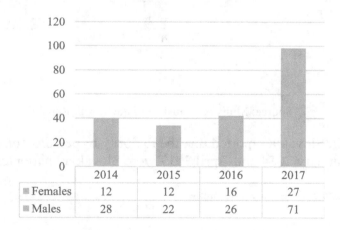

	2014	2015	2016	2017
Females	12	12	16	27
Males	28	22	26	71

Source: National Unit Combating Illegal Migration of the Bureau of Border and Aliens Police of the Presidium of the Police Corps of the Slovak Republic, Ministry of the Interior of the Slovak Republic.

Number of persons prosecuted for trafficking in persons, by sex, 2014 –2017

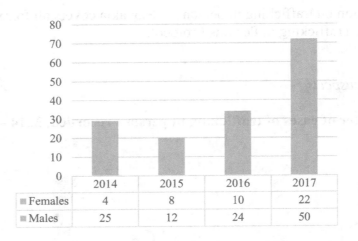

	2014	2015	2016	2017
■ Females	4	8	10	22
■ Males	25	12	24	50

Source: Office of the General Prosecutor, National Unit Combating Illegal Migration
of the Bureau of Border and Aliens Police of the Presidium of the Police Corps of the Slovak Republic.

Number of persons convicted of trafficking in persons, by sex, 2014 –2017

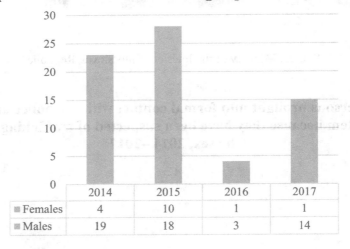

	2014	2015	2016	2017
■ Females	4	10	1	1
■ Males	19	18	3	14

Source: Ministry of Justice of the Slovak Republic.

National officials in Slovakia reported that the majority of persons convicted of trafficking in persons between January 2014 and April 2017 were Slovakian nationals.

Source: Ministry of Justice of the Slovak Republic.

Victims

Number of victims of trafficking in persons detected, by age and sex**, 2014 –2017

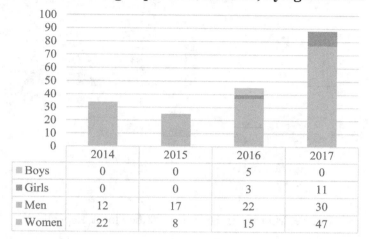

	2014	2015	2016	2017
■ Boys	0	0	5	0
■ Girls	0	0	3	11
■ Men	12	17	22	30
■ Women	22	8	15	47

Source: Ministry of the Interior of the Slovak Republic, National Unit Combating Illegal Migration of the Bureau of Border and Aliens Police of the Presidium of the Police Corps of the Slovak Republic.

**Data refers to participants and non-participants of the Programme for Support and Protection of Victims of Trafficking in Human Beings.

Number of victims of trafficking in persons detected, by form of exploitation**, 2014 –2017

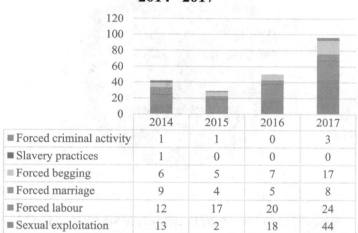

	2014	2015	2016	2017
■ Forced criminal activity	1	1	0	3
■ Slavery practices	1	0	0	0
■ Forced begging	6	5	7	17
■ Forced marriage	9	4	5	8
■ Forced labour	12	17	20	24
■ Sexual exploitation	13	2	18	44

Source: Ministry of the Interior of the Slovak Republic, National Unit Combating Illegal Migration of the Bureau of Border and Aliens Police of the Presidium of the Police Corps of the Slovak Republic.

**Some victims were counted multiple times for being subjected to multiple purposes of trafficking.

The majority of victims identified in the indicated period were citizens of Slovakia. Others were citizens of other Central European countries or from South Asia.

Source: Ministry of the Interior of the Slovak Republic, National Unit Combating Illegal Migration of the Bureau of Border and Aliens Police of the Presidium of the Police Corps of the Slovak Republic.

Identified victims of trafficking, by type of trafficking, 2014 –2017

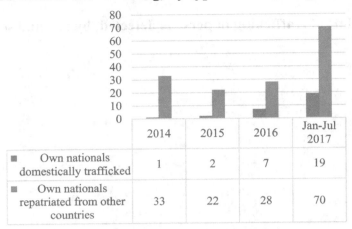

	2014	2015	2016	Jan-Jul 2017
■ Own nationals domestically trafficked	1	2	7	19
■ Own nationals repatriated from other countries	33	22	28	70

Source: Ministry of the Interior of the Slovak Republic.

Countries from which identified victims were repatriated, 2014 –2017

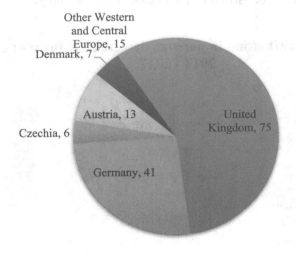

Source: Ministry of the Interior of the Slovak Republic.

The current legislation on trafficking in persons in Slovenia covers all forms of trafficking indicated in the UN Trafficking in Persons Protocol.

Investigations and suspects

Number of cases of trafficking in persons recorded, 2014 – July 2017

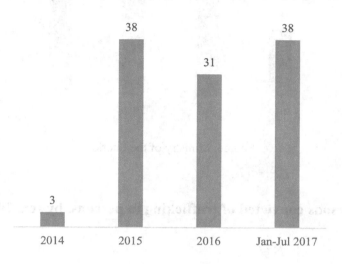

Source: Ministry of the Interior.

Number of persons brought into formal contact with the police and/or criminal justice system because they have been suspected of, arrested for or cautioned for trafficking in persons, by sex**, 2014 – July 2017

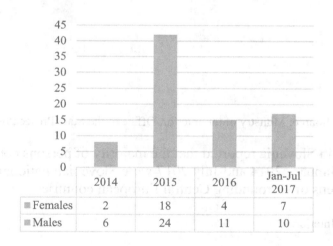

	2014	2015	2016	Jan-Jul 2017
Females	2	18	4	7
Males	6	24	11	10

Source: Ministry of the Interior.

**Note: Formal contact with the police and/or criminal justice system may include persons suspected, arrested, or cautioned at the national level.

Number of persons prosecuted for trafficking in persons, by sex, 2014 – July 2017

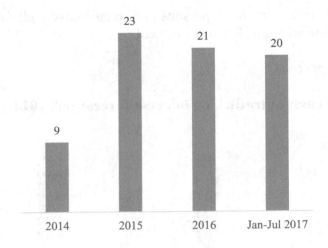

Source: Ministry of the Interior.

Number of persons convicted of trafficking in persons, by sex, 2014 – July 2017

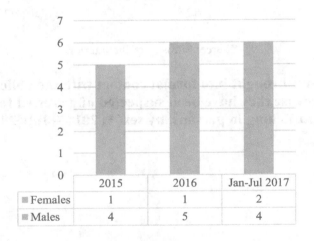

	2015	2016	Jan-Jul 2017
■ Females	1	1	2
■ Males	4	5	4

Source: Ministry of the Interior, Office of the State Prosecutor.

National authorities in Slovenia reported that the majority of persons convicted of trafficking in persons between January 2014 and July 2017 were Slovenian nationals. Other persons convicted were citizens of surrounding Central European countries.

Source: Ministry of the Interior.

Victims

Number of victims of trafficking in persons detected, by age and sex, 2014 – July 2017

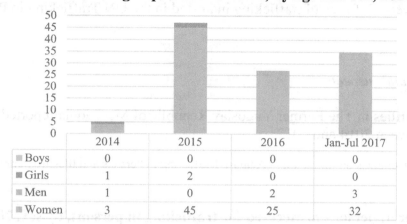

	2014	2015	2016	Jan-Jul 2017
■ Boys	0	0	0	0
■ Girls	1	2	0	0
■ Men	1	0	2	3
■ Women	3	45	25	32

Source: Ministry of the Interior.

Number of victims of trafficking in persons detected, by form of exploitation, 2014 – 2016

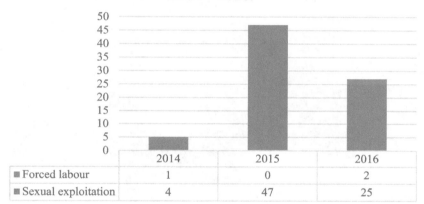

	2014	2015	2016
■ Forced labour	1	0	2
■ Sexual exploitation	4	47	25

Source: Ministry of the Interior.

Citizenships of persons identified as victims of trafficking in persons by state authorities, 2014 – July 2017

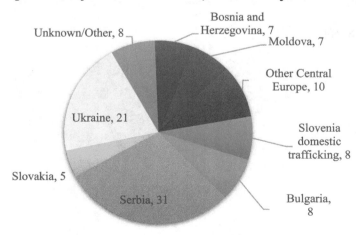

Source: Ministry of the Interior.

−The Former Yugoslav Republic of Macedonia−

The current legislation on trafficking in persons in The Former Yugoslav Republic of Macedonia covers all forms of trafficking indicated in the UN Trafficking in Persons Protocol.

Investigations and suspects

National authorities in The Former Yugoslav Republic of Macedonia reported three cases every year between 2014 and 2017.

Source: National Commission for the Fight Against Trafficking in Persons and Illegal Migration.

Number of persons prosecuted for trafficking in persons, by sex, 2014-2017

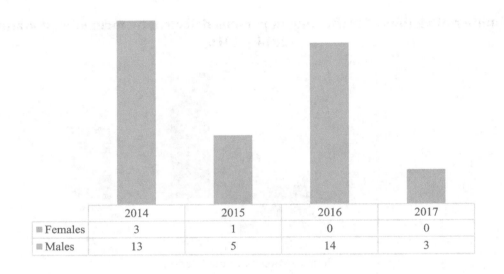

	2014	2015	2016	2017
■ Females	3	1	0	0
■ Males	13	5	14	3

In total 12 persons were convicted of trafficking in persons, of which nine were men and three were women.

Source: Basic Court, Skopje.

Victims

Number of victims of trafficking in persons detected, by age and sex, 2014 – 2017

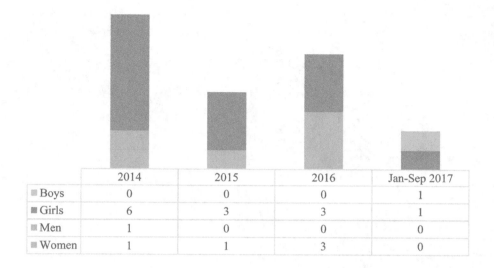

	2014	2015	2016	Jan-Sep 2017
▪ Boys	0	0	0	1
▪ Girls	6	3	3	1
▪ Men	1	0	0	0
▪ Women	1	1	3	0

Source: National Commission for the Fight Against Trafficking in Persons and Illegal Migration.

Number of victims of trafficking in persons detected, by form of exploitation, 2014 – 2017

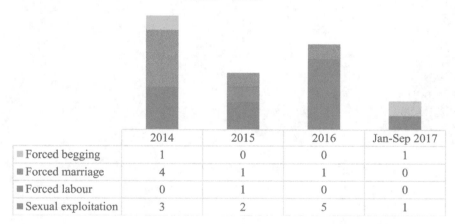

	2014	2015	2016	Jan-Sep 2017
▪ Forced begging	1	0	0	1
▪ Forced marriage	4	1	1	0
▪ Forced labour	0	1	0	0
▪ Sexual exploitation	3	2	5	1

Source: National Commission for the Fight Against Trafficking in Persons and Illegal Migration.

Additional information

The majority of victims were Macedonian citizens. Most victims were trafficked domestically between 2014 and 2017. Victims who were trafficked internationally were repatriated from other Western and Central European countries.

Source: National Commission for the Fight Against Trafficking in Persons and Illegal Migration.

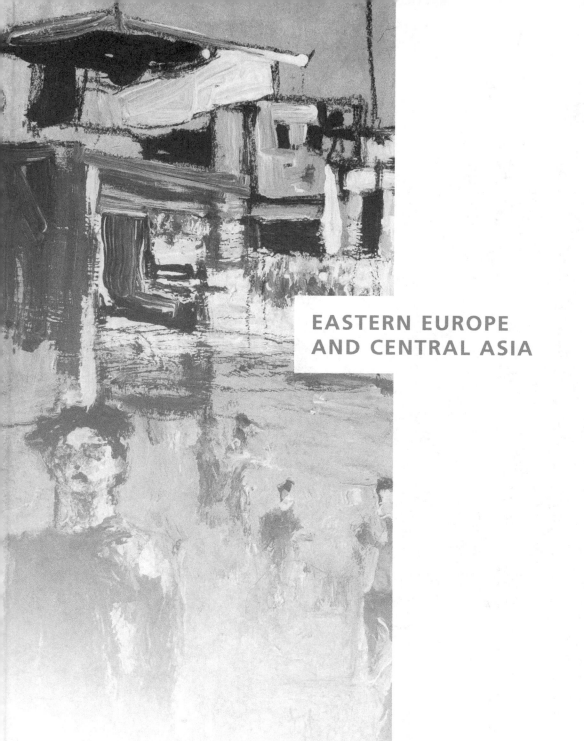

EASTERN EUROPE
AND CENTRAL ASIA

–Armenia–

The current legislation on trafficking in persons in Armenia covers all forms of trafficking indicated in the UN Trafficking in Persons Protocol.

Investigations and suspects

Number of cases of trafficking in persons recorded, 2014 – September 2017

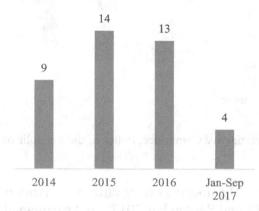

Source: Investigative Committee, Police of the Republic of Armenia.

In 2014, eight females and one male were prosecuted of trafficking in persons. Of these persons, two males and two females were convicted of the crime. In 2015, two males and one female were prosecuted and three males were convicted of trafficking in persons. In 2016, two males and four females were prosecuted. Of these persons, two males and one female were convicted of the crime. In the first few months of 2017, one person was prosecuted for trafficking in persons.

Source: Prosecutor General's Office of the Republic of Republic of Armenia.

Victims

Number of victims of trafficking in persons detected, by age and sex, 2014 – September 2017

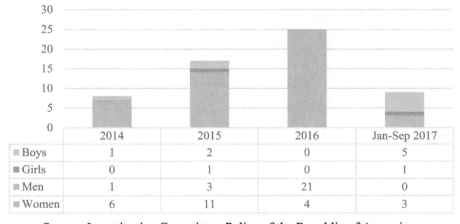

	2014	2015	2016	Jan-Sep 2017
■ Boys	1	2	0	5
■ Girls	0	1	0	1
■ Men	1	3	21	0
■ Women	6	11	4	3

Source: Investigative Committee, Police of the Republic of Armenia.

Number of victims of trafficking in persons detected, by form of exploitation, 2014 – September 2017

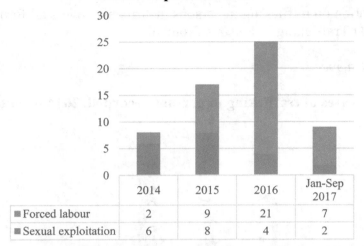

	2014	2015	2016	Jan-Sep 2017
■ Forced labour	2	9	21	7
■ Sexual exploitation	6	8	4	2

Source: Investigative Committee, Police of the Republic of Armenia.

All victims detected by national authorities were citizens of Armenia and Asia. From the period between January 2014 and September 2017, 16 Armenian citizens were domestically trafficked, while during the same period, 39 were repatriated from other countries. The majority of Armenian victims were repatriated from the Russian Federation along with smaller numbers repatriated from other countries.

Source: Investigative Committee, Police of the Republic of Armenia.

The current legislation on trafficking in persons in Azerbaijan covers all forms of trafficking indicated in the UN Trafficking in Persons Protocol.

Investigations and Suspects

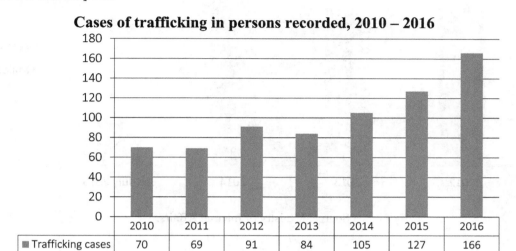

Cases of trafficking in persons recorded, 2010 – 2016

	2010	2011	2012	2013	2014	2015	2016
■ Trafficking cases	70	69	91	84	105	127	166

Source: Ministry of Internal Affairs.

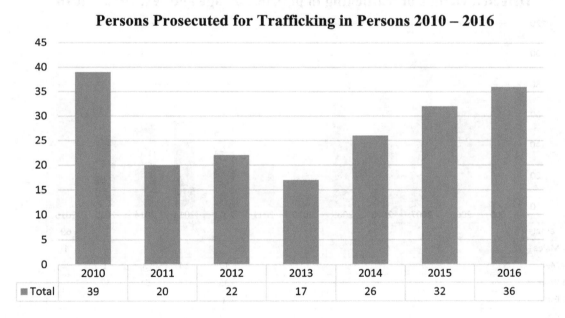

Persons Prosecuted for Trafficking in Persons 2010 – 2016

	2010	2011	2012	2013	2014	2015	2016
■ Total	39	20	22	17	26	32	36

Source: Ministry of Internal Affairs.

Persons Convicted of Trafficking in Persons, by Gender, 2012 – July 2015

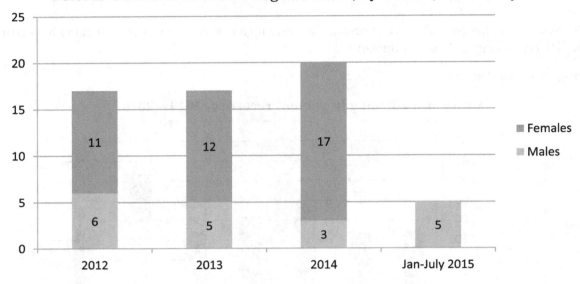

Source: Ministry of Internal Affairs.

Victims

Detected victims of trafficking in persons, by age and sex, 2012 – 2016

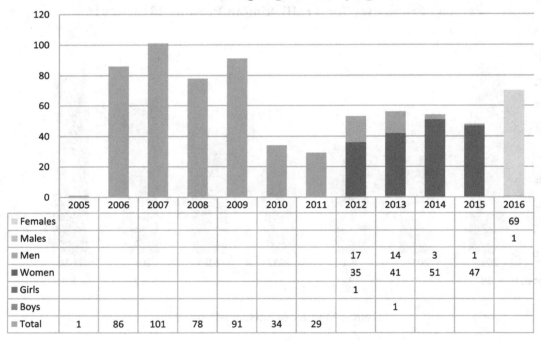

	2005	2006	2007	2008	2009	2010	2011	2012	2013	2014	2015	2016
Females												69
Males												1
Men								17	14	3	1	
Women								35	41	51	47	
Girls								1				
Boys									1			
Total	1	86	101	78	91	34	29					

Source: Ministry of Internal Affairs.

Detected victims of trafficking in persons, by form of exploitation, 2012 – July 2015

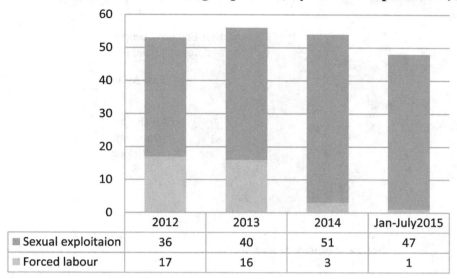

	2012	2013	2014	Jan-July2015
■ Sexual exploitaion	36	40	51	47
▧ Forced labour	17	16	3	1

Source: Ministry of Internal Affairs.

Detected Azerbajani victims trafficked abroad, by country of exploitation, 2012 – July 2015

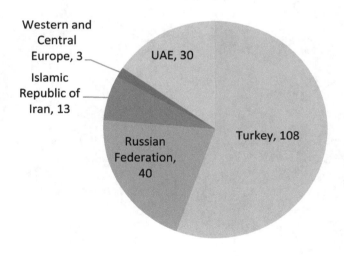

Source: Ministry of Internal Affairs.

Detected victims of trafficking in persons, by country of citizenship, 2012 – July 2015

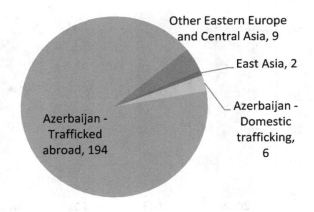

Source: Ministry of Internal Affairs.

In 2016, 70 human trafficking victims were identified. Of these, 69 were females and one was male. The vast majority of them were citizens of Azerbaijan, and only one victim was a foreign national.

Source: Ministry of Internal Affairs.

—Belarus—

The current legislation on trafficking in persons in Belarus covers all forms of trafficking indicated in the UN Trafficking in Persons Protocol.

Investigations and suspects

Number of cases of trafficking in persons recorded, 2014 – June 2017

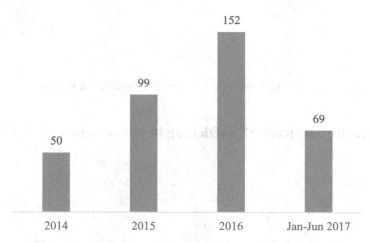

Source: Ministry of the Interior of the Republic of Belarus.

Number of persons brought into formal contact with the police and/or criminal justice system because they have been suspected of, arrested for or cautioned for trafficking in persons **, 2014 – June 2017

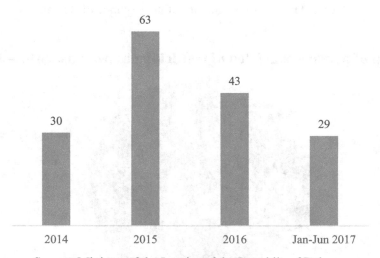

Source: Ministry of the Interior of the Republic of Belarus.

**Note: Formal contact with the police and/or criminal justice system may include persons suspected, arrested, or cautioned at the national level.

Number of persons prosecuted for trafficking in persons, by sex, 2014 – June 2017

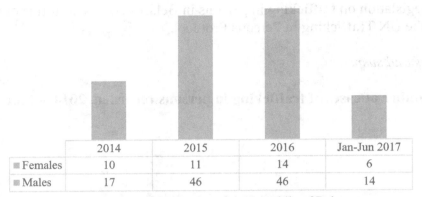

	2014	2015	2016	Jan-Jun 2017
■ Females	10	11	14	6
■ Males	17	46	46	14

Source: Ministry of the Interior of the Republic of Belarus.

Number of persons convicted of trafficking in persons, by sex, 2014 – June 2017

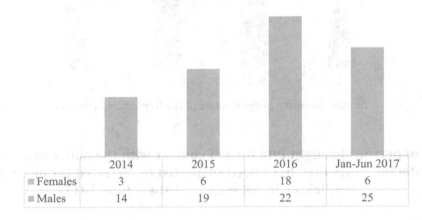

	2014	2015	2016	Jan-Jun 2017
■ Females	3	6	18	6
■ Males	14	19	22	25

Source: Ministry of the Interior of the Republic of Belarus.

Citizenship of persons convicted of trafficking in persons, 2014 – June 2017

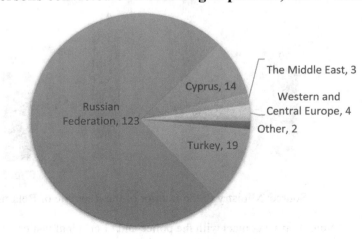

Source: Ministry of the Interior of the Republic of Belarus.

Number of victims of trafficking in persons detected, by age and sex, 2014 – June 2017

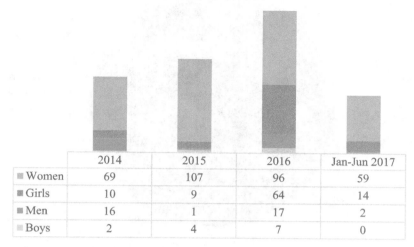

	2014	2015	2016	Jan-Jun 2017
■ Women	69	107	96	59
■ Girls	10	9	64	14
■ Men	16	1	17	2
■ Boys	2	4	7	0

Source: Ministry of the Interior of the Republic of Belarus

The forms of exploitation that are prevalent in Belarus are trafficking for the purposes of sexual exploitation and forced labour. The majority of victims are trafficked for sexual exploitation, with 164 persons trafficked for this purpose in 2016 and 73 persons in the first six months of 2017. Victims trafficked for forced labour purposes numbered 20 in 2016 and two in the first six months of 2017.

Source: Ministry of the Interior of the Republic of Belarus.

The majority of persons identified as victims of trafficking during the period between January 2014 and June 2017 were nationals of Belarus. In 2014, 16 victims from Vietnam were detected, while in 2016 and 2017 the victims were all citizens of countries in Eastern Europe and Central Asia.

Source: Ministry of the Interior of the Republic of Belarus.

Type of trafficking in persons of own nationals, 2014 – June 2017

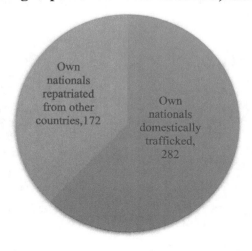

Source: Ministry of the Interior of the Republic of Belarus.

Countries/regions from which own national victims of trafficking in persons were repatriated, 2014 – June 2017

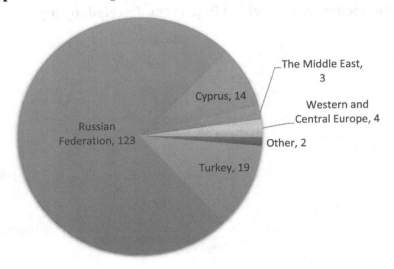

Source: Ministry of the Interior of the Republic of Belarus.

–Georgia–

The current legislation on trafficking in persons in Georgia covers all forms of trafficking indicated in the UN Trafficking in Persons Protocol.

Investigations and suspects

Number of cases of trafficking in persons recorded, 2014 – September 2017

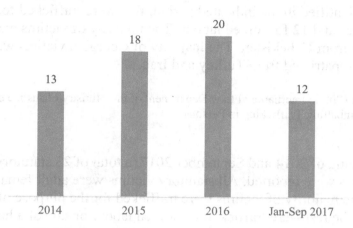

Source: The Secretariat (Public International Law Department of the Ministry of Justice of Georgia) of the Inter-Agency Council on Combatting Trafficking in Persons.

Between the beginning of 2014 and September 2017, a total of 14 persons were prosecuted for trafficking in persons. The majority of these persons were female, totalling nine persons. This trend is the same for convictions. In the indicated period, 15 persons were convicted of trafficking in persons, 10 of which were female. The highest number of convicted persons were from Georgia and Uzbekistan with others from Tajikistan, Kyrgyzstan, Turkey, and Israel.

Source: The Secretariat (Public International Law Department of the Ministry of Justice of Georgia) of the Inter-Agency Council on Combatting Trafficking in Persons.

Victims

Georgian law delineates between two types of trafficking victims: victim of trafficking and statutory victim of trafficking. The difference originates from the authority granting the status. A person who is given the title victim of trafficking is granted this status by the Permanent Group of the Inter-Agency Council on Combatting Trafficking in Persons within 48 hours based on the questionnaires of the mobile group of the State Fund for Protection of and Assistance to Statutory Victims of Trafficking in Persons. A person with the title of statutory victim of trafficking is given this status by law enforcement authorities in accordance with Criminal Procedure Code of Georgia. Both types of victims receive the same free state services and rights. However, each authority maintains separate records.

Source: The Secretariat (Public International Law Department of the Ministry of Justice of Georgia) of the Inter-Agency Council on Combatting Trafficking in Persons.

In 2014, a total of five victims were identified as victims of trafficking in persons, all adults (four male, one female). In 2015, eight adult victims were identified as victims of trafficking in persons (five males, three females), one adult female victim in 2016, and three victims in 2017 (one female child, two adult females).

Source: The Secretariat (Public International Law Department of the Ministry of Justice of Georgia) of the Inter-Agency Council on Combatting Trafficking in Persons.

Of the 17 victims identified in the indicated period, five were trafficked for sexual exploitation purposes and 12 for forced labour. The majority of victims were Georgian citizens with others from Uzbekistan. The majority of Georgian victims were trafficked internationally and repatriated from Turkey and Iraq.

Source: The Secretariat (Public International Law Department of the Ministry of Justice of Georgia) of the Inter-Agency Council on Combatting Trafficking in Persons.

Between the beginning of 2014 and September 2017, a total of 23 statutory victims of trafficking in persons were reported. All statutory victims were adult females except for two female children. The majority of victims were trafficked for the purpose of sexual exploitation, while the rest were trafficked for forced labour or sale of a human being.

Source: The Secretariat (Public International Law Department of the Ministry of Justice of Georgia) of the Inter-Agency Council on Combatting Trafficking in Persons.

In the reporting period, 11 statutory victims of trafficking in persons were from Uzbekistan, seven were citizens of Georgia, and the rest were from other Eastern European and Central Asian countries. The majority of Georgian statutory victims were trafficked domestically.

Source: The Secretariat (Public International Law Department of the Ministry of Justice of Georgia) of the Inter-Agency Council on Combatting Trafficking in Persons.

−Kyrgyzstan−

The current legislation on trafficking in persons in Kyrgyzstan criminalizes trafficking for sexual exploitation and for forced labour under Article 124 of the criminal code and also covers "child adoption for commercial purposes."

Investigations and suspects

Number of cases of trafficking in persons recorded, 2014 – 2017

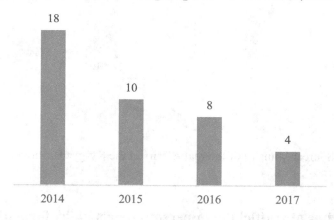

Source: Ministry of Internal Affairs of the Kyrgyz Republic.

Number of persons convicted of trafficking in persons, by sex, 2014 – 2017

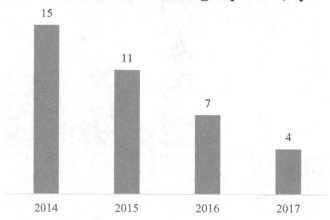

Source: Ministry of Internal Affairs of the Kyrgyz Republic.

Of those persons convicted in 2014, seven were males. In 2016, one person convicted was male. All were citizens of Kyrgyzstan.

Source: Ministry of Internal Affairs of the Kyrgyz Republic.

Victims

Number of victims of trafficking in persons detected, by age, 2014 – 2017

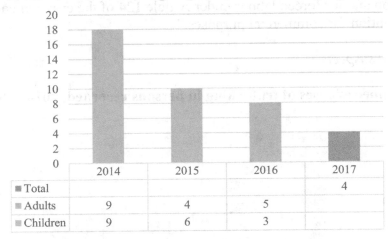

	2014	2015	2016	2017
■ Total				4
■ Adults	9	4	5	
■ Children	9	6	3	

Source: Ministry of Internal Affairs of the Kyrgyz Republic.

Number of victims of trafficking in persons detected, by form of exploitation, 2014 – 2016

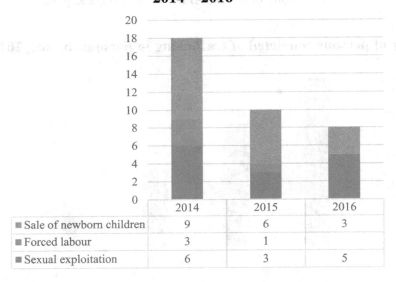

	2014	2015	2016
■ Sale of newborn children	9	6	3
■ Forced labour	3	1	
■ Sexual exploitation	6	3	5

Source: Ministry of Foreign Affairs of the Kyrgyz Republic.

All detected victims in the reporting period were citizens of Kyrgyzstan and were trafficked domestically.

Source: Ministry of Internal Affairs of the Kyrgyz Republic.

−Republic of Moldova−

The current legislation on trafficking in persons in Moldova covers all forms of trafficking indicated in the UN Trafficking in Persons Protocol. The current legislation on trafficking in persons in the Republic of Moldova all forms of trafficking indicated in the UN Trafficking in Persons Protocol. The criminal code delineates between trafficking in human beings (adults) and trafficking in children. Article 165 of the criminal code is used to prosecute trafficking in adults while Article 206 is used to prosecute trafficking in children.

Investigations and suspects

Number of cases of trafficking in persons recorded under Articles 165 and 206, 2014 – June 2017

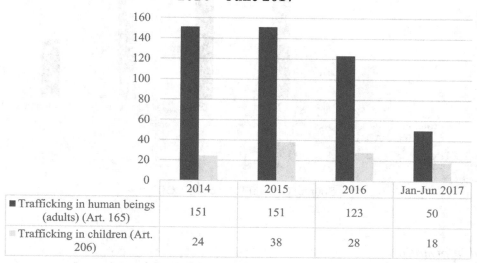

	2014	2015	2016	Jan-Jun 2017
■ Trafficking in human beings (adults) (Art. 165)	151	151	123	50
Trafficking in children (Art. 206)	24	38	28	18

Source: General Prosecutor's Office.

Number of persons brought into formal contact with the police and/or criminal justice system because they have been suspected of, arrested for or cautioned for trafficking in persons**, 2014 – June 2017

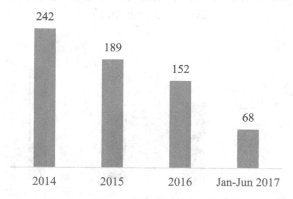

Source: General Prosecutor's Office.

**Note: Formal contact with the police and/or criminal justice system may include persons suspected, arrested, or cautioned at the national level.

In 2014, 123 males and 119 females were brought into formal contact with the police and/or criminal justice system.

Source: General Prosecutor's Office.

Number of persons prosecuted for trafficking in persons under Articles 165 and 206, 2014 – June 2017

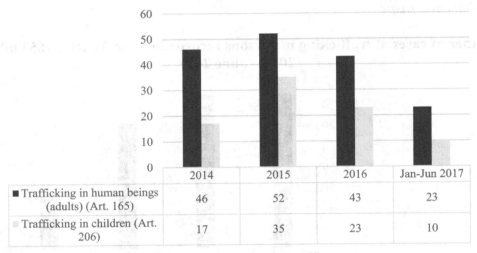

	2014	2015	2016	Jan-Jun 2017
■ Trafficking in human beings (adults) (Art. 165)	46	52	43	23
▢ Trafficking in children (Art. 206)	17	35	23	10

Source: General Prosecutor's Office.

In 2014, 28 males and six females were convicted of trafficking adults. In the same year, 18 males and 11 females were convicted of trafficking in children.

Source: General Prosecutor's Office.

Number of persons convicted of trafficking in persons under Articles 165 and 206, 2014 – June 2017

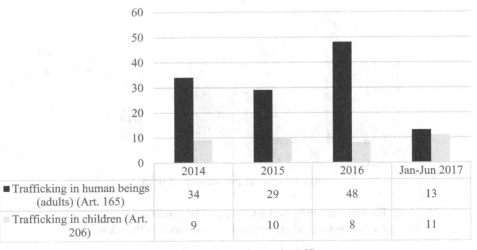

	2014	2015	2016	Jan-Jun 2017
■ Trafficking in human beings (adults) (Art. 165)	34	29	48	13
▢ Trafficking in children (Art. 206)	9	10	8	11

Source: General Prosecutor's Office.

In 2014, nine males and twenty five females were convicted of trafficking adults under Article 165. In the same year, six males and three females were convicted of trafficking in children under Article 206.

Source: General Prosecutor's Office.

National authorities in Moldova reported that the majority of persons convicted of trafficking in persons in 2014 were nationals of Moldova. Additional persons convicted were citizens of Armenia, Bulgaria, and Albania.

Source: General Prosecutor's Office.

Victims

Number of victims of trafficking in persons detected, by age and sex, 2014 – June 2017

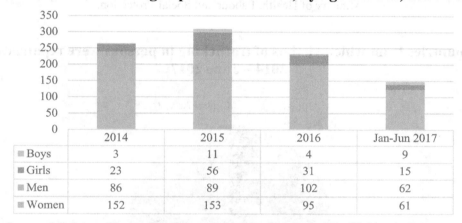

	2014	2015	2016	Jan-Jun 2017
■ Boys	3	11	4	9
■ Girls	23	56	31	15
■ Men	86	89	102	62
■ Women	152	153	95	61

Source: Ministry of Internal Affairs – Centre for Combating Trafficking in Persons.

Number of victims of trafficking in persons detected, by form of exploitation, 2014 – June 2017

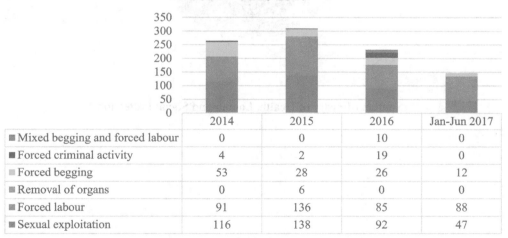

	2014	2015	2016	Jan-Jun 2017
■ Mixed begging and forced labour	0	0	10	0
■ Forced criminal activity	4	2	19	0
■ Forced begging	53	28	26	12
■ Removal of organs	0	6	0	0
■ Forced labour	91	136	85	88
■ Sexual exploitation	116	138	92	47

Source: Ministry of Internal Affairs – Centre for Combating Trafficking in Persons.

The majority of identified victims were citizens of Moldova. A smaller number of victims were citizens of Syria and Germany.

Source: Ministry of Internal Affairs – Centre for Combating Trafficking in Persons.

Type of trafficking experienced by victims of Moldova citizenship, 2014 – June 2017

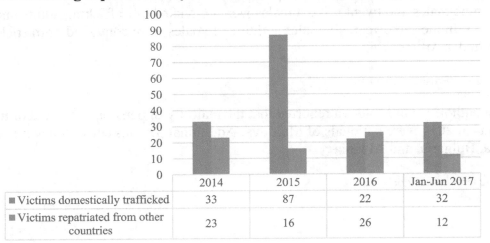

	2014	2015	2016	Jan-Jun 2017
■ Victims domestically trafficked	33	87	22	32
■ Victims repatriated from other countries	23	16	26	12

Source: Ministry of Internal Affairs – Centre for Combating Trafficking in Persons, Ministry of Health, Labour and Social Protection.

Countries from which victims of trafficking in persons were repatriated, 2014 – June 2017

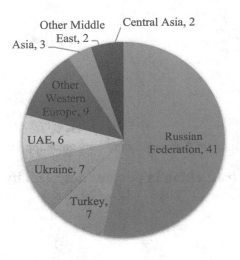

Source: Ministry of Health, Labour and Social Protection.

The Criminal Code of the Russian Federation covers all forms of trafficking indicated in the UN Trafficking in Persons Protocol.

Investigations and suspects

Number of offences of trafficking in persons recorded, 2014 –2017

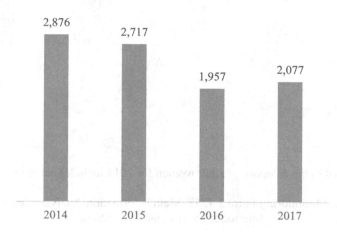

Source: Federal Statistical Monitoring Form 1-EGS. Main Information Analysis Centre of the Ministry of the Interior of the Russian Federation.

Number of persons prosecuted for trafficking in persons, 2014 –2017

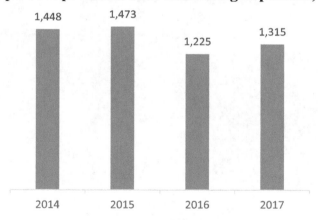

Source: Federal Statistical Monitoring Form 1-EGS. Main Information Analysis Centre of the Ministry of the Interior of the Russian Federation.

Number of victims of trafficking detected, by age and sex, 2014 – 2017

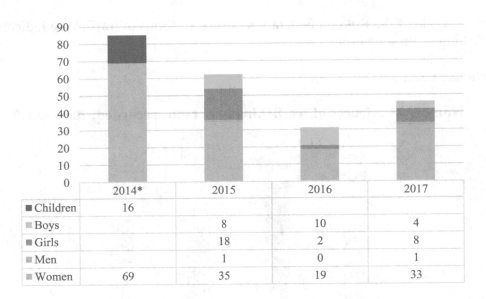

	2014*	2015	2016	2017
■ Children	16			
■ Boys		8	10	4
■ Girls		18	2	8
■ Men		1	0	1
■ Women	69	35	19	33

*Numbers of in the category of adult women for 2014 includes some underage girls

Source: Federal Statistical Monitoring Form 1-EGS. Main Information Analysis Centre of the Ministry of the Interior of the Russian Federation.

The specific offence of trafficking in persons in Tajikistan covers sexual exploitation and forced labour, as well as other forms of trafficking indicated in the UN Trafficking in Persons Protocol.

Investigations and suspects

Number of cases of trafficking in persons recorded, 2014 – 2017

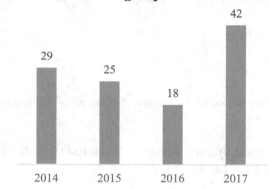

Source: Office of the General Prosecutor of Tajikistan.

Number of persons brought into formal contact with the police and/or criminal justice system because they have been suspected of, arrested for or cautioned for trafficking in persons, by sex, 2014 – 2017**

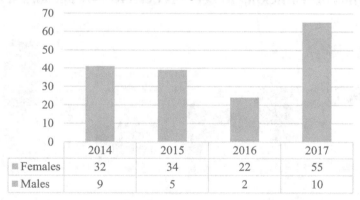

	2014	2015	2016	2017
Females	32	34	22	55
Males	9	5	2	10

Source: Office of the General Prosecutor of Tajikistan.

**Note: Formal contact with the police and/or criminal justice system may include persons suspected, arrested, or cautioned at the national level.

The same number of persons who were brought into formal contact with the police and/or criminal justice system were prosecuted for trafficking in persons during the corresponding years.

Source: Office of the General Prosecutor of Tajikistan.

Number of persons convicted of trafficking in persons, by sex, 2014 – 2017

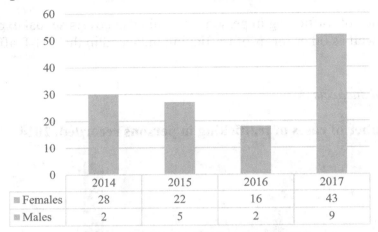

	2014	2015	2016	2017
▪ Females	28	22	16	43
▪ Males	2	5	2	9

Source: Office of the General Prosecutor of Tajikistan.

The national authorities reported that all persons convicted of trafficking in persons in the indicated period were citizens of Tajikistan.

Source: Office of the General Prosecutor of Tajikistan.

Victims

Number of victims of trafficking in persons detected, by age and sex**, 2014 –2017

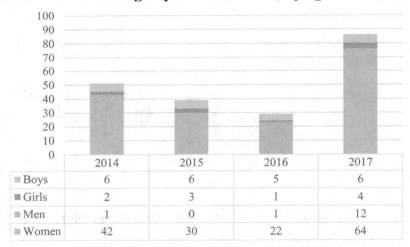

	2014	2015	2016	2017
▪ Boys	6	6	5	6
▪ Girls	2	3	1	4
▪ Men	1	0	1	12
▪ Women	42	30	22	64

Source: Office of the General Prosecutor of Tajikistan.

**National legislation of Tajikistan defines children in terms of human trafficking as "newborns."
However, "children", as defined under article 3 (d) of the UN Protocol, means any person under 18 years of age.

Number of victims of trafficking in persons detected, by form of exploitation, 2014 – 2017

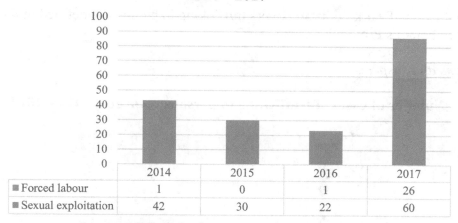

	2014	2015	2016	2017
■ Forced labour	1	0	1	26
■ Sexual exploitation	42	30	22	60

Source: Office of the General Prosecutor of Tajikistan.

All persons detected by national authorities as victims of trafficking in persons were nationals of Tajikistan.

Source: Office of the General Prosecutor of Tajikistan.

Identified victims of trafficking, by type of trafficking, 2014 – 2017

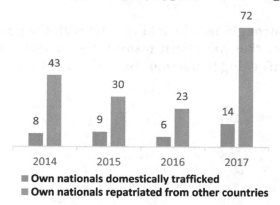

Source: Office of the General Prosecutor of Tajikistan.

Detected victims of trafficking in persons who are citizens of Tajikistan, by country of repatriation, 2014 – 2017

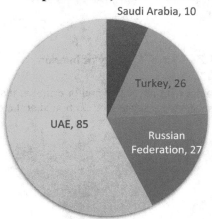

Source: Office of the General Prosecutor of Tajikistan.

The Criminal Code of Turkmenistan covers trafficking in persons as defined in the UN Trafficking in Persons Protocol.

Investigations and suspects

Number of cases of trafficking in persons recorded, 2014 – 2017

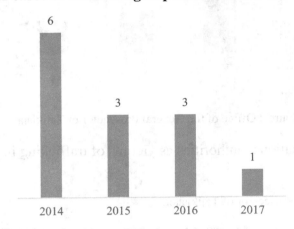

Source: Ministry of Interior

Number of persons brought into formal contact with the police and/or criminal justice system because they have been suspected of, arrested for or cautioned for trafficking in persons, by sex**, 2014 – 2017

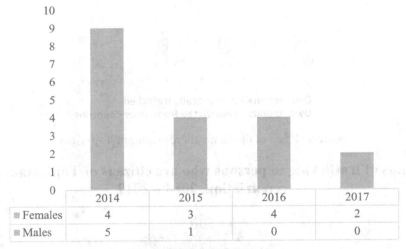

	2014	2015	2016	2017
▪ Females	4	3	4	2
▪ Males	5	1	0	0

Source: Ministry of Interior

**Note: Formal contact with the police and/or criminal justice system may include persons suspected, arrested, or cautioned at the national level.

Number of persons prosecuted for trafficking in persons, by sex, 2014 –2017

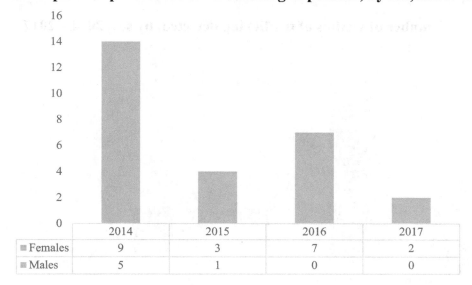

	2014	2015	2016	2017
■ Females	9	3	7	2
■ Males	5	1	0	0

Source: Ministry of Interior

Number of persons convicted of trafficking in persons, by sex, 2014 – 2017

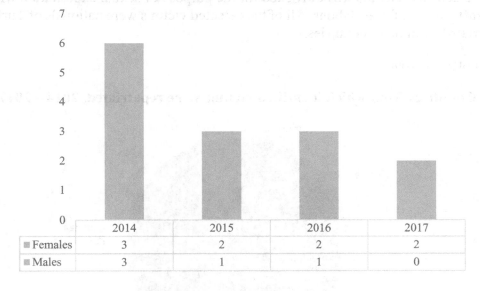

	2014	2015	2016	2017
■ Females	3	2	2	2
■ Males	3	1	1	0

Source: Ministry of Interior

All of the convicted persons were nationals of Turkmenistan.

Source: Ministry of Interior

Victims

Number of victims of trafficking detected, by sex, 2014 – 2017

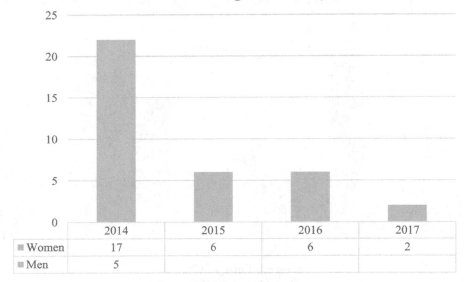

	2014	2015	2016	2017
■ Women	17	6	6	2
■ Men	5			

Source: Ministry of Interior

Most of the detected victims was trafficked for the purpose of sexual exploitation with a lower number trafficked for forced labour. All of the detected victims were nationals of Turkmenistan and repatriated from other countries.

Source: Ministry of Interior

Countries from which identified victims were repatriated, 2014 – 2017

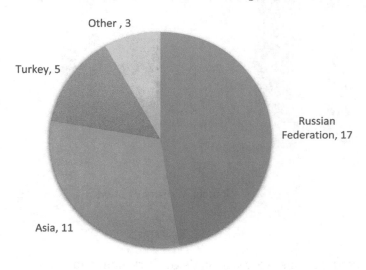

Source: Ministry of Interior

The current legislation on trafficking in persons in Ukraine covers all forms of trafficking indicated in the UN Trafficking in Persons Protocol.

Investigations and suspects

Number of cases of trafficking in persons recorded, 2014 – July 2017

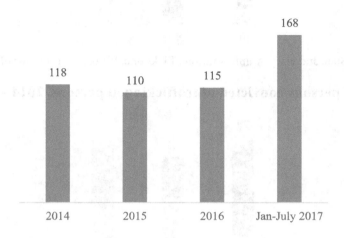

Source: The Consolidated Report of Criminal Offences.

Number of persons brought into formal contact with the police and/or criminal justice system because they have been suspected of, arrested for or cautioned for trafficking in persons, by sex**, 2014 – July 2017

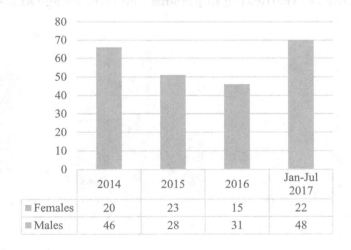

	2014	2015	2016	Jan-Jul 2017
Females	20	23	15	22
Males	46	28	31	48

Source: The Report on Perpetrators of Criminal Offences.

**Note: Formal contact with the police and/or criminal justice system may include persons suspected, arrested, or cautioned at the national level.

Number of persons prosecuted for trafficking in persons, 2014 – June 2017

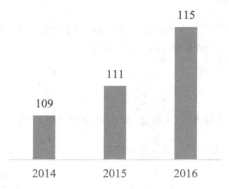

Source: State Judiciary Administration of Ukraine, Ministry of Interior of Ukraine

Number of persons convicted of trafficking in persons, 2014 – June 2017

Source: State Judiciary Administration of Ukraine, Ministry of Interior of Ukraine

Victims

Number of victims of trafficking in persons detected, by age and sex, 2014 –2017

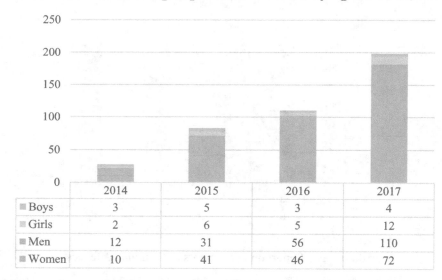

	2014	2015	2016	2017
Boys	3	5	3	4
Girls	2	6	5	12
Men	12	31	56	110
Women	10	41	46	72

Source: Database of the Ministry of Social Policy of Ukraine

Number of victims of trafficking in persons detected by type of exploitation 2014 –2017

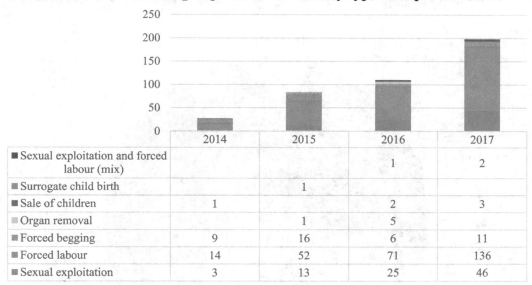

	2014	2015	2016	2017
■ Sexual exploitation and forced labour (mix)			1	2
■ Surrogate child birth		1		
■ Sale of children	1		2	3
■ Organ removal		1	5	
■ Forced begging	9	16	6	11
■ Forced labour	14	52	71	136
■ Sexual exploitation	3	13	25	46

Source: Database of the Ministry of Social Policy of Ukraine.

Identified victims of trafficking, by type of trafficking, 2014 –2017

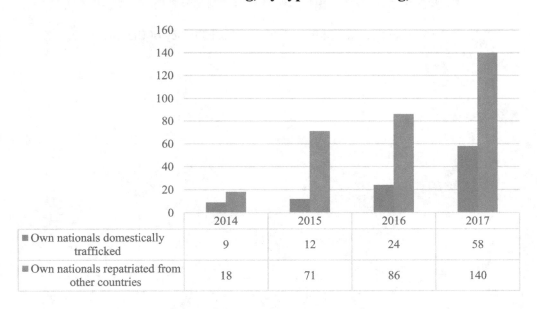

	2014	2015	2016	2017
■ Own nationals domestically trafficked	9	12	24	58
■ Own nationals repatriated from other countries	18	71	86	140

Source: Database of the Ministry of Social Policy of Ukraine

Countries from which identified victims were repatriated, 2014 – 2017

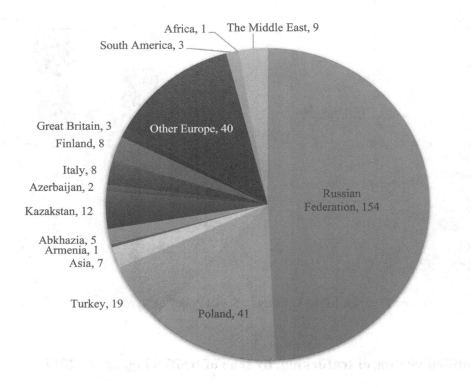

Source: Database of the Ministry of Social Policy of Ukraine

The current legislation on trafficking in persons in Uzbekistan covers all forms of trafficking indicated in the UN Trafficking in Persons Protocol.

Investigations and suspects

Number of cases of trafficking in persons recorded, 2014 – 2017

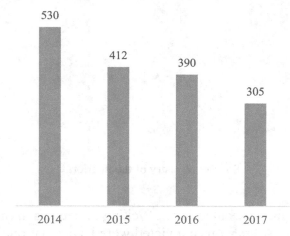

Source: Ministry of the Interior.

Number of persons brought into formal contact with the police and/or criminal justice system because they have been suspected of, arrested for or cautioned for trafficking in persons, by sex**, 2014 – 2017

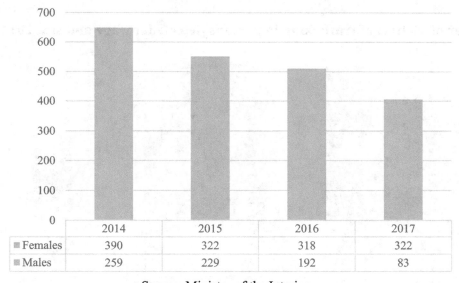

	2014	2015	2016	2017
▪ Females	390	322	318	322
▪ Males	259	229	192	83

Source: Ministry of the Interior.

**Note: Formal contact with the police and/or criminal justice system may include persons suspected, arrested, or cautioned at the national level.

Number of persons prosecuted for trafficking in persons, by sex, 2014 – 2017

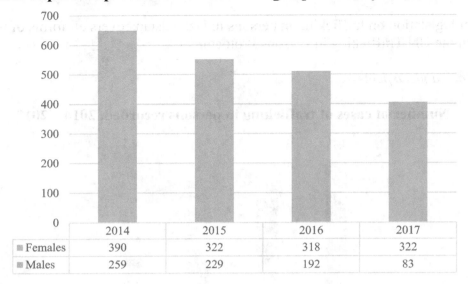

	2014	2015	2016	2017
▪ Females	390	322	318	322
▪ Males	259	229	192	83

Source: Ministry of the Interior.

The same number of persons prosecuted for trafficking in persons in the indicated years were also convicted of the crime. All persons convicted were Uzbek nationals.

Source: Ministry of the Interior.

Victims

Number of victims of trafficking in persons detected, by age and sex, 2014 – 2017

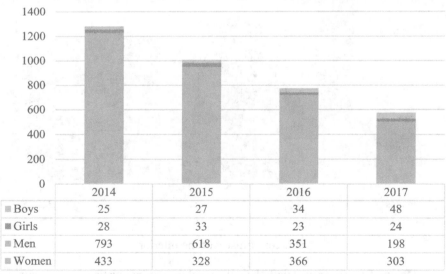

	2014	2015	2016	2017
▪ Boys	25	27	34	48
▪ Girls	28	33	23	24
▪ Men	793	618	351	198
▪ Women	433	328	366	303

Source: Ministry of the Interior.

Number of victims of trafficking in persons detected, by form of exploitation, 2014 – 2017

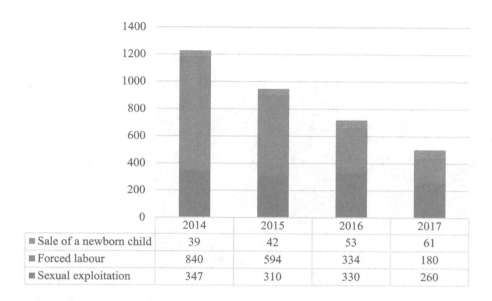

	2014	2015	2016	2017
▪ Sale of a newborn child	39	42	53	61
▪ Forced labour	840	594	334	180
▪ Sexual exploitation	347	310	330	260

Source: Ministry of the Interior.

All detected victims in the indicated period were citizens of Uzbekistan.

Source: Ministry of the Interior.

WEST AND SOUTH ASIA

—Afghanistan—

The current legislation on trafficking in persons in Afghanistan covers all forms of trafficking indicated in the UN Trafficking in Persons Protocol.

Investigations and Suspects

According to the Human Rights Council, more than 60 per cent of trafficking in women and children takes place inside Afghanistan, while cross-border trafficking occurs in 40 per cent of cases.

Source: UN General Assembly.

In 2015, five cases of buying and selling of women for the purpose or under pretext of marriage were recorded under the EVAW law.

Source: Ministry of Women's Affairs.

Victims

UNAMA continued to receive reports of recruitment and use of children by Anti-Government Elements and Afghan national security forces as co-chair of the United Nations Country Task Force on Monitoring and Reporting (CTFMR). They recorded 57 incidents involving the recruitment or use of 89 boys in 2016.

CTFMR documented 64 boys recruited or used by Taliban, 10 boys recruited or used by Daesh/ISKP, and five boys recruited by unidentified Anti-Government Elements, mainly to plant IEDs, transport explosives, carry out suicide attacks, and spy.

Source: UNAMA.

–Bangladesh–

The current legislation on trafficking in persons in Bangladesh covers all forms of trafficking indicated in the UN Trafficking in Persons Protocol.

Investigation and Suspects

The Bangladesh Police recorded more than 1,000 cases of human trafficking between September 2016 and February 2018. A total 2,100 people were arrested, with one conviction.

Source: Bangladesh Police.

Victims

A total of about 1,100 victims were identified between September 2016 and February 2018.

Victims of Trafficking in Persons, by sex, September 2016 – February 2018

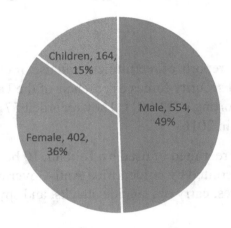

Source: Bangladesh Police

In 2014, the RRRI task Force / MoHA received applications for the repatriation of 1,821 trafficked victims from different countries, especially from India. Out of them, MoHA issued repatriation orders for 970 victims.

Source: Government of the People's Republic of Bangladesh.

–Bhutan–

The current legislation on trafficking in persons in Bhutan adopts a wider definition of trafficking than the one indicated in the UN Trafficking in Persons Protocol.

Investigations and Suspects

The Royal Bhutan Police registered 20 cases under "criminal attempt to trafficking of a person" in 2016. Of these, three cases were under hearing before courts.

Source: Office of the Attorney General.

In the year 2013, India passed the Criminal Law (Amendment) Ordinance introducing section 370A criminalizing trafficking in persons according to the UN Trafficking in Persons Protocol definition. The Immoral Traffic Prevention Act (ITPA) was used, and it is still vastly used to prosecute some forms of trafficking for sexual exploitation. Other articles of the criminal code are also used to prosecute trafficking for sexual exploitation, including 'buying girls for prostitution,' 'selling of girls for prostitution,' 'importation of girls,' and 'procuration of minor girls'. Trafficking for forced labour is prosecuted under other offences, including the Child Labour Prohibition Act and the laws prohibiting bonded labour.

Investigations and Suspects

In 2015, a total of 6,877 cases related to human trafficking were recorded. Of these, 3,087 referred to procuration of minor girls, six to importation of girls from foreign countries, 111 to selling of minors for prostitution, 11 to buying of minors from prostitution, while the rest referred to Immoral trafficking and human trafficking under sections 370 and 370A, as shown below.

Cases Registered for Immoral Trafficking and Human Trafficking, 2014 – 2015

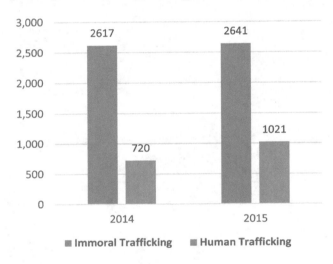

Source: National Crime Records Bureau.

A total of 824 cases under 370 and 370A of the criminal code ended in convictions. 1,497 people, (1,331 males and 166 females) were charged for human trafficking, while 7601 people (5380 males and 2221 females) were charged for immoral trafficking during 2015.

221 cases (about 20% of the total) of child trafficking under section 370 and 370A of the Indian Penal Code were registered in the country during 2015. Out of 5,003 cases relating to child trafficking, trials have been completed in 384 cases during 2015. A total of 55 cases under child trafficking ended in conviction, and a total of 95 persons have been convicted under various crimes relating to child trafficking.

Source: National Crime Records Bureau.

–Maldives–

In December 2013, national authorities introduced the offence of trafficking in persons in the Maldives. The anti-trafficking bill criminalizes sexual exploitation and forced labour. Previously, the Maldives did not have an anti-trafficking legislation in place. Article 25 (a) of the Constitution prohibits slavery, servitude, and forced labour. Article 3(a) of the Employment Act (2008) prohibits forced labour.

Investigations and Suspects

Between June 2016 and May 2017, there were eight registered human trafficking cases in the Maldives. Out of 17 offenders, 10 where charged and three were convicted. 11 offenders were from Bangladesh and five from the Maldives.

Source: Prosecutor Generals' Office, Maldives.

Victims

Between June 2016 and May 2017, 12 victims were identified: three females and nine males mainly from Bangladesh and a smaller number from Kenya.

Source: Prosecutor Generals' Office, Maldives.

The current legislation on trafficking in persons in Nepal covers all forms of trafficking indicated in the UN Trafficking in Persons Protocol definition.

Investigations and Suspects

Between 2015 and 2016, the police recorded 395 cases of trafficking in persons, 130 of which ended in convictions.

Trafficking in Persons Cases and Convictions, 2011 – 2016

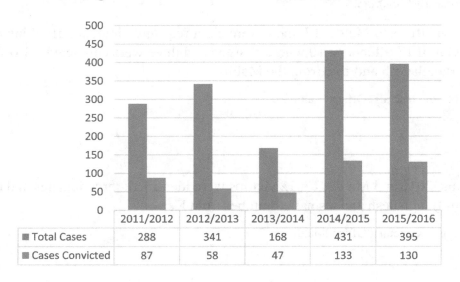

	2011/2012	2012/2013	2013/2014	2014/2015	2015/2016
■ Total Cases	288	341	168	431	395
■ Cases Convicted	87	58	47	133	130

Source: Nepal Police.

Victims

Victims of Trafficking in Persons, by age, 2015 – 2016

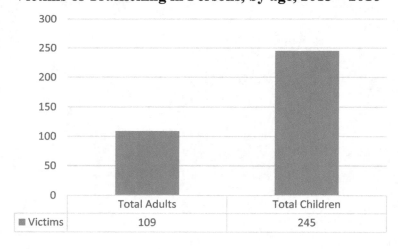

	Total Adults	Total Children
■ Victims	109	245

Source: Nepal Police.

Overall, 350 victims were identified to be female, and two to be male.

Source: Nepal Police.

<h1 align="center">–Pakistan–</h1>

The Prevention and Control of Human Trafficking Ordinance (PACHTO) was used to prosecute some forms of international trafficking. In addition, the authorities made use of other offences to prosecute some trafficking cases. In June 2018, the Senate approved the Prevention of Trafficking in Persons Act, 2018 criminalizing trafficking in persons according to the UN Trafficking in Persons Protocol definition.

Investigations and suspects

The Federal Investigation Agency of Pakistan recorded 4384 human smuggling and human trafficking arrests between 2014 and 2016.

Number of Human Smuggling/Trafficking Arrests, 2014 – 2016

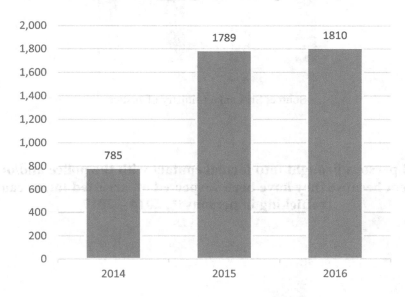

Source: Federal Investigation Agency.

−Sri Lanka−

The current legislation on trafficking in persons in Sri Lanka covers all forms of trafficking indicated in the UN Trafficking in Persons Protocol.

Investigations and suspects

Number of cases of trafficking in persons recorded, 2014 – 2017

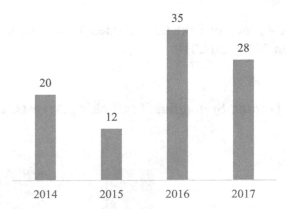

Source: Sri Lanka Ministry of Justice

Number of persons brought into formal contact with the police and/or criminal justice system because they have been suspected of, arrested for or cautioned for trafficking in persons**, 2014 – 2017

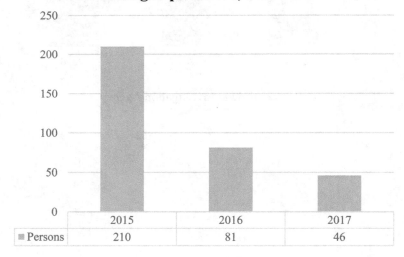

	2015	2016	2017
■ Persons	210	81	46

Source: Sri Lanka Ministry of Justice

**Note: Formal contact with the police and/or criminal justice system may include persons suspected, arrested, or cautioned at the national level.

Number of persons prosecuted for trafficking in persons, 2014 – 2017

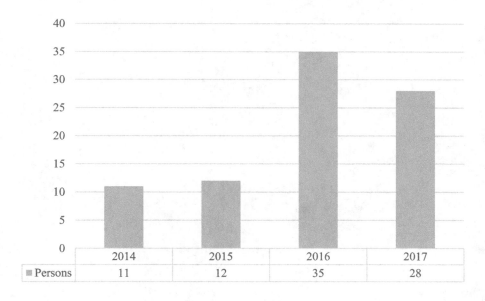

	2014	2015	2016	2017
Persons	11	12	35	28

Source: Sri Lanka Ministry of Justice

Number of persons convicted of trafficking in persons, 2014 – 2017

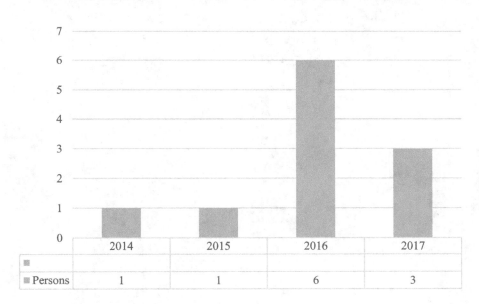

	2014	2015	2016	2017
Persons	1	1	6	3

Source: Sri Lanka Ministry of Justice

EAST ASIA
AND THE PACIFIC

The current legislation on trafficking in persons in Australia covers all forms of trafficking indicated in the UN Trafficking in Persons Protocol.

Investigations and suspects

Between 2014 and 2017*, 15 persons were newly prosecuted for trafficking in persons. During the same period, three persons, all male, were convicted. As of 30 June 2017, there were 17 ongoing cases that commenced between 2014 and 2016.

Source: Commonwealth Director of Public Prosecutions and Australian Federal.
*Data from 2017 is derived from the period between 1 January 2017 and 30 June 2017.

Victims

Number of victims of trafficking in persons referred to the Support for Trafficked People Program, by age and sex, 2014 – 2017

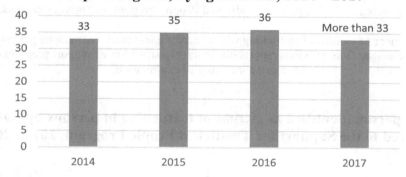

	2014	2015	2016	2017
Men	5	8	less than 5	less than 5
Boys		0	0	less than 5
Girls		10	10	8
Women	25	17	21	25
Unknown/unrecorded	less than 5	0	0	less than 5

Source: Department of Social Services and Australian Red Cross.

**The information provided about victims of trafficking in persons in Australia is based on the number of suspected trafficked persons referred to the Support for Trafficked People Program. For privacy reasons, Australia does not report on the number of victims of trafficking where there are less than five persons per category.

Number of victims of trafficking in person referred to the Support for Trafficked People Program, by form of exploitation, 2014 –2017

	2014	2015	2016	2017
Sexual exploitation	12	less than 5	less than 5	less than 5
Forced labour	7	14	7	7
Domestic servitude	6	4	9	8
Forced marriages	less than 5	14	14	15
Other	less than 5		less than 5	less than 5
Debt bondage	less than 5			

Source: Department of Social Services and Australian Red Cross.

**The information provided about victims of trafficking in persons in Australia is based on the number of suspected
trafficked persons referred to the Support for Trafficked People Program. For privacy reasons, Australia does not
report on the number of victims of trafficking where there are less than five persons per category. Some
statistics may have changed from previous reports due to a reclassification of support program clients to a more
appropriate category of exploitation.

Citizenships of person identified as victims of trafficking in persons by state authorities referred to the Support for Trafficked People Program, 2014 - 2017

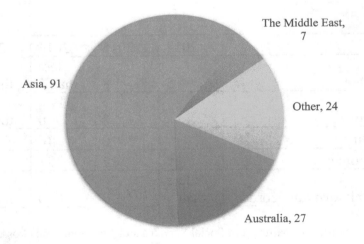

Source: Department of Social Services and Australian Red Cross

**The information provided about victims of trafficking in persons in Australia is based on
the number of suspected trafficked persons referred to the Support for Trafficked People Program.

−Brunei Darussalam−

The current legislation on trafficking in persons in Brunei Darussalam was adopted in 2004 and covers all forms of trafficking indicated in the UN Trafficking in Persons Protocol. However, Brunei Darussalam is not a party to the UN Trafficking in Persons Protocol.

Investigations and suspects

The national authorities commenced prosecution against two males and two females in 2016. Of these four persons, two males and one female were convicted of trafficking in persons in the court of first instance.

Source: Attorney General's Chambers.

Victims

The national authorities reported one victim in 2016. The victim was trafficked for the purpose of sexual exploitation and was from Asia.

Source: Attorney General's Chambers.

−Cambodia−

The current legislation on trafficking in persons in Cambodia covers all forms of trafficking indicated in the UN Trafficking in Persons Protocol.

Number of repatriated victims of trafficking in persons, by countries of return and sex, 2014

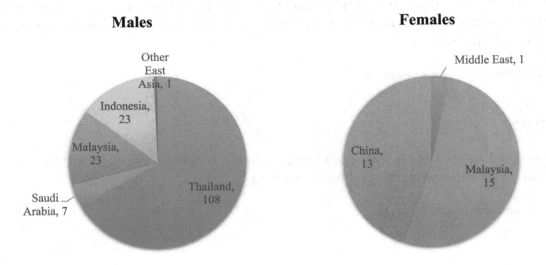

Males

Females

Source: National Committee for Counter Trafficking.

Number of repatriated victims of trafficking in persons, by forms of exploitation, 2014

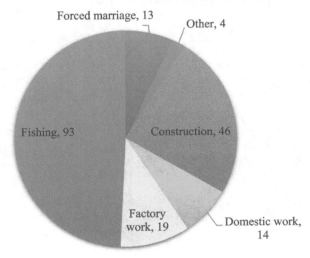

Source: National Committee for Counter Trafficking.

—Indonesia—

The current legislation on trafficking in persons in Indonesia covers all forms of exploitation indicated in the UN Trafficking Protocol.

Investigations and suspects

The Criminal Investigation Police reported 875 cases of trafficking in persons between 2012 and 2015, successfully closing 435. In 2015, 89 cases were reported and 58 were resolved by the police. The Attorney General's Office reported receiving 565 cases of trafficking in persons between 2012 and 2015, 423 of which were prosecuted. In 2015 alone, the Attorney General's Office received 95 cases, and prosecuted 18.

Source: Secretariat of the Task Force on Prevention and Handling of the Crime of Trafficking in Persons.

In 2016, IOM Indonesia and the Ministry of Marine Affairs and Fisheries reported that eight defendants were found guilty of trafficking in persons and forced labour within the fishing industry in one district. IOM also reported that, with its assistance, 1,500 victims of trafficking returned to their home countries.

Source: IOM Indonesia.

Victims

In 2015, 441 victims were identified by the network of Safe Homes and Trauma Centres (RPTC). Of those identified, 243 were males and 198 were females.

Source: Secretariat of the Task Force on Prevention and Handling of the Crime of Trafficking in Persons.

In the same year, IOM identified 283 Indonesian victims of trafficking within the fishing industry.

Source: IOM Indonesia.

–Japan–

The current legislation on trafficking in persons in Japan covers all forms of trafficking indicated in the UN Trafficking in Persons Protocol.

Investigations and suspects

In 2014, 32 cases of trafficking in persons were recorded by national authorities. In 2015 and 2016, 44 cases were recorded each year.

Source: National Police Agency

Number of persons brought into formal contact with the police and/or criminal justice system because they have been identified as an offender and treated as a suspect, by sex, 2014 – 2016

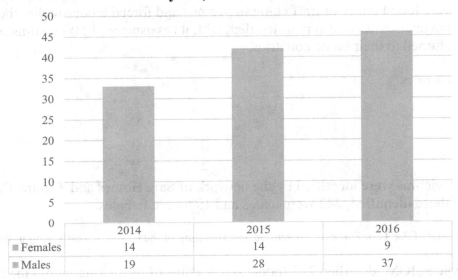

	2014	2015	2016
Females	14	14	9
Males	19	28	37

Source: National Police Agency.

Number of persons prosecuted for trafficking in persons, by sex**, 2014 – 2016

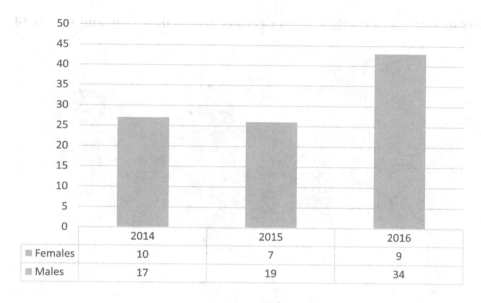

	2014	2015	2016
Females	10	7	9
Males	17	19	34

Source: Ministry of Justice.
**This data includes persons who were prosecuted under the Penal Code and under other laws such as the Prostitution Prevention Law and Employment Security Act.

Number of persons convicted of trafficking in persons, by sex, 2014 – 2016

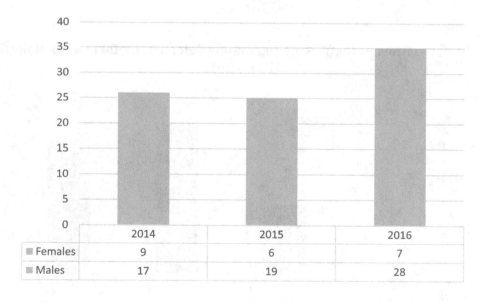

	2014	2015	2016
Females	9	6	7
Males	17	19	28

Source: Ministry of Justice.

The majority of persons convicted of trafficking in persons were nationals of Japan. Others convicted were from Thailand, the Philippines, China, and Brazil.

Source: Ministry of Justice.

Victims

Number of victims of trafficking in persons detected, by age and sex, 2014 – 2016

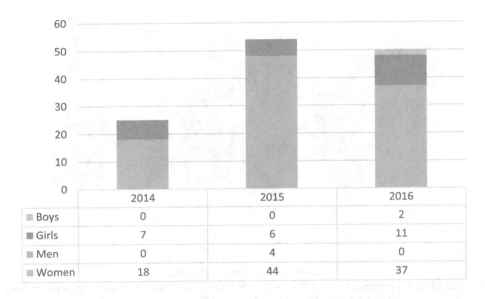

	2014	2015	2016
▪ Boys	0	0	2
▪ Girls	7	6	11
▪ Men	0	4	0
▪ Women	18	44	37

Source: Cabinet Secretariat, National Police Agency, Ministry of Justice, Ministry of Health, Labour and Welfare, and Ministry of Foreign Affairs

Number of victims of trafficking in persons detected, by form of exploitation, 2014 – 2016

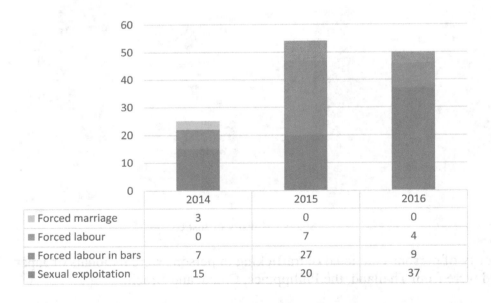

	2014	2015	2016
▪ Forced marriage	3	0	0
▪ Forced labour	0	7	4
▪ Forced labour in bars	7	27	9
▪ Sexual exploitation	15	20	37

Source: National Police Agency, Ministry of Justice.

Citizenships of persons identified as victims of trafficking in persons by state authorities, 2014 – 2016

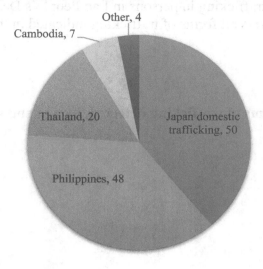

Source: National Police Agency, Ministry of Justice.

The current legislation on trafficking in persons in Lao People's Democratic Republic was introduced in 2015 and covers all forms of trafficking indicated in the UN Trafficking in Persons Protocol.

Victims

Number of victims of trafficking detected, by age and sex, 2011 - 2015

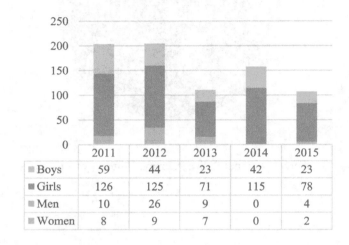

	2011	2012	2013	2014	2015
■ Boys	59	44	23	42	23
■ Girls	126	125	71	115	78
■ Men	10	26	9	0	4
■ Women	8	9	7	0	2

Source: Ministry of Labour and Social Welfare.

−Malaysia−

The current legislation on trafficking in persons in covers all forms of trafficking indicated in the UN Trafficking in Persons Protocol.

Investigations and suspects

Number of cases of trafficking in persons recorded, 2016 –2017

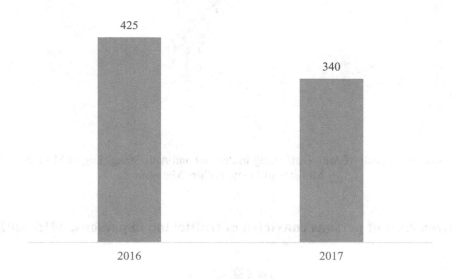

Source: Council of Anti-Trafficking in Persons and Anti-Smuggling of Migrants, Ministry of Home Affairs Malaysia.

Number of persons prosecuted for trafficking in persons, by sex, 2016 – 2017

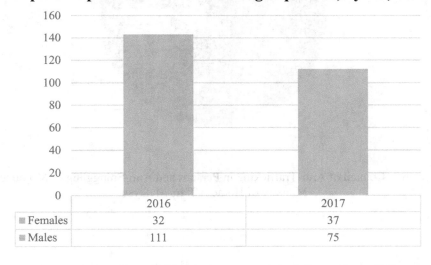

	2016	2017
Females	32	37
Males	111	75

Source: Council of Anti-Trafficking in Persons and Anti-Smuggling of Migrants, Ministry of Home Affairs Malaysia.

Number of persons convicted of trafficking in persons, by sex, 2015 –2017

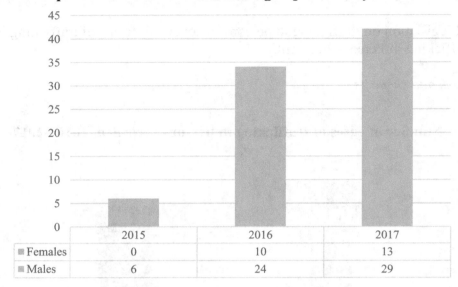

	2015	2016	2017
▪ Females	0	10	13
▪ Males	6	24	29

Source: Council of Anti-Trafficking in Persons and Anti-Smuggling of Migrants, Ministry of Home Affairs Malaysia

Citizenships of persons convicted of trafficking in persons, 2015 –2017

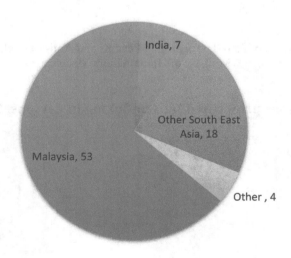

Source: Council of Anti-Trafficking in Persons and Anti-Smuggling of Migrants, Ministry of Home Affairs Malaysia

Victims

Number of victims of trafficking in persons detected, by age and sex, 2014 –2017

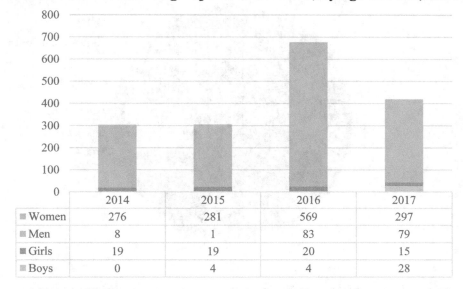

	2014	2015	2016	2017
■ Women	276	281	569	297
■ Men	8	1	83	79
■ Girls	19	19	20	15
■ Boys	0	4	4	28

Source: Council of Anti-Trafficking in Persons and Anti-Smuggling of Migrants, Ministry of Home Affairs Malaysia.

Number of victims of trafficking in persons detected by form of exploitation, 2017

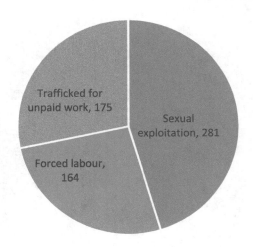

Trafficked for unpaid work, 175

Sexual exploitation, 281

Forced labour, 164

Source: Council of Anti-Trafficking in Persons and Anti-Smuggling of Migrants, Ministry of Home Affairs Malaysia.

Citizenships of persons identified as victims of trafficking in persons by state authorities, 2014 –2017

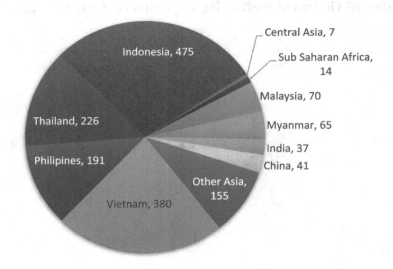

Indonesia, 475

Central Asia, 7

Sub Saharan Africa, 14

Malaysia, 70

Myanmar, 65

Thailand, 226

India, 37

Philipines, 191

China, 41

Other Asia, 155

Vietnam, 380

Source: Council of Anti-Trafficking in Persons and Anti-Smuggling of Migrants, Ministry of Home Affairs Malaysia.

The current legislation on trafficking in persons in Mongolia covers all forms of trafficking indicated in the UN Trafficking in Persons Protocol.

Investigations and suspects

Number of cases of trafficking in persons recorded, 2014 – September 2017

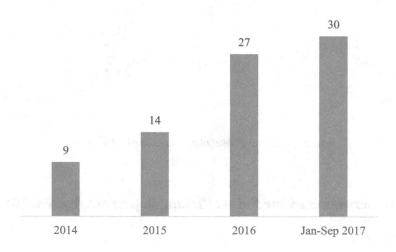

Source: General Police Department of Mongolia.

Number of persons brought into formal contact with the police and/or criminal justice system because they have been suspected of, arrested for or cautioned for trafficking in persons, by sex**, 2014 – September 2017

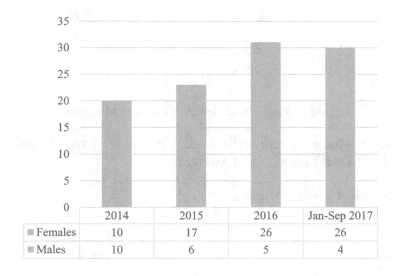

	2014	2015	2016	Jan-Sep 2017
Females	10	17	26	26
Males	10	6	5	4

Source: General Police Department of Mongolia.

**Note: Formal contact with the police and/or criminal justice system may include persons suspected, arrested, or cautioned at the national level.

Number of persons prosecuted for trafficking in persons, by sex, 2014 – September 2017

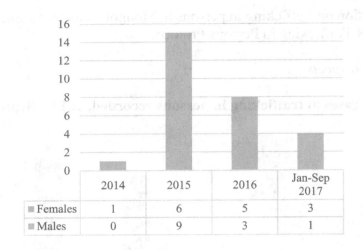

	2014	2015	2016	Jan-Sep 2017
■ Females	1	6	5	3
■ Males	0	9	3	1

Source: General Prosecutor's Office of Mongolia.

Number of persons convicted of trafficking in persons, by sex, 2014 – 2016

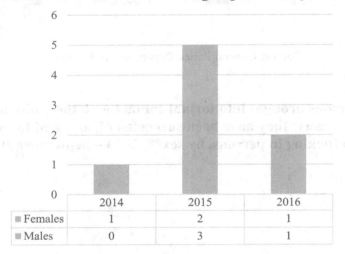

	2014	2015	2016
■ Females	1	2	1
■ Males	0	3	1

Source: The Judicial General Council of Mongolia.

National authorities in Mongolia reported that all persons convicted of trafficking in persons between 2014 and 2016 were nationals of Mongolia.

Source: The Judicial General Council of Mongolia.

Number of victims of trafficking in persons detected, by age and sex, 2014 – September 2017

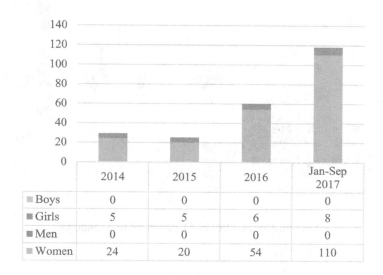

	2014	2015	2016	Jan-Sep 2017
■ Boys	0	0	0	0
■ Girls	5	5	6	8
■ Men	0	0	0	0
■ Women	24	20	54	110

Source: General Police Department of Mongolia.

Number of victims of trafficking in persons detected, by form of exploitation, 2014 – September 2017

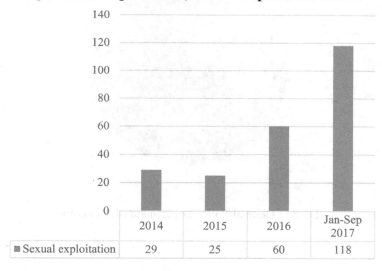

	2014	2015	2016	Jan-Sep 2017
■ Sexual exploitation	29	25	60	118

Source: General Police Department of Mongolia.

All victims identified by national authorities were citizens of Mongolia in the indicated period.

Source: General Police Department of Mongolia.

Type of trafficking experienced by citizens of Mongolia, 2014 - September 2017

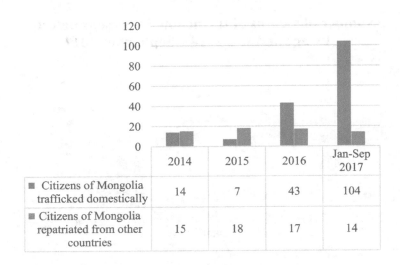

	2014	2015	2016	Jan-Sep 2017
■ Citizens of Mongolia trafficked domestically	14	7	43	104
■ Citizens of Mongolia repatriated from other countries	15	18	17	14

Source: General Police Department of Mongolia.

Countries from which identified victims were repatriated, 2014 - September 2017

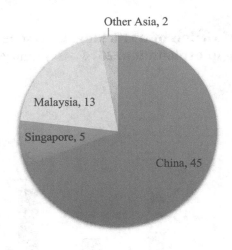

Source: General Police Department of Mongolia.

The current legislation on trafficking in persons in Myanmar covers all forms of trafficking indicated in the UN Trafficking in Persons Protocol.

Investigations and suspects

Number of cases of trafficking in persons recorded, 2015 – April 2018

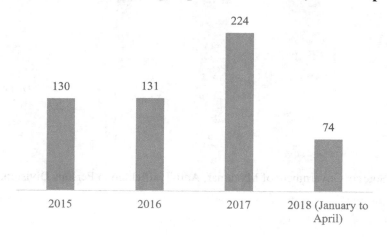

Source: Government of Myanmar, Anti-Trafficking in Persons Division

Number of persons brought into formal contact with the police and/or criminal justice system because they have been suspected of, arrested for or cautioned for trafficking in persons, by sex**, 2015 – April 2018

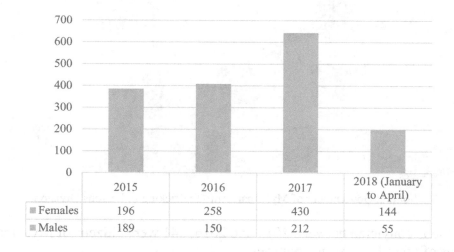

	2015	2016	2017	2018 (January to April)
■ Females	196	258	430	144
■ Males	189	150	212	55

Source: Government of Myanmar, Anti-Trafficking in Persons Division.

**Note: Formal contact with the police and/or criminal justice system may include persons suspected, arrested, or cautioned at the national level.

Number of persons prosecuted for trafficking in persons, by sex, 2014 – April 2018

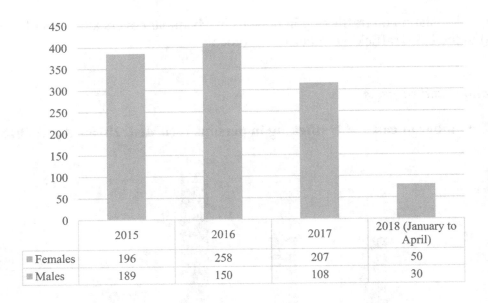

	2015	2016	2017	2018 (January to April)
■ Females	196	258	207	50
■ Males	189	150	108	30

Source: Government of Myanmar, Anti-Trafficking in Persons Division.

Number of persons convicted of trafficking in persons, by sex, 2015 – April 2018

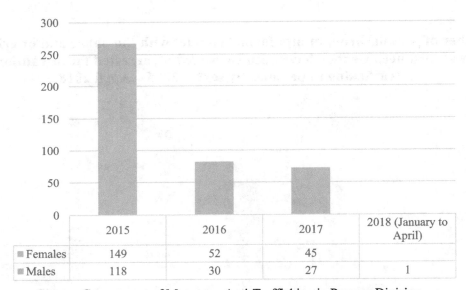

	2015	2016	2017	2018 (January to April)
■ Females	149	52	45	
■ Males	118	30	27	1

Source: Government of Myanmar, Anti-Trafficking in Persons Division.

Of those persons convicted between 2015 and 2016, 341 were citizens of Myanmar, eight were citizens of other East Asian countries.

Source: Government of Myanmar, Anti-Trafficking in Persons Division.

Victims

Number of victims of trafficking in persons detected, by age and sex, 2015 – April 2018

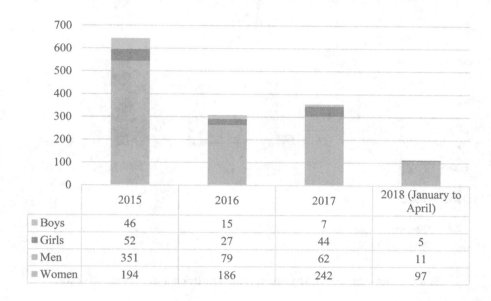

	2015	2016	2017	2018 (January to April)
■ Boys	46	15	7	
■ Girls	52	27	44	5
■ Men	351	79	62	11
■ Women	194	186	242	97

Source: Government of Myanmar, Anti-Trafficking in Persons Division.

Number of victims of trafficking in persons detected, by form of exploitation, 2015 – April 2018

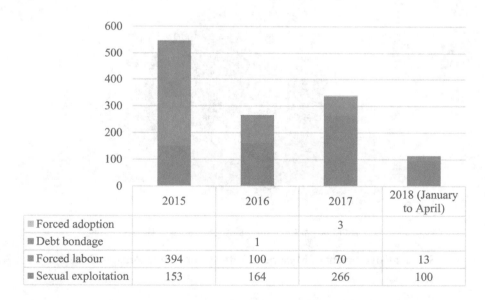

	2015	2016	2017	2018 (January to April)
■ Forced adoption			3	
■ Debt bondage		1		
■ Forced labour	394	100	70	13
■ Sexual exploitation	153	164	266	100

Source: Government of Myanmar, Anti-Trafficking in Persons Division.

In the reporting period, 1,418 detected victims were all citizens of Myanmar

Source: Government of Myanmar, Anti-Trafficking in Persons Division

Identified victims of trafficking, by type of trafficking, 2015 – April 2018

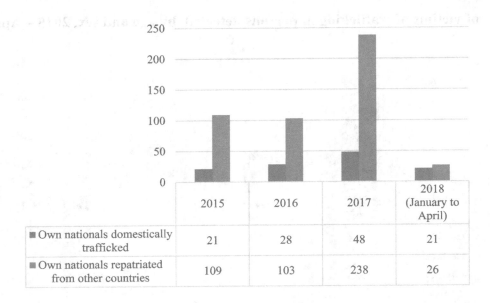

	2015	2016	2017	2018 (January to April)
■ Own nationals domestically trafficked	21	28	48	21
■ Own nationals repatriated from other countries	109	103	238	26

Source: Government of Myanmar, Anti-Trafficking in Persons Division.

Countries from which identified victims were repatriated, 2014 – April 2018

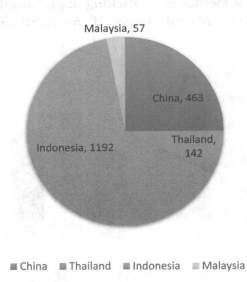

Malaysia, 57
China, 463
Thailand, 142
Indonesia, 1192

■ China ■ Thailand ■ Indonesia ■ Malaysia

Source: Government of Myanmar, Anti-Trafficking in Persons Division.

−New Zealand−

Trafficking in persons is criminalized in New Zealand under different legislations; Section 98D - Human trafficking is a crime under the Crimes Act 1961; Section 98 - Dealing in Slaves is a crime under the Crimes Act 1961; Section 98AA - Dealing in People under 18 for sexual exploitation, removal of body parts, or engagement in forced labour is a crime under the Crimes Act 1961.

Investigations and suspects

In 2015, two men were charged with arranging by deception the entry of foreign nationals into New Zealand. In November 2017, people trafficking charges were laid against a couple arranging by deception the entry of two South Asian citizens, as well as for other offences related to the exploitation of workers on temporary entry visas, the provision of false and misleading information to an immigration officer, aiding and abetting to breach visa conditions, and attempting to pervert the course of justice. The first person to be convicted of people trafficking was sentenced in December 2016.

Source: Immigration New Zealand.

Victims

In 2015, national authorities recorded 18 identified victims, all adult males. In 2016, 19 victims were identified: 13 males and six females. During 2017, four adult males were identified as victims of trafficking in persons.

Source: Immigration New Zealand.

All victims identified were trafficked for forced labour purposes. Identified victims were citizens of South Asian countries and from the Pacific islands.

Source: Immigration New Zealand.

−People's Republic of China−

The People's Republic of China criminalizes trafficking in persons under Articles 240 (abducting and trafficking of women or children), 241 (purchase of women and children), 242(2) (obstruction of rescuing victims), 262 (abduction of children under 14), 358 (forced prostitution), and 359 (harbouring prostitution or seducing others into prostitution).

Investigations and suspects

Recorded number of trafficking in persons crimes, 2014 – 2017**

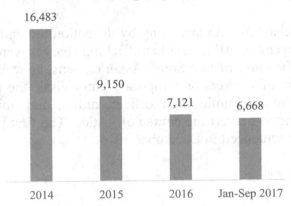

Source: The Government of the People's Republic of China

** In accordance with the following legal provisions: Articles 240, 241, 242(2) and 262 of the Criminal Law of the People's Republic of China.

Number of persons prosecuted for trafficking in persons, by sex, 2014 – 2017**

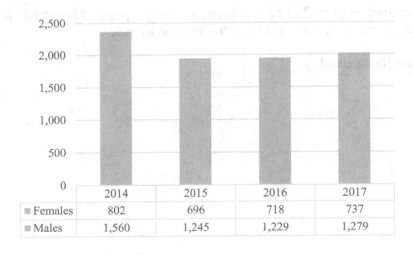

	2014	2015	2016	2017
■ Females	802	696	718	737
■ Males	1,560	1,245	1,229	1,279

Source: The Government of the People's Republic of China

** In accordance with the following legal provisions: Articles 240, 241, 242(2) and 262 of the Criminal Law of the People's Republic of China

−Republic of Korea−

The current legislation on trafficking in the Republic of Korea persons in covers all forms of trafficking indicated in the UN Trafficking in Persons Protocol.

Investigations and suspects

Number of cases of trafficking in persons and related crimes recorded, 2014 – July 2017

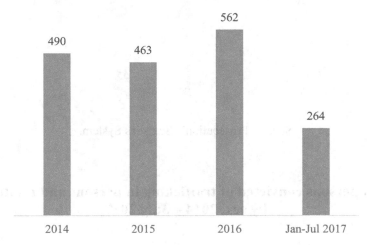

Source: Prosecution's Statistics System.

Number of persons brought into formal contact with the police and/or criminal justice system because they have been suspected of trafficking in persons and related crimes, by sex, 2014 – July 2017

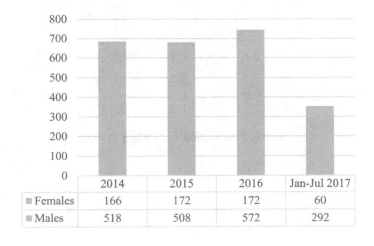

	2014	2015	2016	Jan-Jul 2017
Females	166	172	172	60
Males	518	508	572	292

Source: Prosecution's Statistics System.

Number of persons prosecuted for trafficking in persons and related crimes, by sex, 2014 – July 2017

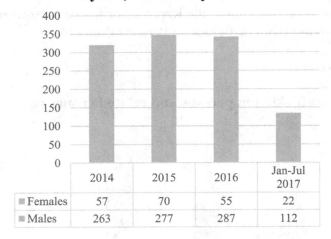

	2014	2015	2016	Jan-Jul 2017
■ Females	57	70	55	22
■ Males	263	277	287	112

Source: Prosecution's Statistics System.

Number of persons convicted of trafficking in persons and related crimes, by sex, 2014 – July 2017

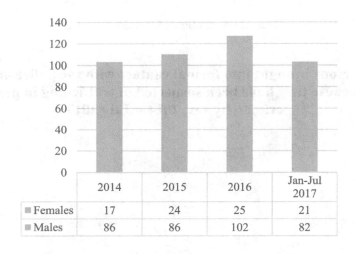

	2014	2015	2016	Jan-Jul 2017
■ Females	17	24	25	21
■ Males	86	86	102	82

Source: Prosecution's Statistics System.

−Singapore−

The current legislation on trafficking in persons in Singapore covers all forms of trafficking indicated in the UN Trafficking in Persons Protocol. Singapore's Prevention of Human Trafficking Act came into force in 2015. Prior to 2015, various elements of the UN Trafficking in Persons Protocol were prosecuted under different criminal statutes.

Investigations and suspects

Number of cases of trafficking in persons recorded, 2015 – August 2017

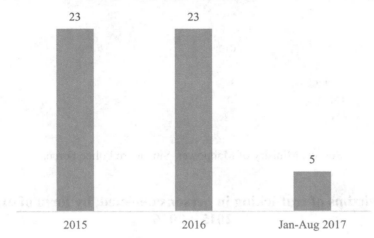

Source: The Ministry of Manpower, Singapore Police Force.

In 2015, 11 persons were brought into formal contact with the police and/or criminal justice system because they were suspected of, arrested for or cautioned for trafficking in persons. Seven of these persons were males and four were females. In 2016, one female and five males were brought into formal contact.

Source: Ministry of Manpower, Singapore Police Force.

In 2014, four males were prosecuted for trafficking in persons. The following year, three males and two females were prosecuted for trafficking in persons. During the first months of 2017, one male was prosecuted. Of those prosecuted in 2016, three males were convicted. In 2017, one male was convicted of trafficking in persons.

Source: Ministry of Manpower, Singapore Police Force.

Victims

Number of victims of trafficking in persons detected, by age and sex, 2015 – 2016

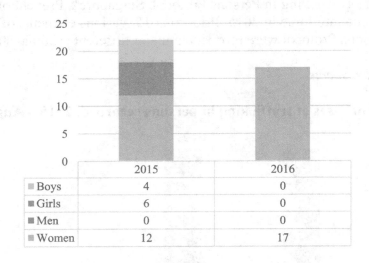

	2015	2016
■ Boys	4	0
■ Girls	6	0
■ Men	0	0
■ Women	12	17

Source: Ministry of Manpower, Singapore Police Force.

Number of victims of trafficking in persons detected, by form of exploitation, 2015 – 2016

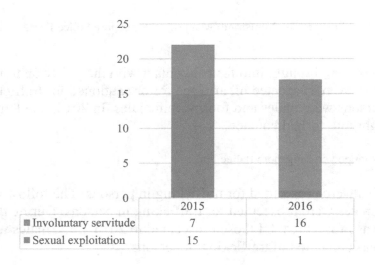

	2015	2016
■ Involuntary servitude	7	16
■ Sexual exploitation	15	1

Source: Ministry of Manpower, Singapore Police Force.

The current legislation on trafficking in persons in Thailand covers all forms of trafficking indicated in the UN Trafficking in Persons Protocol.

Investigations and suspects

Number of cases of trafficking in persons recorded, 2014 – April 2018

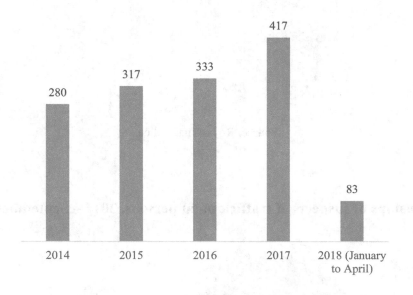

Source: Royal Thai Police and Office of the Attorney General.

Number of persons prosecuted for trafficking in persons, by sex, 2014 – September 2017

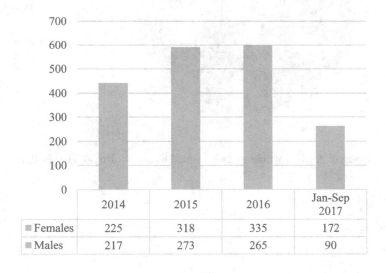

	2014	2015	2016	Jan-Sep 2017
■ Females	225	318	335	172
■ Males	217	273	265	90

Source: Royal Thai Police.

Number of persons convicted of trafficking in persons, by sex, 2014 – September 2017

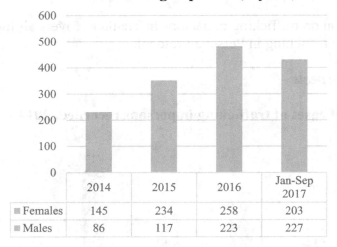

	2014	2015	2016	Jan-Sep 2017
■ Females	145	234	258	203
■ Males	86	117	223	227

Source: Royal Thai Police.

Citizenships of suspects of trafficking in persons, 2014 – September 2017

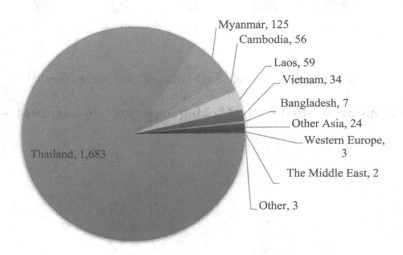

Source: Anti-Trafficking in Persons Division – Royal Thai Police.

Victims

Number of victims of trafficking in persons detected, by age and sex, 2014 – July 2017

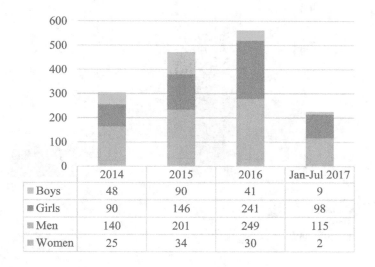

	2014	2015	2016	Jan-Jul 2017
■ Boys	48	90	41	9
■ Girls	90	146	241	98
■ Men	140	201	249	115
■ Women	25	34	30	2

Source: Division of Anti-Trafficking in Persons –
Ministry of Social Development and Human Security.

Number of victims of trafficking in persons detected, by form of exploitation, 2014 – July 2017

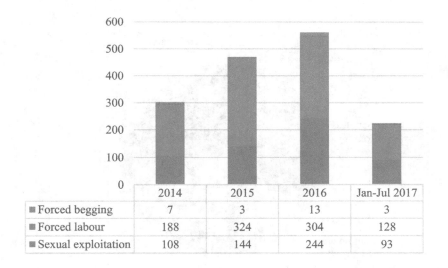

	2014	2015	2016	Jan-Jul 2017
■ Forced begging	7	3	13	3
■ Forced labour	188	324	304	128
■ Sexual exploitation	108	144	244	93

Source: Division of Anti-Trafficking in Persons –
Ministry of Social Development and Human Security.

Number of trafficking in persons legal cases, by form of exploitation, 2017 – April 2018

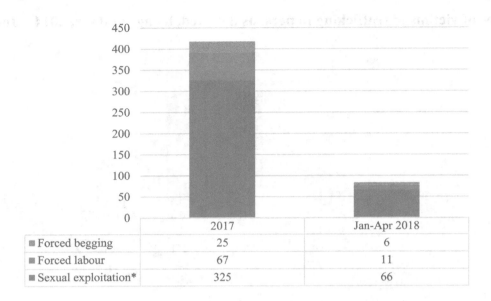

	2017	Jan-Apr 2018
■ Forced begging	25	6
■ Forced labour	67	11
■ Sexual exploitation*	325	66

Source: Office of the Attorney General of Thailand

Citizenships of persons identified as victims of trafficking in persons by state authorities, 2014 – July 2017

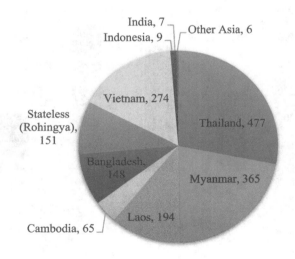

India, 7
Indonesia, 9
Other Asia, 6
Vietnam, 274
Stateless (Rohingya), 151
Thailand, 477
Bangladesh, 148
Myanmar, 365
Cambodia, 65
Laos, 194

Source: Division of Anti-Trafficking in Persons –
Ministry of Social Development and Human Security.

Identified victims of trafficking, by type of trafficking, 2014 – July 2017

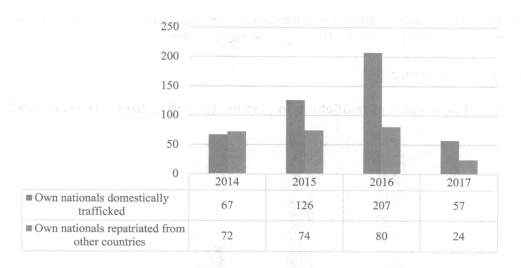

	2014	2015	2016	2017
■ Own nationals domestically trafficked	67	126	207	57
■ Own nationals repatriated from other countries	72	74	80	24

Source: Division of Anti-Trafficking in Persons –
Ministry of Social Development and Human Security.

Countries from which identified victims were repatriated, 2014 – July 2017

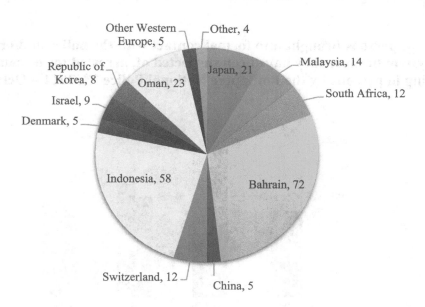

Source: Division of Anti-Trafficking in Persons –
Ministry of Social Development and Human Security.

The current legislation on trafficking in persons in the Philippines covers all forms of trafficking indicated in the UN Trafficking in Persons Protocol.

Investigations and suspects

Number of cases of trafficking in persons recorded, 2014 – October 2017

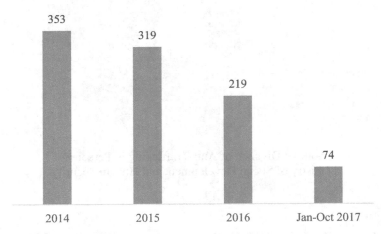

Source: Inter-Agency Council Against Trafficking.

Number of persons brought into formal contact with the police and/or criminal justice system because they have been suspected of, arrested for or cautioned for trafficking in persons by the Philippine National Police **, 2014 – October 2017

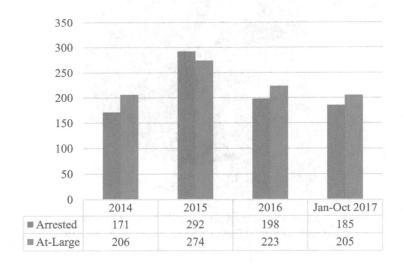

	2014	2015	2016	Jan-Oct 2017
■ Arrested	171	292	198	185
■ At-Large	206	274	223	205

Source: Philippine National Police – Women and Children Protection Centre.

**Note: Formal contact with the police and/or criminal justice system may include persons suspected, arrested, or cautioned at the national level.

Number of persons brought into formal contact with the police and/or criminal justice system because they have been suspected of, arrested for or cautioned for trafficking in persons by the National Bureau of Investigation, 2014 – October 2017

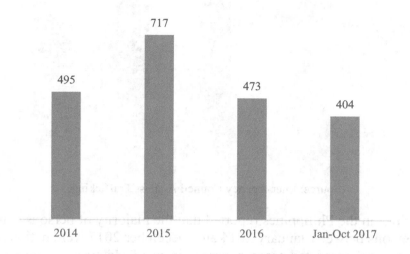

Source: National Bureau of Investigation – Anti-Human Trafficking Division.

Number of persons prosecuted for trafficking in persons, by sex, 2014 – September 2017

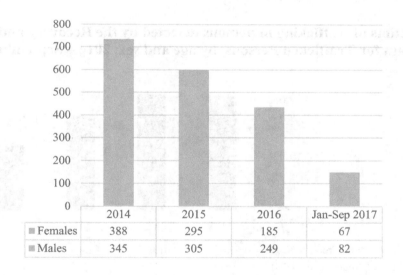

	2014	2015	2016	Jan-Sep 2017
■ Females	388	295	185	67
■ Males	345	305	249	82

Source: Inter-Agency Council Against Trafficking.

Number of persons convicted of trafficking in persons, by sex, 2014 – December 2017

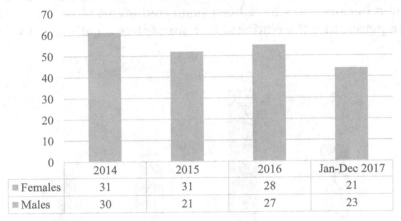

	2014	2015	2016	Jan-Dec 2017
Females	31	31	28	21
Males	30	21	27	23

Source: Inter-Agency Council Against Trafficking.

National authorities in the Philippines reported that the majority of persons convicted of trafficking in persons between January 2014 and December 2017 were nationals of the Philippines. Additional convicted persons were citizens of Malaysia, Switzerland, the Republic of Korea, the United States of America, and Germany.

Source: Inter-Agency Council Against Trafficking.

Victims

Number of victims of trafficking in persons detected by the Recovery and Reintegration Program for Trafficked Persons, by age and sex, 2014 – September 2017

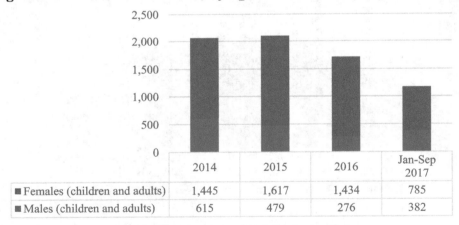

	2014	2015	2016	Jan-Sep 2017
Females (children and adults)	1,445	1,617	1,434	785
Males (children and adults)	615	479	276	382

Source: Department of Social Welfare and Development.

Additional information
The majority of victims detected by the Recovery and Reintegration Program were adults.

Source: Department of Social Welfare and Development.

Number of victims of trafficking in persons detected by the Philippine National Police – Women and Children Protection Center, by age and sex, 2014 – October 2017

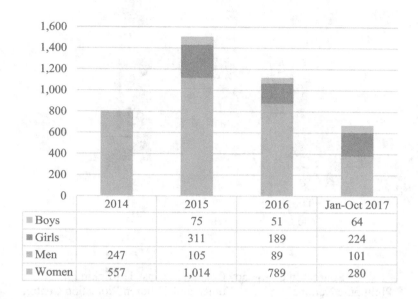

	2014	2015	2016	Jan-Oct 2017
■ Boys		75	51	64
■ Girls		311	189	224
■ Men	247	105	89	101
■ Women	557	1,014	789	280

Source: Philippine National Police – Women and Children Protection Centre.

Number of victims of trafficking in persons detected by the National Bureau of Investigation – Anti-Human Trafficking Division, by age and sex, 2014 – September 2017

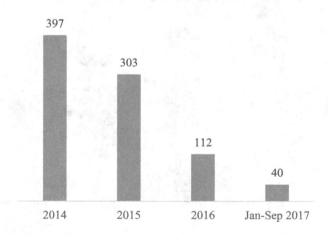

Source: National Bureau of Investigation – Human Trafficking Division.

Number of victims of trafficking in persons detected by the Anti-Trafficking Task Force, by age and sex, 2014 – October 2017

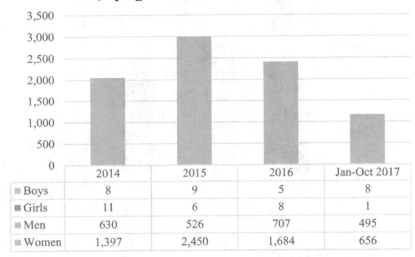

	2014	2015	2016	Jan-Oct 2017
Boys	8	9	5	8
Girls	11	6	8	1
Men	630	526	707	495
Women	1,397	2,450	1,684	656

Source: Inter-Agency Council Against Trafficking,
Philippine National Police – Women and Children Protection Centre,
and Department of Social Welfare and Development.

Number of victims of trafficking in persons assisted in prosecution of cases, by age and sex, 2014 – October 2017

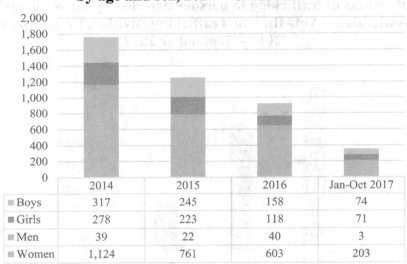

	2014	2015	2016	Jan-Oct 2017
Boys	317	245	158	74
Girls	278	223	118	71
Men	39	22	40	3
Women	1,124	761	603	203

Source: Inter-Agency Council Against Trafficking.

Number of victims of trafficking in persons assisted in prosecution of cases, by form of exploitation, 2014 – October 2017

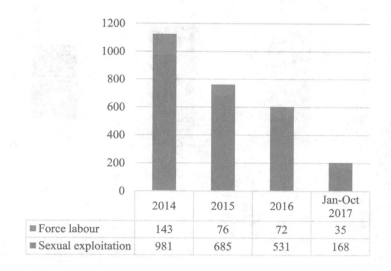

	2014	2015	2016	Jan-Oct 2017
■ Force labour	143	76	72	35
■ Sexual exploitation	981	685	531	168

Source: Inter-Agency Council Against Trafficking.

Number of victims of trafficking in detected by the Philippine National Police – Women and Children Protection Centre, by form of exploitation, 2014 – October 2017

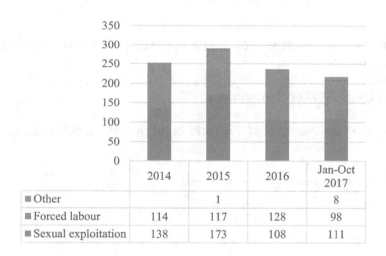

	2014	2015	2016	Jan-Oct 2017
■ Other		1		8
■ Forced labour	114	117	128	98
■ Sexual exploitation	138	173	108	111

Source: Philippine National Police – Women and Children Protection Centre.

Number of victims of trafficking in detected by the Recovery and Reintegration Program for Trafficked Persons, by form of exploitation, 2014 – September 2017

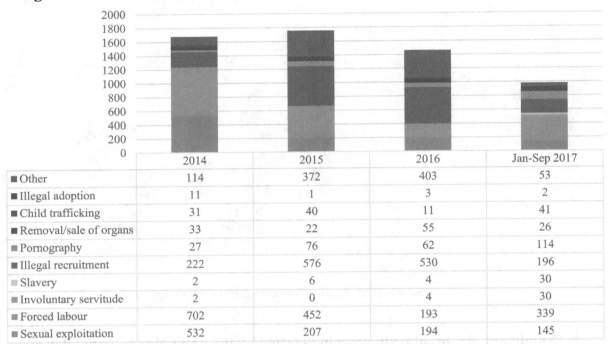

	2014	2015	2016	Jan-Sep 2017
▪ Other	114	372	403	53
▪ Illegal adoption	11	1	3	2
▪ Child trafficking	31	40	11	41
▪ Removal/sale of organs	33	22	55	26
▪ Pornography	27	76	62	114
▪ Illegal recruitment	222	576	530	196
▪ Slavery	2	6	4	30
▪ Involuntary servitude	2	0	4	30
▪ Forced labour	702	452	193	339
▪ Sexual exploitation	532	207	194	145

Source: Department of Social Welfare and Development.

The majority of victims were citizens of the Philippines. Other detected victims were citizens of China, Ukraine, and Indonesia.

Source: Inter-Agency Council Against Trafficking.

Between January 2014 and September 27, forty eight persons were repatriated to the Philippines.

Source: Inter-Agency Council Against Trafficking.

−Timor Leste−

The current legislation on trafficking in persons in Timor Leste covers all forms of trafficking indicated in the UN Trafficking in Persons Protocol. Articles 163, 164, and 165 of the penal code refer to trafficking offences and were introduced in 2009.

Investigations and suspects

In 2015, 5 cases of trafficking in persons were recorded, and in 2016 and 2017, 3 cases were recorded each year. In the years of 2015 and 2017, 2 persons per year were brought into formal contact with the police and/or criminal justice system by either being suspected, cautioned, or arrested for trafficking in persons.

In total, prosecution for trafficking in persons was commenced against 2 persons in 2015 and 1 person in 2016. In 2017, 2 females and one male were prosecuted. Between 2015 and 2017, one person was convicted of trafficking in persons each year.

Source: Police Scientific Criminal Investigation.

Victims

In the period between 2015 and 2017 about 40 females were identified by state authorities as victims of trafficking in persons. Most were identified as victims of sexual exploitation. All of the detected victims of trafficking in persons in the period between 2015 and 2017 were Asian citizens.

Source: Police Scientific Criminal Investigation.

The current legislation on trafficking in persons in Viet Nam covers all forms of trafficking indicated in the UN Trafficking in Persons Protocol. The offence of trafficking in persons is codified at Article 119 of the criminal code. Authorities also use the law prohibiting "fraudulently exchanging or appropriating children" under Article 120 of the criminal code to prosecute trafficking cases.

Investigations and suspects

Number of cases of trafficking in persons recorded under Articles 119 and 120, 2012 – June 2015

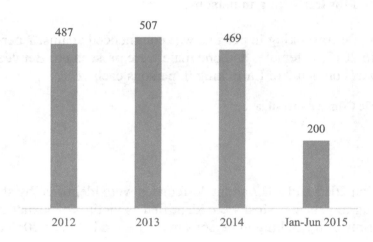

Source: Steering Committee on Preventing and Combating Criminals.

Number of persons prosecuted for trafficking in persons under Articles 119 and 120, 2012 – June 2015

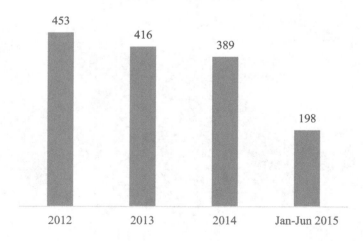

Source: The Supreme People's Procuracy of Viet Nam.

Number of persons convicted of trafficking in persons, by level of conviction and article of the criminal code used, 2012 – June 2015

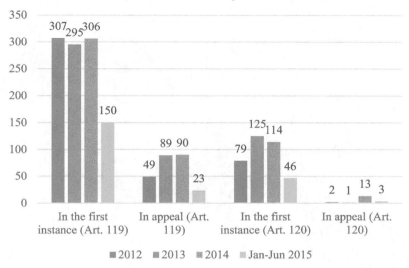

Source: The Supreme People's Court of Viet Nam.

Victims

Number of victims of trafficking in persons detected, 2012 – June 2015

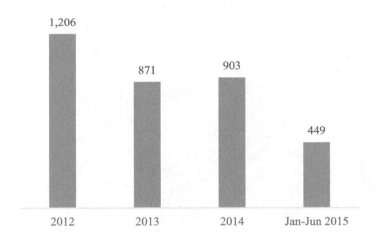

Source: Steering Committee on Preventing and Combating Criminals.

All detected victims between January 2012 and June 2015 were citizens of Viet Nam. When trafficked internationally, victims were repatriated from countries in East Asia.

Source: Steering Committee on Preventing and Combating Criminals, Department of the Ministry of Public Security of Viet Nam.

NORTH AMERICA

−Canada−

The current legislation on trafficking in persons in Canada covers all forms of trafficking indicated in the UN Trafficking in Persons Protocol.

Investigations and suspects

Number of offences of trafficking in persons recorded, 2014 – August 2017

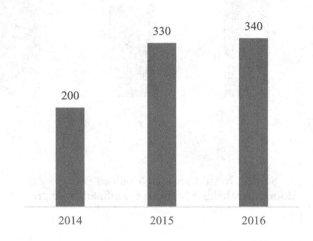

Source: The Uniform Crime Reporting Survey.

Number of persons brought into formal contact with the police and/or criminal justice system because they have been suspected of, arrested for or cautioned for trafficking in persons, by sex**, 2014 – 2016

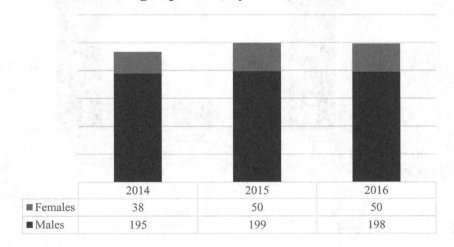

	2014	2015	2016
■ Females	38	50	50
■ Males	195	199	198

Source: The Uniform Crime Reporting Survey and Royal Canadian Mounted Police – Human Trafficking National Coordination Centre.

**Note: Formal contact with the police and/or criminal justice system may include persons suspected, arrested, or cautioned at the national level.

Number of persons prosecuted for trafficking in persons, by sex, 2014 – 2016

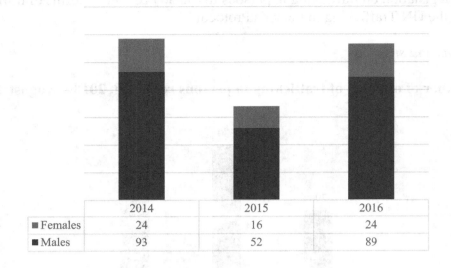

	2014	2015	2016
■ Females	24	16	24
■ Males	93	52	89

Source: Royal Canadian Mounted Police –
Human Trafficking National Coordination Centre.

Number of persons convicted of trafficking in persons, by sex, 2014 – 2016

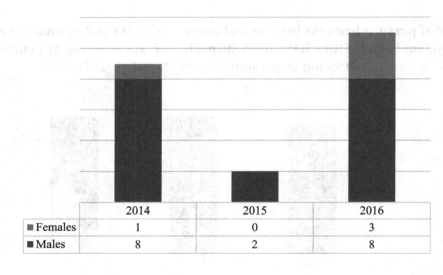

	2014	2015	2016
■ Females	1	0	3
■ Males	8	2	8

Source: Royal Canadian Mounted Police –
Human Trafficking National Coordination Centre.

The Royal Canadian Mounted Police – Human Trafficking National Coordination Centre reported that the majority of persons convicted of trafficking in persons between 2014 and September were Canadian nationals. According to reports, there are numerous offenders whose citizenship is unknown.

Source: The Royal Canadian Mounted Police – Human Trafficking National Coordination Centre

Victims

Number of victims of trafficking in persons detected, by age and sex, 2014 – 2016

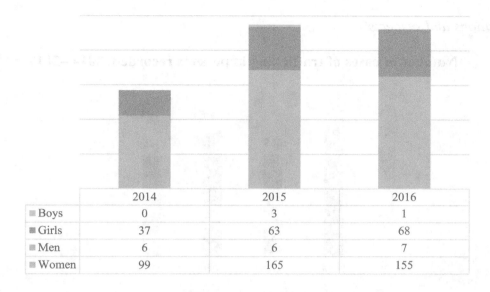

	2014	2015	2016
▪ Boys	0	3	1
▪ Girls	37	63	68
▪ Men	6	6	7
▪ Women	99	165	155

Source: The Uniform Crime Reporting Survey and
Royal Canadian Mounted Police – Human Trafficking National Coordination Centre.

Number of victims of trafficking in persons detected, by form of exploitation, 2014 – 2016

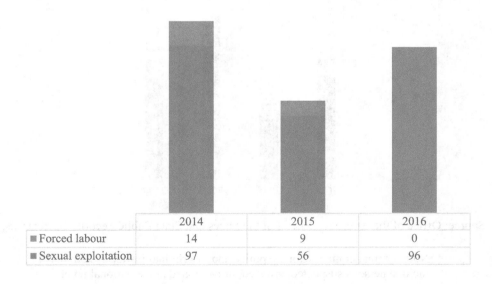

	2014	2015	2016
▪ Forced labour	14	9	0
▪ Sexual exploitation	97	56	96

Source: Royal Canadian Mounted Police –
Human Trafficking National Coordination Centre.

−Mexico−

The current legislation on trafficking in persons in Mexico covers all forms of trafficking indicated in the UN Trafficking in Persons Protocol.

Investigations and suspects

Number of cases of trafficking in persons recorded, 2014 –2017

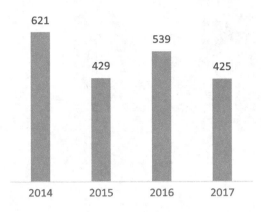

Source: National Commission of Superior Courts of Justice of the United Mexican States.

Number of persons brought into formal contact with the police and/or criminal justice system because they have been suspected of, arrested for or cautioned for trafficking in persons **, 2014 –2017

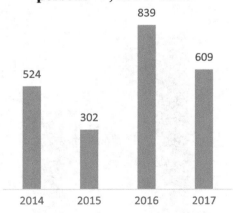

Source: Office of the Attorney General of the States and State Public Security Secretariats.

**Note: Formal contact with the police and/or criminal justice system may include persons suspected, arrested, or cautioned at the national level.

Number of persons prosecuted for trafficking in persons, by sex, 2014 –2017

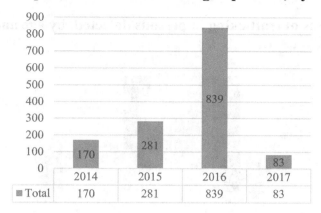

	2014	2015	2016	2017
■ Total	170	281	839	83

Source: National Commission of Superior Courts of Justice of the United Mexican States.

Number of persons convicted of trafficking in persons, by sex, 2014 –2017

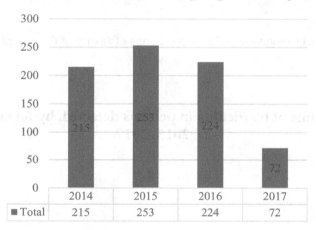

	2014	2015	2016	2017
■ Total	215	253	224	72

Source: Comisión Nacional de Tribunales Superiores de Justicia de los Estados Unidos Mexicanos (CONATRIB), Consejo de la Judicatura Federal (CJF) y Secretariado Ejecutivo del Sistema Nacional de Seguridad Pública (SESNSP).

Citizenships of persons convicted of trafficking in persons, 2014 – September 2017

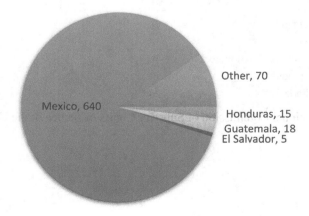

Source: National Commission of Superior Courts of Justice of the United Mexican States.

Victims

Number of victims of trafficking in persons detected, by age and sex, 2015 -2017

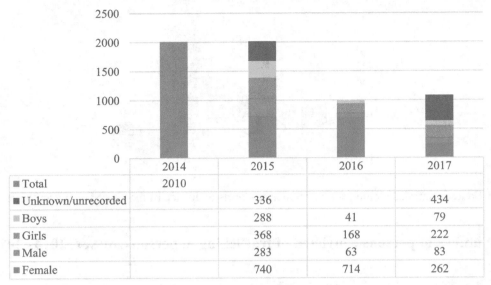

	2014	2015	2016	2017
■ Total	2010			
■ Unknown/unrecorded		336		434
■ Boys		288	41	79
■ Girls		368	168	222
■ Male		283	63	83
■ Female		740	714	262

Source: National Commission of Superior Courts of Justice of the United Mexican States.

Number of victims of trafficking in persons detected, by forms of exploitation, 2015 -2017

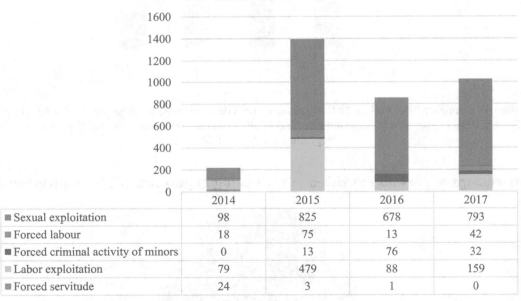

	2014	2015	2016	2017
■ Sexual exploitation	98	825	678	793
■ Forced labour	18	75	13	42
■ Forced criminal activity of minors	0	13	76	32
■ Labor exploitation	79	479	88	159
■ Forced servitude	24	3	1	0

Source: National Commission of Superior Courts of Justice of the United Mexican States.

Citizenships of persons identified as victims of trafficking in persons by state authorities**, 2014 – September 2017

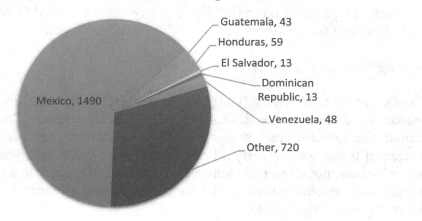

Source: National Commission of Superior Courts of Justice of the United Mexican States.

−United States of America−

The current legislation on trafficking in persons in the United States of America covers sex trafficking and forced labour.

Investigations and suspects

The Departments of Justice (DOJ), Homeland Security (DHS), and State (DOS) are the primary investigating agencies for federal trafficking offenses. The United States has no formal mechanism to track prosecutions at the state and local levels. While the Federal Bureau of Investigation (FBI) collects data on state and local human trafficking investigations, not all jurisdictions participate. In 2016, participating state and local jurisdictions reported a total of 654 human trafficking offences resulting in arrest or solved for crime reporting purposes.

Source: The U.S. Department of State Trafficking in Persons Report, 2016, 2017.

Number of cases investigated by federal government agencies, October 2013 - September 2016**

	Oct 2013-Sep 2014	Oct 2014-Sep 2015	Oct 2015-Sep 2016
■ Department of Homeland Security	987	1,034	1,029
▨ Department of Justice	835	802	843
■ Department of State	154	175	288

Source: The U.S. Department of State Trafficking in Persons Report, 2016, 2017.

**Note: Statistics are taken per fiscal year in the United States, which spans the period between October 1 and September 30.

Additional information

In addition, DOJ funds Enhanced Collaborative Model (ECM) anti-trafficking taskforces. In the period between October 1, 2013 and September 30, 2014, these taskforces, which include participation from other federal partners, reported initiating 1,083 investigations. From October 1, 2014 to September 30, 2015, the taskforces investigated 1,011 cases and 982 cases between October 1, 2015 and September 30, 2016.

The Department of Defense (DOD) investigates trafficking in persons cases involving U.S. military, DoD civilians, and Defense contractor personnel. DoD reported investigating 14 cases involving U.S. military in 2014, 10 cases in 2015, and 13 cases in 2016.

The Department of the Interior investigated one trafficking in persons case in 2016.

Source: The U.S. Department of State Trafficking in Persons Report, 2016, 2017.

**Number of persons prosecuted for trafficking in persons,
October 1, 2013– September 30, 2016****

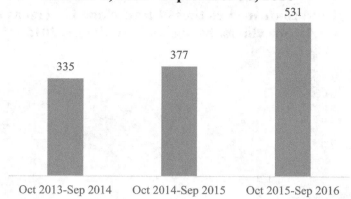

Source: The U.S. Department of State Trafficking in Persons Report, 2016, 2017.

**These prosecutions represent federal human trafficking prosecutions initiated by DOJ. Data includes defendants charged under trafficking-specific criminal statutes and related non-trafficking criminal statutes. The data does not include child sex trafficking cases brought under non-trafficking statutes.

Additional information

The number of persons prosecuted for trafficking in persons does not correlate to the number of cases prosecuted as there may have been multiple defendants in a case. In 2014, DOJ brought 208 prosecutions, 257 in 2015, and 241 in 2016.

Source: The U.S. Department of State Trafficking in Persons Report, 2016, 2017.

**Number of persons convicted of trafficking in persons,
October 1, 2013 – September 30, 2016****

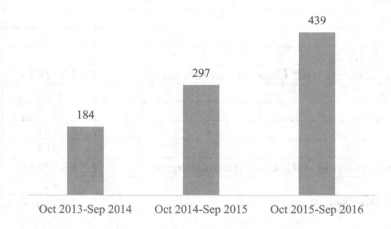

Source: The U.S. Department of State Trafficking in Persons Report, 2016, 2017.

**These convictions represent federal human trafficking convictions secured by the Department of Justice. Data includes defendants charged under trafficking-specific criminal statutes and related non-trafficking criminal. The data does not include child sex trafficking cases brought under non-trafficking statutes.

Victims

Number of potential and confirmed victims of trafficking in persons detected by DOJ-funded victim service providers, by age and sex, July 1, 2015 – June 30, 2017

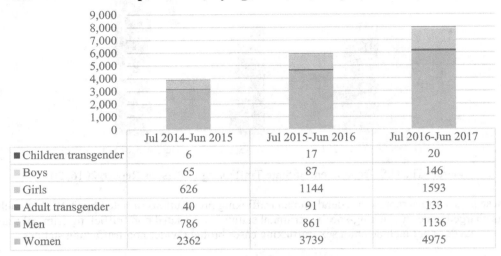

	Jul 2014-Jun 2015	Jul 2015-Jun 2016	Jul 2016-Jun 2017
■ Children transgender	6	17	20
■ Boys	65	87	146
■ Girls	626	1144	1593
■ Adult transgender	40	91	133
■ Men	786	861	1136
■ Women	2362	3739	4975

Source: Department of Justice Office for Victims of Crime.

Number of victims of trafficking in persons assisted by HHS, FY 2016 and FY 2017 **

Adult Certification Letters Issued	**FY 2016**	**FY 2017**
Male	155	165
Female	288	281
Labor Trafficking	324	333
Sex Trafficking	78	77
Labor and Sex Trafficking	41	35
Minor Eligibility Letters Issued	**FY 2016**	**FY 2017**
Male	195	288
Female	137	221
Labor Trafficking	243	370
Sex Trafficking	74	105
Labor and Sex Trafficking	15	34
Foreign Victims Assisted with Case Management	**FY 2016**	**FY 2017**
Adults	1168	1043
Minors	256	57
Male	591	453
Female	812	630
Domestic Victims Assisted with Case Management	**FY 2016**	**FY 2017**
Total	341	636
Victims Assisted through Hotline	**FY 2016**	**FY 2017**
Adults	4771	5469
Minors	2294	2742
Male	913	1205
Female	6237	7185

Source: Department of Health and Human Services Office on Trafficking in Persons

**Record-keeping systems used by DOJ and HHS did not allow for cross-referencing to determine which victims were served by both agencies.

Additional information

The Department of Health and Human Services (HHS) issued Certification and Eligibility Letters for foreign victims to be eligible for services and benefits to the same extent as refugees, provided grant funding for comprehensive case management for foreign and domestic trafficking victims, and funded capacity-building grants for community-based organizations and child welfare systems to respond to trafficking. In FY 2016, HHS issued 775 total adult and child letters and 955 in FY 2017.

In addition, HHS funds the Trafficking Victims Assistance Program (TVAP), awarding grants to three NGOs to provide comprehensive case management services to foreign national victims and their qualified family members through a nationwide network of NGO sub-recipients. In FY 2016, there were 1,424 persons served through this program and 1,531 served in FY 2017.

DOJ provides funding to develop, expand, or strengthen victim service programs for both domestic and foreign trafficking victims: as of May 2018, DOJ funding supported approximately 115 awards with this goal across the United States. During FY 2017, DOJ made new awards to 19 victim service providers offering comprehensive and specialized services across the United States, totalling approximately $16.2 million, compared with $19.7 million in FY 2017 and $13.8 million in FY 2016.

Source: Department of Justice Office for Victims of Crime and the Department of Health and Human Services.

The United States provides trafficking-specific immigration options through Continued Presence and T non-immigrant status, which is also temporary, but which includes a potential to adjust to lawful permanent resident status. T non-immigrant status is available for victims and eligible family members. In FY 2016, 1,736 victims and eligible family members were approved. In FY 2017, 1,336 victims and eligible family members were approved. T-non-immigrants can also apply to adjust to lawful permanent residents if they meet certain eligibility requirements.

Source: United States Citizenship and Immigration Services.

Number of potential and confirmed victims of trafficking in persons detected by DOJ-funded victim service providers, by form of exploitation, July 1, 2015-June 30, 2017

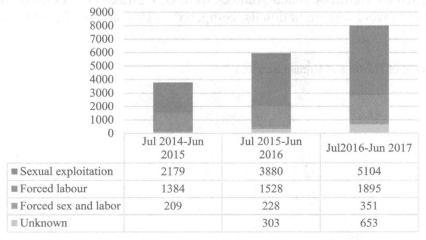

	Jul 2014-Jun 2015	Jul 2015-Jun 2016	Jul2016-Jun 2017
Sexual exploitation	2179	3880	5104
Forced labour	1384	1528	1895
Forced sex and labor	209	228	351
Unknown		303	653

Source: Department of Justice Office for Victims of Crime.

Citizenships of persons identified as potential and confirmed victims of trafficking in persons by DOJ-funded victim service providers by state authorities, July 2016 – June 2017

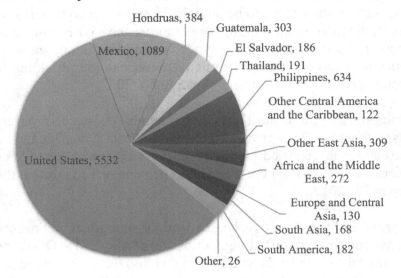

Source: Department of Justice Office for Victims of Crime.

Additional information

In 2017, HHS issued Certification and Eligibility letters to foreign victims, both adults and children, from approximately 63 countries. The majority of victims originated from Honduras, Guatemala, Mexico, El Salvador, and the Philippines. In 2016, letters were issued to victims from 60 countries. The majority of victims originated from the Philippines, Mexico, Guatemala, Honduras, India, El Salvador and Thailand.

Source: Department of Health and Human Services.

In FY 2017, Department of Health and Human Services Office on Trafficking in Persons reported that 57% potential victims of human trafficking assisted through the National Human Trafficking Hotline were U.S. citizens and lawful permanent residents and 43% were foreign nationals, compared to 55% and 45% respectively in FY 2016. In FY 2017, 20% of victims identified by victim outreach grantees were U.S. citizens or lawful permanent residents and 80% were foreign nationals, compared to 10% and 90% respectively in FY 2016.

Source: Department of Health and Human Services

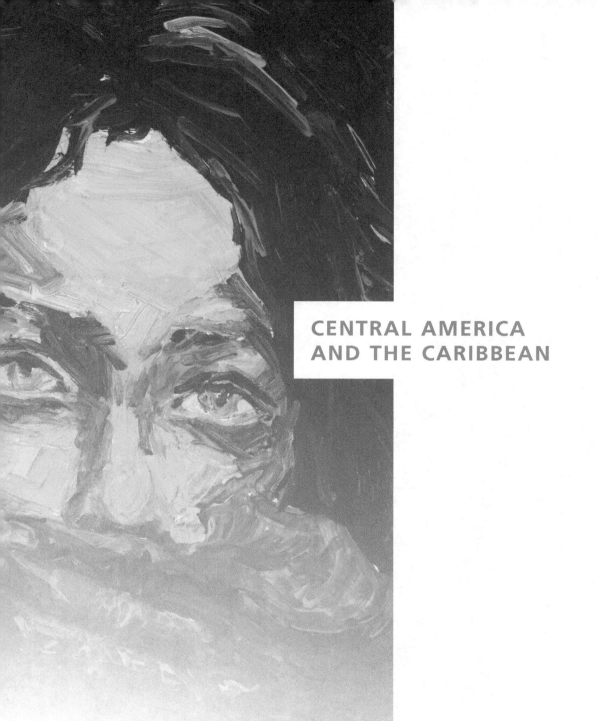

**CENTRAL AMERICA
AND THE CARIBBEAN**

−The Caribbean Islands−

This section covers Antigua and Barbuda, The Bahamas, Grenada, Jamaica, and The Republic of Trinidad and Tobago. The current legislation on trafficking in persons in Antigua and Barbuda, The Bahamas, Grenada, Jamaica, and in The Republic of Trinidad and Tobago cover all forms of trafficking indicated in the UN Trafficking in Persons Protocol. The Prevention of Trafficking in Persons Act of Grenada was introduced in July 2014.

Investigations and victims

In 2015, the Directorate of Gender Affairs in Antigua and Barbuda reported two female perpetrators of trafficking.

Source: DoGa: Directorate of Gender Affairs, Gender Based Violence Statistics 2011-2015.

As of 2017, there have been no reported trafficking in persons cases or victims in Grenada.

Source: Criminal Investigation Department of Grenada.

Between 2014 and 2015, the Jamaican Constabulary Force Trafficking in Persons Unit conducted 31 raids, launching 35 new trafficking in persons investigations. Five persons were arrested and charged, while 18 others were arrested and charged for offences akin to human trafficking.

Source: National Task Force against Trafficking in Persons.

In the period between April 2017 and March 2018, there were 42 ongoing investigations of trafficking in persons in The Republic of Trinidad and Tobago. There were 7 charges, of which 3 were in reference to the trafficking in Persons Act, and 4 in relation to other sexual offences.

Source: Permanent Mission of the Republic of Trinidad and Tobago to the Office of the United Nations, Vienna.

Victims

In Antigua and Barbuda, seven female human trafficking victims were identified in 2014, while six female and two male victims were identified in 2015.

Source: DoGa: Directorate of Gender Affairs, Gender Based Violence Statistics 2011-2015.

In the same period in The Republic of Trinidad and Tobago, 16 victims were identified, of which 13 were Venezuelans, 2 were Trinidad and Tobago citizens and one from other countries.

Source: Permanent Mission of the republic of Trinidad and Tobago to the Office of the United Nations, Vienna.

−Costa Rica−

The current legislation on trafficking in persons in Costa Rica covers all forms of trafficking indicated in the UN Trafficking in Persons Protocol.

Investigations and suspects

Number of cases of trafficking in persons recorded, 2014 – September 2017

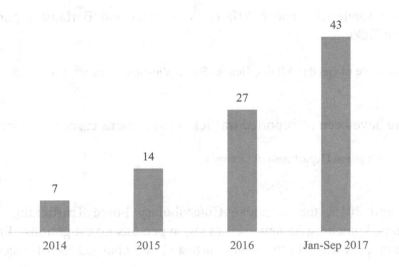

Source: Deputy Prosecutor's Office against Trafficking in Persons.

Number of persons brought into formal contact with the police and/or criminal justice system because they have been arrested for trafficking in persons, by sex, 2016 – September 2017

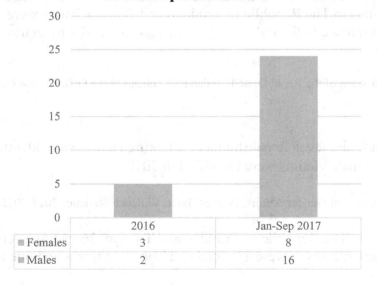

	2016	Jan-Sep 2017
■ Females	3	8
■ Males	2	16

Source: Deputy Prosecutor's Office against Trafficking in Persons.

Number of persons prosecuted for trafficking in persons, by sex, 2016 – September 2017

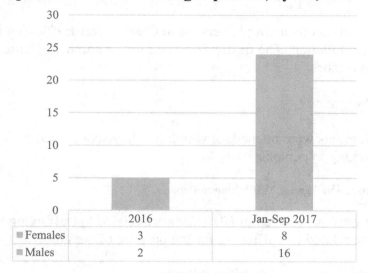

	2016	Jan-Sep 2017
▪ Females	3	8
▪ Males	2	16

Source: Deputy Prosecutor's Office against Trafficking in Persons.

Of those prosecuted in 2016, one male was convicted of trafficking in persons. In the first nine months of 2017, 10 persons were convicted, five males and five females. The majority of those convicted in 2017 were nationals of Costa Rica with citizens of other Central American countries.

Source: Deputy Prosecutor's Office against Trafficking in Persons.

Victims

In 2016, five adult female victims of trafficking in persons for sexual exploitation were detected. In 2017, a total of 60 victims were identified – 23 girls, 30 women, and seven men. Of those victims detected in 2017, 53 were trafficked for sexual exploitation, 14 for organ removal, seven for a mix of forced labour and sexual exploitation, and two for illegal adoption. In 2014, victims were repatriated from the United States and Spain.

Source: Deputy Prosecutor's Office against Trafficking in Persons.

The current legislation on trafficking in persons in Cuba covers trafficking in persons for the purpose of sexual exploitation. The trafficking of minors is another offense, which legislation calls "corruption of minors."

Investigations and suspects

In 2016, 14 investigations were opened, of which two have concluded with criminal sentences for trafficking in persons.

Source: National Commission Against Trafficking in Persons.

A total of 21 cases were prosecuted in 2016. 20 were related to trafficking for sexual exploitation and one related to trafficking for the purpose of begging.

Source: National Commission Against Trafficking in Persons.

Victims

The majority of detected victims were trafficked for the purpose of sexual exploitation in 2016 with others trafficked for the purpose of corruption of minors.

Source: National Commission Against Trafficking in Persons.

Cuban victims trafficked internationally were identified in South America, Western and Southern Europe, North America and Sub Saharan Africa.

Source: National Commission Against Trafficking in Persons.

In 2016, 20 Cubans were identified as victims of trafficking in Turkey. In the same year, six Cuban children were identified as victims of trafficking in the United States.

Source: National Commission Against Trafficking in Persons.

The current legislation on trafficking in persons in the Dominican Republic covers all forms of trafficking indicated in the UN Trafficking in Persons Protocol.

Investigations and suspects

The Dominican Republic recorded eight cases of trafficking in persons in 2014 and 2016, 15 cases in 2015, while during the first nine months of 2017, 12 cases were recorded.

Source: Annual Report of the Special Prosecutor's Office against the Illicit Trafficking of Migrants and Trafficking in Persons.

Number of persons brought into formal contact with the police and/or criminal justice system because they have been suspected of, arrested for or cautioned for trafficking in persons, by sex**, 2015 – September 2017

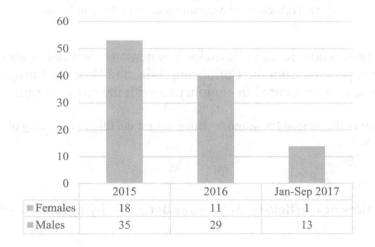

	2015	2016	Jan-Sep 2017
▪ Females	18	11	1
▪ Males	35	29	13

Source: Annual Report of the Special Prosecutor's Office against the
Illicit Trafficking of Migrants and Trafficking in Persons.

**Note: Formal contact with the police and/or criminal justice system may
include persons suspected, arrested, or cautioned at the national level.

In 2014, 66 persons were suspected of, arrested for or cautioned for trafficking in persons. The same number of persons who were brought into formal contact with the police and/or criminal justice system were prosecuted for the crime in corresponding years.

Source: Annual Report of the Special Prosecutor's Office against the Illicit Trafficking of Migrants and Trafficking in Persons.

Number of persons convicted of trafficking in persons, by sex, 2014 – September 2017

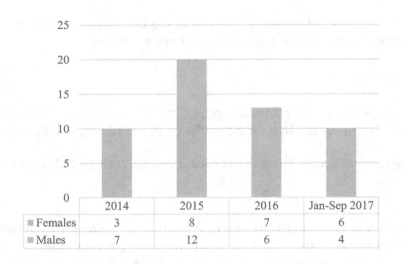

	2014	2015	2016	Jan-Sep 2017
■ Females	3	8	7	6
■ Males	7	12	6	4

Source: Annual Report of the Special Prosecutor's Office against the
Illicit Trafficking of Migrants and Trafficking in Persons.

The majority of persons convicted of trafficking in persons were nationals of the Dominican Republic with three persons from the Caribbean, Asia, and Western Europe. The charge of pimping was also sought or secured in conjunction with the crime of trafficking in persons.

Source: Annual Report of the Special Prosecutor's Office against the Illicit Trafficking of Migrants and Trafficking in Persons.

Victims

Number of victims of trafficking in persons detected, by age, 2014 – September 2017

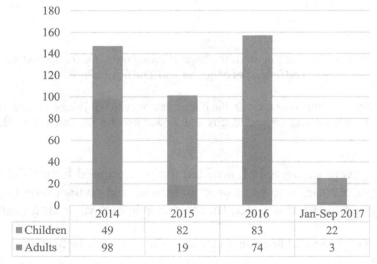

	2014	2015	2016	Jan-Sep 2017
■ Children	49	82	83	22
■ Adults	98	19	74	3

Source: Annual Report of the Special Prosecutor's Office against the
Illicit Trafficking of Migrants and Trafficking in Persons.

Additional information
The majority of victims detected by national authorities in the indicated period, as shown by the chart above, were minors under the age of eighteen. Of these children, the majority were female, with 48 identified minor female victims in 2014 and 63 in 2016. Females were also

the majority of victims in the adult category, with 70 identified adult female victims in 2014 and 74 in 2016. 101 were nationals of the Dominican Republic and 82 were of unknown citizenships.

Source: Source: Annual Report of the Special Prosecutor's Office against the
Illicit Trafficking of Migrants and Trafficking in Persons.

Number of victims of trafficking in persons detected, by form of exploitation, 2014 – September 2017

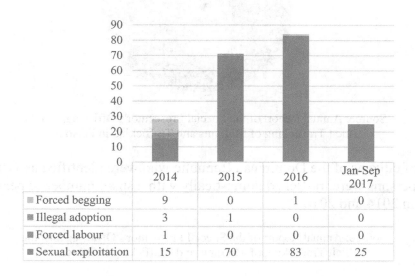

	2014	2015	2016	Jan-Sep 2017
■ Forced begging	9	0	1	0
■ Illegal adoption	3	1	0	0
■ Forced labour	1	0	0	0
■ Sexual exploitation	15	70	83	25

Source: Annual Report of the Special Prosecutor's Office against the
Illicit Trafficking of Migrants and Trafficking in Persons.

Citizenships of persons identified as victims of trafficking in persons by state authorities, 2014 – September 2017

Colombia, 22

Other, 1

Venezuela, 38

Dominican Repuiblic, 429

Source: Annual Report of the Special Prosecutor's Office against the
Illicit Trafficking of Migrants and Trafficking in Persons.

The majority of citizens of the Dominican Republic who were identified as victims of trafficking in persons were trafficked domestically with a small number of persons reported as repatriated in 2014 and 2016.

Source: Annual Report of the Special Prosecutor's Office against the
Illicit Trafficking of Migrants and Trafficking in Persons.

−El Salvador−

The current legislation on trafficking in persons in El Salvador covers all forms of trafficking indicated in the UN Trafficking in Persons Protocol.

Investigations and suspects

Number of cases of trafficking in persons recorded, 2014 – June 2017

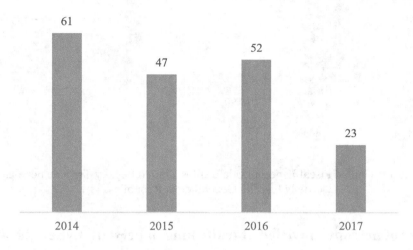

Source: Unidad Fiscal Especializada Delitos Tráfico Ilegal y Trata de personas de la Fiscalía General de la República.

Number of persons brought into formal contact with the police and/or criminal justice system because they have been suspected of, arrested for or cautioned for trafficking in persons, by sex**, 2014 –2017

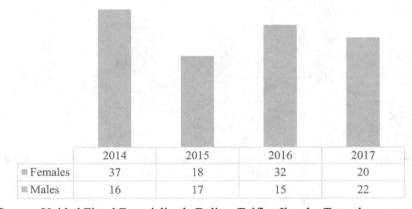

	2014	2015	2016	2017
Females	37	18	32	20
Males	16	17	15	22

Source: Unidad Fiscal Especializada Delitos Tráfico Ilegal y Trata de personas de la Fiscalía General de la República.

**Note: Formal contact with the police and/or criminal justice system may include persons suspected, arrested, or cautioned at the national level.

Number of persons prosecuted for trafficking in persons, by sex, 2014 –2017

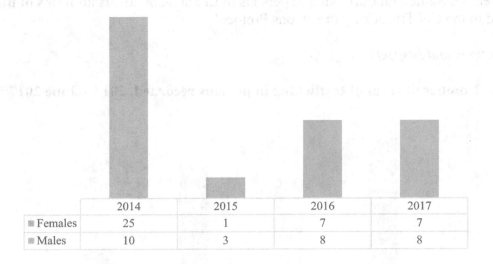

	2014	2015	2016	2017
▪ Females	25	1	7	7
▪ Males	10	3	8	8

Source: Unidad Fiscal Especializada Delitos Tráfico Ilegal y Trata de personas
de la Fiscalía General de la República.

Number of persons convicted of trafficking in persons, by sex, 2014 –2017

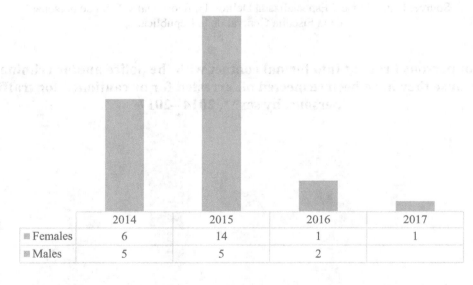

	2014	2015	2016	2017
▪ Females	6	14	1	1
▪ Males	5	5	2	

Source: Unidad Fiscal Especializada Delitos Tráfico Ilegal y Trata de personas
de la Fiscalía General de la República.

Most of the convicted persons was from El Salvador with very few from other countries in Central America.

Source: Unidad Fiscal Especializada Delitos Tráfico Ilegal y Trata de Personas de la Fiscalía General de la República.

Victims

Number of victims of trafficking in persons detected, by age and sex, 2014 –2017

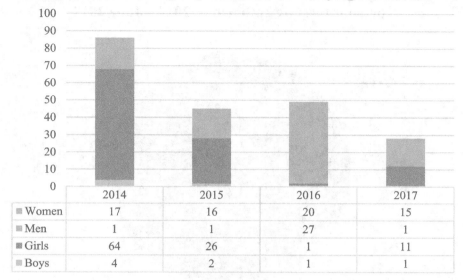

	2014	2015	2016	2017
■ Women	17	16	20	15
■ Men	1	1	27	1
■ Girls	64	26	1	11
■ Boys	4	2	1	1

Source: Unidad Fiscal Especializada Delitos Tráfico Ilegal y Trata de Personas
de la Fiscalía General de la República.

Number of victims of trafficking in persons detected, by form of exploitation, 2014 –June 2017

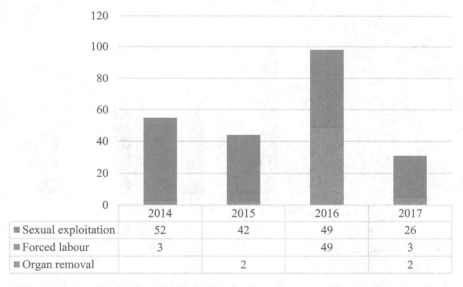

	2014	2015	2016	2017
■ Sexual exploitation	52	42	49	26
■ Forced labour	3		49	3
■ Organ removal		2		2

Source: Unidad Fiscal Especializada Delitos Tráfico Ilegal y Trata de Personas
de la Fiscalía General de la República.

Citizenships of persons identified as victims of trafficking in persons by state authorities, 2014 – June 2017

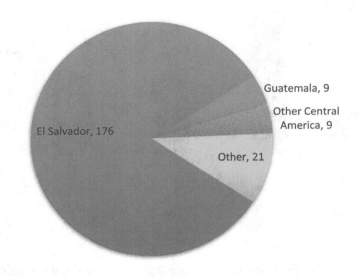

Source: Unidad Fiscal Especializada Delitos Tráfico Ilegal y Trata de Personas de la Fiscalía General de la República.

Identified victims of trafficking, by type of trafficking, 2014 – September 2017

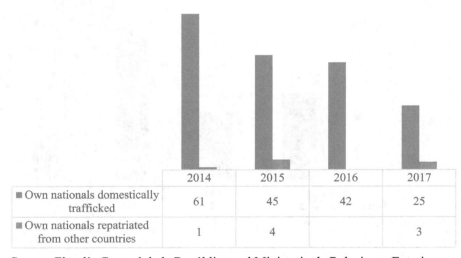

	2014	2015	2016	2017
■ Own nationals domestically trafficked	61	45	42	25
■ Own nationals repatriated from other countries	1	4		3

Source: Fiscalía General de la República y el Ministerio de Relaciones Exteriores.

The detected victims, which was trafficked internationally, was repatriated from countries in Central America, South Korea and Italy.

Source: Dirección General de Migración y Extranjería y el Ministerio de Relaciones Exteriores.

The current legislation on trafficking in persons in Guatemala covers all forms of trafficking indicated in the UN Trafficking in Persons Protocol.

Investigations and suspects

Number of cases of trafficking in persons recorded, 2014 – November 2017

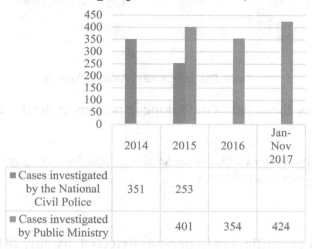

	2014	2015	2016	Jan-Nov 2017
■ Cases investigated by the National Civil Police	351	253		
■ Cases investigated by Public Ministry		401	354	424

Source: Public Ministry – Prosecutor's Office of the Section Against Trafficking in Persons, National Civil Police – Section Against Trafficking in Persons.

In 2014, 84 persons had formal contact with the police and/or criminal justice system because they were suspected, arrested, or cautioned for trafficking in persons. In 2015, 79 persons were arrested for the crime by the National Civil Police. In 2016, 91 persons, 47 men and 44 women, were arrested. In 2017, 62 persons were accused of trafficking in persons, while 58 persons were arrested for the offence.

Source: Public Ministry – Prosecutor's Office of the Section Against Trafficking in Persons, National Civil Police – Section Against Trafficking in Persons.

In 2014, 65 persons were prosecuted for trafficking in persons. In 2015, 105 persons were prosecuted.

Source: Public Ministry, Judicial Agency.

Number of persons convicted of trafficking in persons, 2014 – November 2017

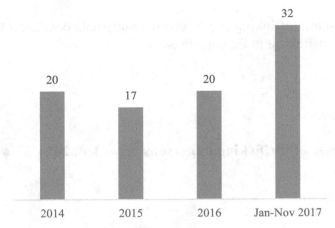

Source: Public Ministry, Judicial Agency.

The majority of persons convicted of trafficking in persons in the indicated period were citizens of Guatemala.

Source: Public Ministry – Prosecutor's Office of the Section Against Trafficking in Persons, National Civil Police – Section Against Trafficking in Persons.

Victims

Number of victims of trafficking in persons detected, by age, 2014 – November 2017

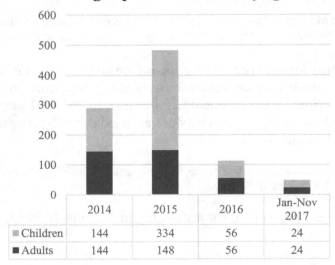

	2014	2015	2016	Jan-Nov 2017
Children	144	334	56	24
Adults	144	148	56	24

Source: Public Ministry, Judicial Agency, Secretary of Social Welfare of the Presidency, Secretariat Against Sexual Violence, Exploitation, and Trafficking in Persons, Alliance Association, Children's Shelter Association, and Survivors Foundation.

Number of victims of trafficking in persons detected, by form of exploitation, 2014 – November 2017

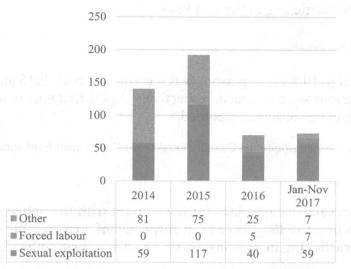

	2014	2015	2016	Jan-Nov 2017
■ Other	81	75	25	7
■ Forced labour	0	0	5	7
■ Sexual exploitation	59	117	40	59

Source: Office of the Attorney General of the Nation, Judicial Agency.

Citizenships of persons identified as victims of trafficking in persons by state authorities, 2014 – 2015

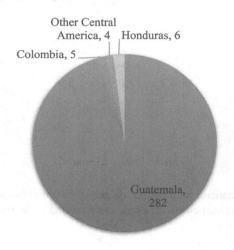

Source: Public Ministry, National Civil Police.

The majority of victims of trafficking in persons who were citizens of Guatemala were trafficked domestically. Those victims who were trafficked internationally were repatriated from Central America, Western Europe, and North America.

Source: Ministry of Foreign Affairs.

−Honduras−

The current legislation on trafficking in persons in Honduras covers all forms of trafficking indicated in the UN Trafficking in Persons Protocol.

Investigations and suspects

In 2014, one case of trafficking in persons was recorded. In both 2015 and 2016, eight cases of trafficking in persons were recorded, respectively. In the first nine months of 2017, two cases of trafficking in persons were recorded.

Source: Public Ministry, Inter-institutional Commission Against Commercial Exploitation and Trafficking in Persons (CICESCT).

Number of persons brought into formal contact with the police and/or criminal justice system because they have been suspected of, arrested for or cautioned for trafficking in persons, by sex, 2014 – September 2017**

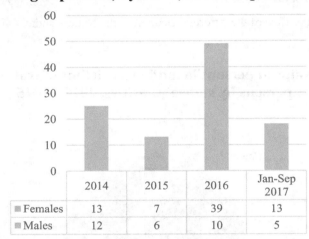

	2014	2015	2016	Jan-Sep 2017
Females	13	7	39	13
Males	12	6	10	5

Source: Public Ministry.

**Note: Formal contact with the police and/or criminal justice system may include persons suspected, arrested, or cautioned at the national level.

Number of persons prosecuted for trafficking in persons, by sex, 2014 – September 2017

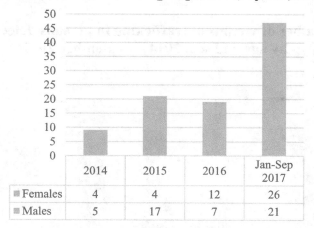

	2014	2015	2016	Jan-Sep 2017
Females	4	4	12	26
Males	5	17	7	21

Source: Public Ministry.

Number of persons convicted of trafficking in persons, by sex, 2014 – September 2017

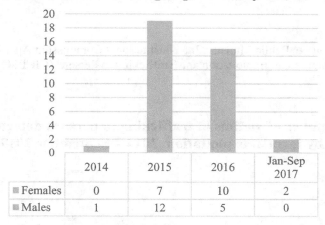

	2014	2015	2016	Jan-Sep 2017
Females	0	7	10	2
Males	1	12	5	0

Source: Public Ministry.

All persons convicted of trafficking in persons in the indicated period were Honduran nationals.

Source: Public Ministry.

Victims

Number of victims of trafficking in persons detected, by age and sex, 2014 – September 2017

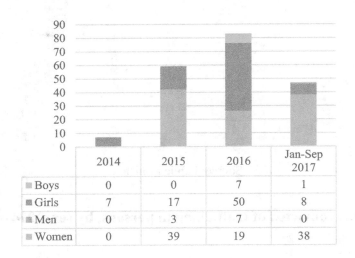

	2014	2015	2016	Jan-Sep 2017
Boys	0	0	7	1
Girls	7	17	50	8
Men	0	3	7	0
Women	0	39	19	38

Source: Public Ministry, Inter-institutional Commission Against Commercial Exploitation and Trafficking in Persons (CICESCT).

Number of victims of trafficking in persons detected, by form of exploitation, 2014 – September 2017

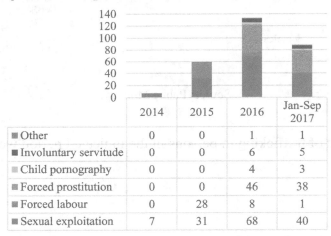

	2014	2015	2016	Jan-Sep 2017
Other	0	0	1	1
Involuntary servitude	0	0	6	5
Child pornography	0	0	4	3
Forced prostitution	0	0	46	38
Forced labour	0	28	8	1
Sexual exploitation	7	31	68	40

Source: Public Ministry, Inter-institutional Commission Against Commercial Exploitation and Trafficking in Persons (CICESCT).

The majority of identified victims of trafficking in persons in the indicated period were citizens of Honduras. Others were from other Central American countries.

Source: Public Ministry, Inter-institutional Commission Against Commercial Exploitation and Trafficking in Persons (CICESCT).

Identified victims of trafficking, by type of trafficking, 2014 – September 2017

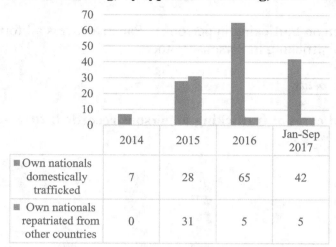

	2014	2015	2016	Jan-Sep 2017
■ Own nationals domestically trafficked	7	28	65	42
■ Own nationals repatriated from other countries	0	31	5	5

Source: Ministry of Foreign Affairs, Inter-institutional Commission Against Commercial Exploitation and Trafficking in Persons (CICESCT).

Most Honduran victims who were trafficked internationally were repatriated from Mexico. Others were repatriated from other Central American countries or Europe.

Source: Ministry of Foreign Affairs and International Cooperation (SRECI).

—Panama—

The current legislation on trafficking in persons in Panama covers all forms of trafficking indicated in the UN Trafficking in Persons Protocol.

Investigations and suspects

Number of cases of trafficking in persons recorded, 2014 – July 2017

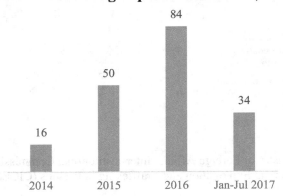

Source: Family Prosecutor's Office, Public Ministry,
Police Information Directorate – Foreign Affairs and Immigration Section, and National Police of Panama.

Number of persons brought into formal contact with the police and/or criminal justice system because they have been suspected of, arrested for or cautioned for trafficking in persons, by sex**, 2014 – July 2017

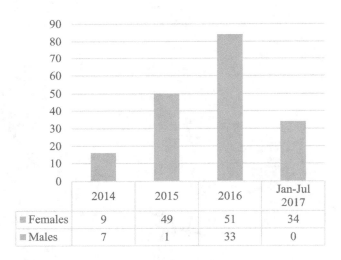

	2014	2015	2016	Jan-Jul 2017
Females	9	49	51	34
Males	7	1	33	0

Source: Family Prosecutor's Office, Public Ministry,
Police Information Directorate – Foreign Affairs and Immigration Section, and National Police of Panama.
**Note: Formal contact with the police and/or criminal justice system may
include persons suspected, arrested, or cautioned at the national level.

Number of persons prosecuted for trafficking in persons, by sex, 2014 – July 2017

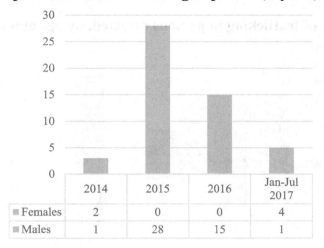

	2014	2015	2016	Jan-Jul 2017
■ Females	2	0	0	4
■ Males	1	28	15	1

Source: Specialized Prosecutor's Office against Organized Crime.

Number of persons convicted of trafficking in persons, by sex, 2014 – July 2017

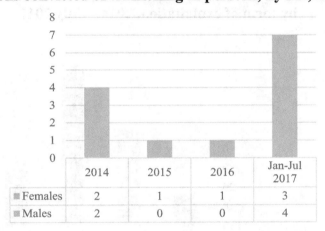

	2014	2015	2016	Jan-Jul 2017
■ Females	2	1	1	3
■ Males	2	0	0	4

Source: Specialized Prosecutor's Office against Organized Crime.

The persons convicted of trafficking in persons between January 2014 and July 2017 were citizens of Panama, other Central American and Caribbean countries, and South American countries.

Source: Specialized Prosecutor's Office against Organized Crime.

Victims

Number of victims of trafficking in persons detected, by age and sex, 2014 – July 2017

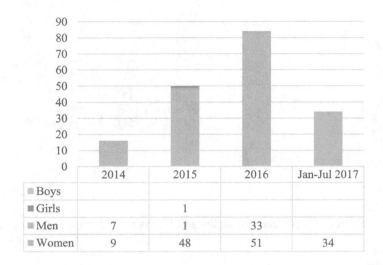

	2014	2015	2016	Jan-Jul 2017
■ Boys				
■ Girls		1		
■ Men	7	1	33	
■ Women	9	48	51	34

Source: Family Prosecutor's Office, Public Ministry,
Police Information Directorate – Foreign Affairs and Immigration Section, and National Police of Panama.

Number of victims of trafficking in persons detected, by form of exploitation, 2014 – July 2017

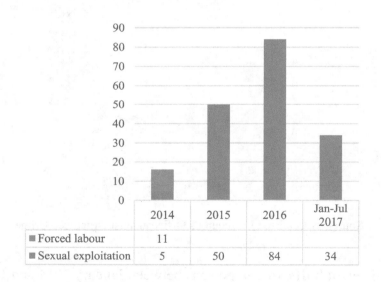

	2014	2015	2016	Jan-Jul 2017
■ Forced labour	11			
■ Sexual exploitation	5	50	84	34

Source: Family Prosecutor's Office, Public Ministry,
Police Information Directorate – Foreign Affairs and Immigration Section, and National Police of Panama.

Citizenships of persons identified as victims of trafficking in persons by state authorities, 2014 – July 2017

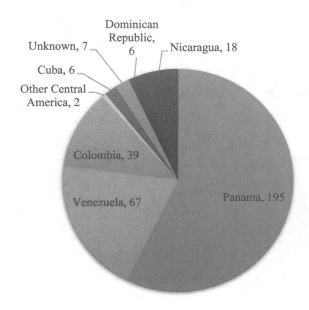

Source: Family Prosecutor's Office, Public Ministry,
Police Information Directorate – Foreign Affairs and Immigration Section, and National Police of Panama.

The majority of victims of trafficking in persons who were citizens of Panama were trafficked domestically in the indicated period.

Source: Family Prosecutor's Office, Public Ministry, Police Information Directorate – Foreign Affairs and Immigration Section, and National Police of Panama.

SOUTH AMERICA

The current legislation on trafficking in persons in Argentina covers all forms of trafficking indicated in the UN Trafficking in Persons Protocol.

Investigations and suspects

Number of cases of trafficking in persons recorded, 2014 – September 2017

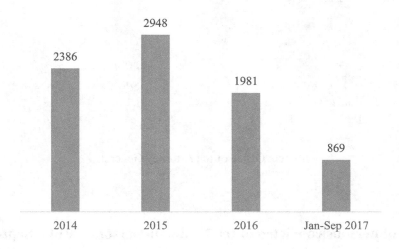

Source: Public Prosecutor's Office of the Nation.

Number of persons prosecuted for trafficking in persons, by sex, 2014 –September 2017

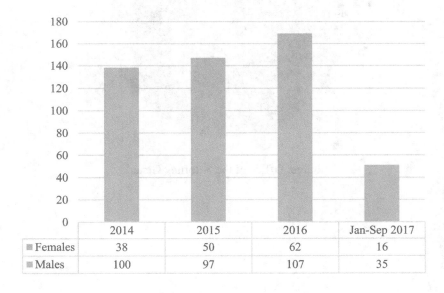

	2014	2015	2016	Jan-Sep 2017
Females	38	50	62	16
Males	100	97	107	35

Source: Office of Trafficking and Exploitation of Persons.

Number of persons convicted of trafficking in persons, by sex, 2014 – September 2017

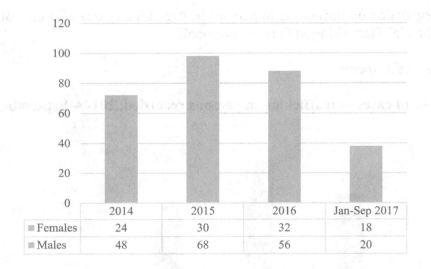

	2014	2015	2016	Jan-Sep 2017
■ Females	24	30	32	18
■ Males	48	68	56	20

Source: Office of the Attorney General.

Citizenships of persons convicted of trafficking in persons, 2014 – September 2017

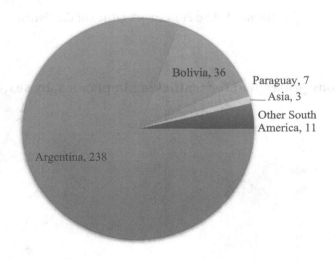

Source: Office of the Attorney General.

Victims

Number of victims of trafficking in persons detected, by age and sex, 2014 – September 2017

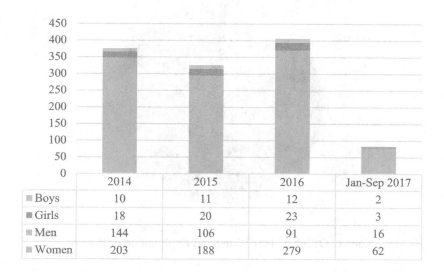

	2014	2015	2016	Jan-Sep 2017
Boys	10	11	12	2
Girls	18	20	23	3
Men	144	106	91	16
Women	203	188	279	62

Source: Office of Trafficking and Exploitation of Persons.

Number of victims of trafficking in persons detected, by form of exploitation, 2014 – September 2017

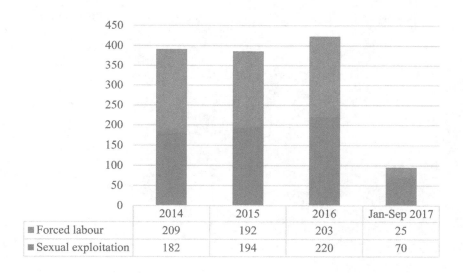

	2014	2015	2016	Jan-Sep 2017
Forced labour	209	192	203	25
Sexual exploitation	182	194	220	70

Source: Office of Trafficking and Exploitation of Persons.

One additional victim was trafficked for the purpose of forced marriage during the first eight months of 2017.

Source: Office of Trafficking and Exploitation of Persons.

Citizenships of persons identified as victims of trafficking in persons by state authorities, 2014 – September 2017

Source: Office of Trafficking and Exploitation of Persons.

The current legislation on trafficking in persons in The Plurinational State of Bolivia covers all forms of trafficking indicated in the UN Trafficking in Persons Protocol.

Investigations and suspects

Number of persons brought into formal contact with the police and/or criminal justice system because they have been suspected of, arrested for or cautioned for trafficking in persons, by sex**, 2014 – August 2017

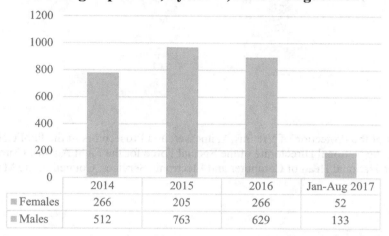

	2014	2015	2016	Jan-Aug 2017
Females	266	205	266	52
Males	512	763	629	133

Source: Director of the Protection of Victims, Witnesses, and Prosecutors of the Public Ministry – FEVAP, and The National Directorate of the Special Force for the Fight Against Crime

**Note: Formal contact with the police and/or criminal justice system may include persons suspected, arrested, or cautioned at the national level.

Number of persons prosecuted for trafficking in persons, by sex, 2014 – August 2017

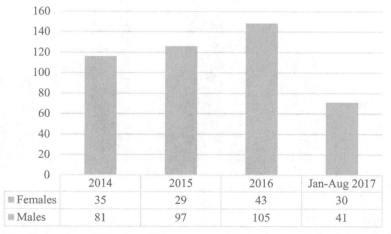

	2014	2015	2016	Jan-Aug 2017
Females	35	29	43	30
Males	81	97	105	41

Source: Director of the Protection of Victims, Witnesses, and Prosecutors of the Public Ministry – FEVAP, The National Directorate of the Special Force for the Fight Against Crime, and The National Head of Computer and Electronic Services, Council of the Magistracy.

Number of persons convicted of trafficking in persons, by sex, 2014 – August 2017

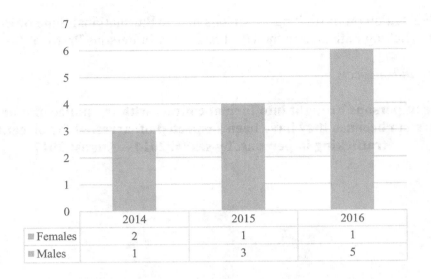

	2014	2015	2016
■ Females	2	1	1
■ Males	1	3	5

Source: Director of the Protection of Victims, Witnesses, and Prosecutors of the Public Ministry – FEVAP,
The National Directorate of the Special Force for the Fight Against Crime,
and The National Head of Computer and Electronic Services, Council of the Magistracy.

Victims

**Number of victims of trafficking in persons detected, by age and sex,
2014 – August 2017**

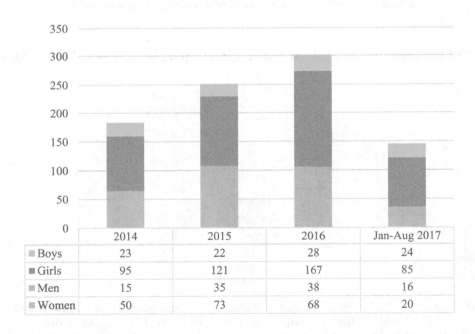

	2014	2015	2016	Jan-Aug 2017
■ Boys	23	22	28	24
■ Girls	95	121	167	85
■ Men	15	35	38	16
■ Women	50	73	68	20

Source: Director of the Protection of Victims, Witnesses, and Prosecutors of the Public Ministry – FEVAP.

Number of victims of trafficking in persons detected, by form of exploitation, 2014 – August 2017

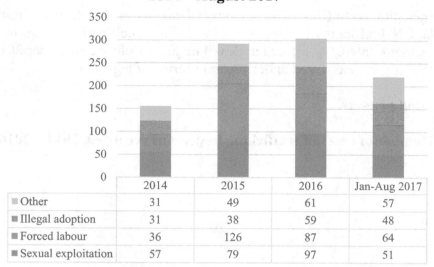

	2014	2015	2016	Jan-Aug 2017
▪ Other	31	49	61	57
▪ Illegal adoption	31	38	59	48
▪ Forced labour	36	126	87	64
▪ Sexual exploitation	57	79	97	51

Source: Director of the Protection of Victims, Witnesses, and Prosecutors of the Public Ministry – FEVAP.

On the whole, the majority of detected victims in the indicated period were nationals of Bolivia. The remaining 21 victims were from surrounding South American countries, Central America, and Asia. In 2014, the majority of victims from Bolivia were internationally trafficked.

Source: Director of the Protection of Victims, Witnesses, and Prosecutors of the Public Ministry – FEVAP.

Detected Bolivian victims of trafficking in persons, by country of repatriation, 2014 – August 2017

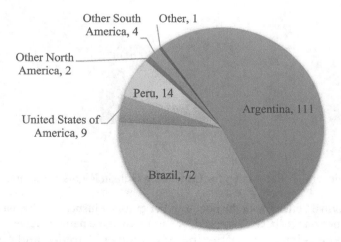

Source: Director of the Protection of Victims, Witnesses, and Prosecutors of the Public Ministry – FEVAP and Official General Director of Consular Affairs.

−Brazil−

The current legislation on trafficking in persons in Brazil covers all forms of trafficking indicated in the UN Trafficking in Persons Protocol. The specific offence criminalizing trafficking in persons entered into force in Brazil in 2016. Before September 2016, different aspects of trafficking were covered under separate forms of legislation.

Investigations and suspects

Number of cases of trafficking in persons recorded, 2014 – 2016

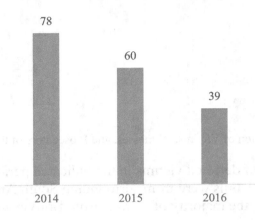

Source: Federal Police Action for Combating Human Rights Violators.

Number of persons brought into formal contact with the police and/or criminal justice system because they have been suspected of, arrested for or cautioned for trafficking in persons **, 2014 – 2016

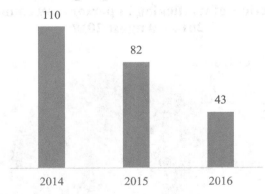

Source: Federal Police Action for Combating Human Rights Violators.

**Note: Formal contact with the police and/or criminal justice system may include persons suspected, arrested, or cautioned at the national level.

In 2014, 39 persons were convicted of trafficking in persons (31 males and eight females).

Source: Federal Police Action for Combating Human Rights Violators.

Victims

Number of victims of trafficking in persons detected, by age and sex, 2015 – June 2017

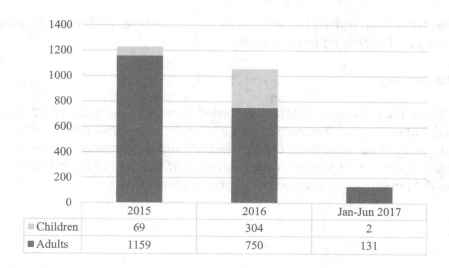

	2015	2016	Jan-Jun 2017
Children	69	304	2
Adults	1159	750	131

Source: Report of the Network of Nuclei and Stations to Combat Trafficking in Persons.

In 2014, Brazilian authorities reported 44 victims trafficked for the purpose of sexual exploitation, 26female adults, and 18 female children. In 2015, authorities reported 101 victims trafficked for the same purpose, 51 female adults and 50 female children. For the same purpose in 2016, authorities reported 75 victims, 33 female adults and 42 female children.

Source: Federal Police Action for Combating Human Rights Violators.

The current legislation on trafficking in persons in Chile covers all forms of trafficking indicated in the UN Trafficking in Persons Protocol.

Investigations and suspects

In 2014 and 2015, the national authorities recorded four cases per year. In 2016, six cases were recorded. Nine persons, five men and four women, were prosecuted for both 2014 and 2015. In 2016, 14 persons were prosecuted, five men and nine women. Between 2016 and the first six months of 2017, five persons were convicted of trafficking in persons in the court of first instance. All persons convicted were of foreign citizens.

Source: Ministry of the Public.

Victims

Number of victims of trafficking in persons detected, by age and sex, 2014 – 2016

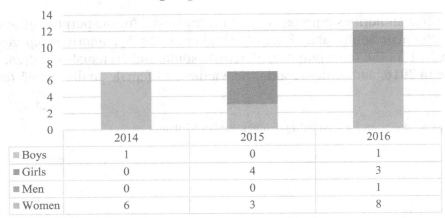

	2014	2015	2016
■ Boys	1	0	1
■ Girls	0	4	3
■ Men	0	0	1
■ Women	6	3	8

Source: Ministry of the Public, Investigation Police of Chile, and the Carabineros of Chile.

Number of victims of trafficking in persons detected, by form of exploitation, 2014 – 2016

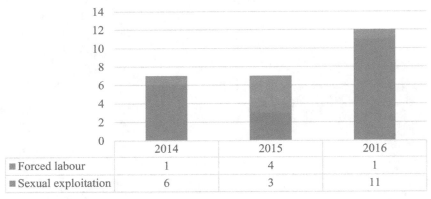

	2014	2015	2016
■ Forced labour	1	4	1
■ Sexual exploitation	6	3	11

Source: Ministry of the Public, Investigation Police of Chile, and the Carabineros of Chile.

In the period between 2014 and 2016, the majority of victims were of foreign citizens, including victims from South America, Sub-Saharan Africa, Asia, and Eastern Europe.

Source: Ministry of the Public, Investigation Police of Chile, and the Carabineros of Chile.

−Colombia−

The current legislation on trafficking in persons in Colombia covers all forms of trafficking indicated in the UN Trafficking in Persons Protocol.

Investigations and suspects

In 2016, there were 194 cases of trafficking in persons recorded and in 2016, 82 were recorded.

Source: Office of the Attorney General of the Nation.

Number of persons brought into formal contact with the police and/or criminal justice system because they have been suspected of, arrested for or cautioned for trafficking in persons, by sex, 2014 – July 2017**

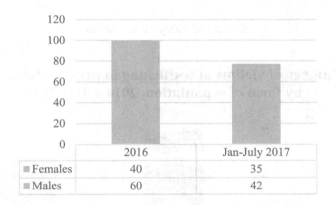

	2016	Jan-July 2017
■ Females	40	35
■ Males	60	42

Source: Office of the Attorney General of the Nation.

**Note: Formal contact with the police and/or criminal justice system may include persons suspected, arrested, or cautioned at the national level.

In 2016, 42 persons captured or were issued an arrest warrant for the crime of trafficking in persons by the Office of the Attorney General of the Nation. In the same year, 22 persons were charged with the crime of trafficking in persons, 17 males and five females. In the beginning of 2017, one male and one female were charged.

Source: Office of the Attorney General of the Nation.

In 2016, six males and five females were accused of trafficking in persons and in 2017, one male and three female. Of those accused, two males and three females were convicted in 2016. In 2017, three males and three females were convicted of trafficking in persons. All convicted persons were citizens of Colombia.

Source: Office of the Attorney General of the Nation.

Victims

Number of victims of trafficking in persons detected, by age and sex, 2014 – July 2017

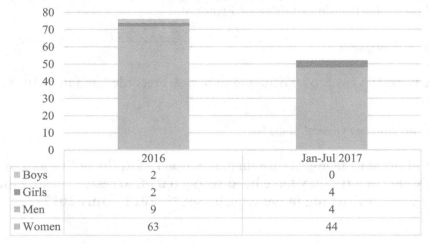

	2016	Jan-Jul 2017
■ Boys	2	0
■ Girls	2	4
■ Men	9	4
■ Women	63	44

Source: Ministry of the Interior.

Number of victims of trafficking in persons detected, by form of exploitation, 2014 – July 2017

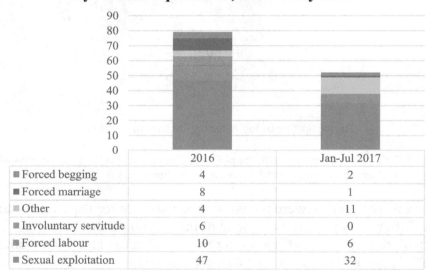

	2016	Jan-Jul 2017
■ Forced begging	4	2
■ Forced marriage	8	1
■ Other	4	11
■ Involuntary servitude	6	0
■ Forced labour	10	6
■ Sexual exploitation	47	32

Source: Ministry of the Interior.

The majority of victims in the indicated period were citizens of Colombia. Others were citizens of other South American countries.

Source: Ministry of the Interior.

Between January 2016 and July 2017, 98 identified victims were repatriated from other countries, while 22 were domestically trafficked according to the Ministry of the Interior. According to the Ministry of Foreign Affairs, 62 identified victims were repatriated from other countries in the indicated period.

Source: Ministry of the Interior.

Countries from which victims of trafficking were repatriated, according to the Ministry of the Interior, 2016 - July 2017

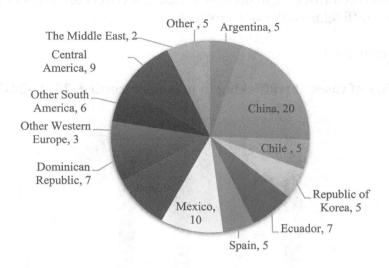

Other, 5 • Argentina, 5
The Middle East, 2
Central America, 9
Other South America, 6
Other Western Europe, 3
Dominican Republic, 7
Peru, 9
Mexico, 10
Spain, 5
China, 20
Chile, 5
Republic of Korea, 5
Ecuador, 7

Source: The Ministry of the Interior.

Countries from which victims of trafficking were repatriated, according to the Ministry of Foreign Affairs, 2016 - July 2017

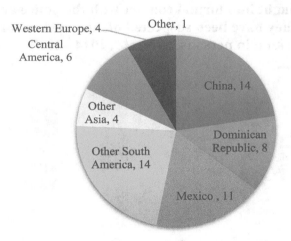

Western Europe, 4 • Other, 1
Central America, 6
Other Asia, 4
Other South America, 14
China, 14
Dominican Republic, 8
Mexico , 11

Source: The Ministry of Foreign Affairs.

−Ecuador−

The current legislation on trafficking in persons in Ecuador covers all forms of trafficking indicated in the UN Trafficking in Persons Protocol.

Investigations and suspects

Number of cases of trafficking in persons recorded, 2014 −2017

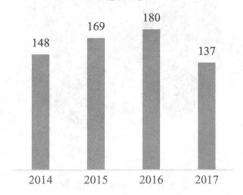

Source: Ministry of Interior.

Number of persons brought into formal contact with the police and/or criminal justice system because they have been suspected of, arrested for or cautioned for trafficking in persons, by sex**, 2014 −2017

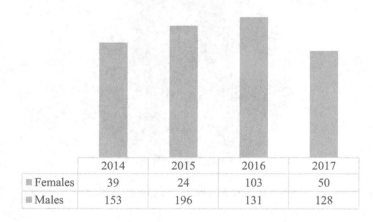

	2014	2015	2016	2017
Females	39	24	103	50
Males	153	196	131	128

Source: Ministry of Interior.

**Note: Formal contact with the police and/or criminal justice system may include persons suspected, arrested, or cautioned at the national level.

Number of persons prosecuted for trafficking in persons, by sex, 2014 –2017

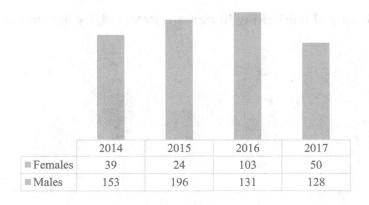

	2014	2015	2016	2017
■ Females	39	24	103	50
■ Males	153	196	131	128

Source: Ministry of Interior.

Number of persons convicted of trafficking in persons, by sex, 2014 –2017

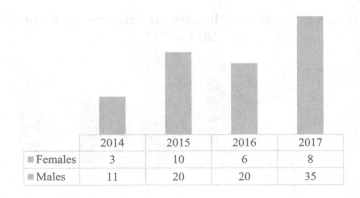

	2014	2015	2016	2017
■ Females	3	10	6	8
■ Males	11	20	20	35

Source: Ministry of Interior.

Citizenships of persons convicted of trafficking in persons, 2014 –2017

Ecuador, 91

Other, 22

Source: Ministry of Interior.

Victims

Number of victims of trafficking in persons detected, by age and sex, 2014 –2017

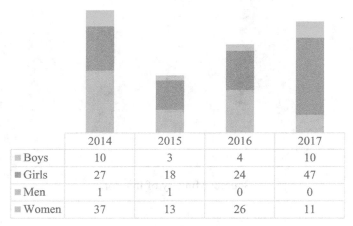

	2014	2015	2016	2017
▪ Boys	10	3	4	10
▪ Girls	27	18	24	47
▪ Men	1	1	0	0
▪ Women	37	13	26	11

Source: Ministry of Interior.

Number of victims of trafficking in persons detected, by form of exploitation, 2014 –2017

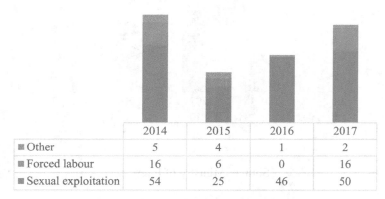

	2014	2015	2016	2017
▪ Other	5	4	1	2
▪ Forced labour	16	6	0	16
▪ Sexual exploitation	54	25	46	50

Source: Source: Ministry of Interior.

Citizenships of persons identified as victims of trafficking in persons by state authorities, 2014 –2017

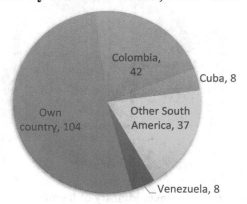

Source: Source: Ministry of Interior.

Identified victims of trafficking, by type of trafficking, 2014 –2017

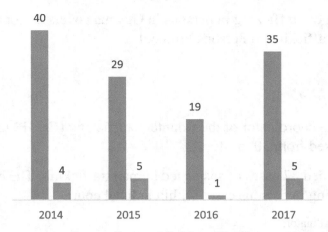

Source: Source: Ministry of Interior.

Of the detected victims that were trafficked internationally, 15 victims, were reported repatriated from South American countries.

Source: Source: Ministry of Interior

–Guyana–

The current legislation on trafficking in persons in Guyana covers all forms of exploitation indicated in the UN Trafficking in Persons Protocol.

Investigations and Suspects

According to the acting coordinator of the Counter Trafficking (C-TIP) unit, between 2015 and 2016 cases increased from 30 to 41.

In 2017, Guyana recorded 47 cases of suspected human trafficking. The country has convicted two trafficking in persons cases within judicial court.

Source: C-TIP Acting Coordinator.

Victims

Between 2015 and 2016, the number of victims increased from 65 to 103. In 2017, the trafficking cases recorded accounted for 110 alleged victims.

Source: C-TIP Acting Coordinator.

The current legislation on trafficking in persons in Paraguay covers all forms of trafficking indicated in the UN Trafficking in Persons Protocol.

Investigations and suspects

Number of cases of trafficking in persons recorded, 2014 – September 2017

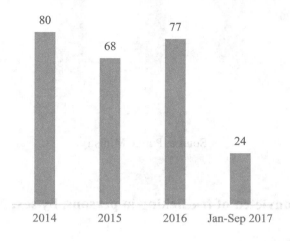

Source: Public Ministry.

Number of persons brought into formal contact with the police and/or criminal justice system because they have been suspected of, arrested for or cautioned for trafficking in persons, by sex**, 2014 – September 2017

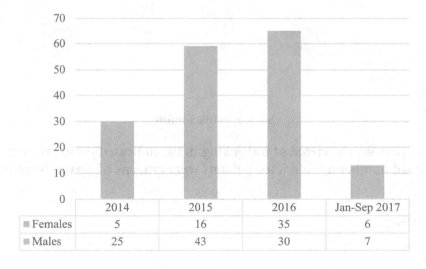

	2014	2015	2016	Jan-Sep 2017
Females	5	16	35	6
Males	25	43	30	7

Source: Public Ministry.

**Note: Formal contact with the police and/or criminal justice system may include persons suspected, arrested, or cautioned at the national level.

Number of persons prosecuted for trafficking in persons, by sex, 2014 – September 2017

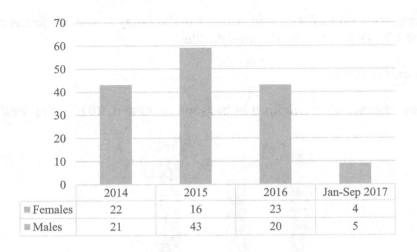

	2014	2015	2016	Jan-Sep 2017
▪ Females	22	16	23	4
▪ Males	21	43	20	5

Source: Public Ministry.

Number of persons convicted of trafficking in persons, by sex, 2014 – September 2017

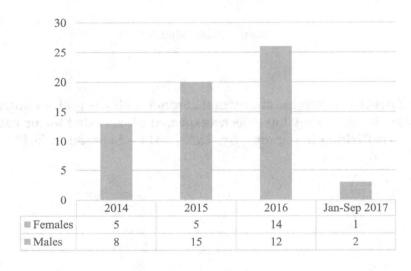

	2014	2015	2016	Jan-Sep 2017
▪ Females	5	5	14	1
▪ Males	8	15	12	2

Source: Public Ministry.

The majority of persons convicted of trafficking in the indicated period were nationals of Paraguay. A small number of convicted persons were citizens of Spain, Argentina, and Colombia.

Source: Public Ministry.

Number of victims of trafficking in persons detected, by age and sex, 2014 – September 2017

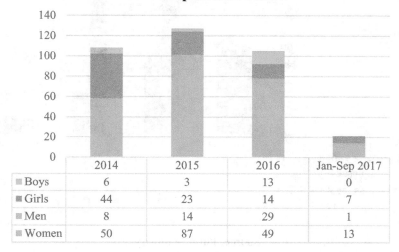

	2014	2015	2016	Jan-Sep 2017
Boys	6	3	13	0
Girls	44	23	14	7
Men	8	14	29	1
Women	50	87	49	13

Source: Public Ministry.

Number of victims of trafficking in persons detected, by form of exploitation, 2014 – September 2017

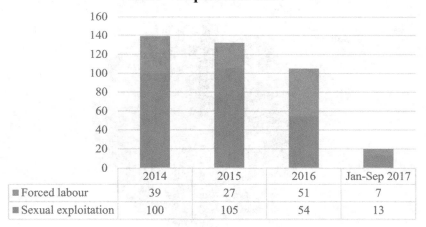

	2014	2015	2016	Jan-Sep 2017
Forced labour	39	27	51	7
Sexual exploitation	100	105	54	13

Source: Public Ministry.

Most identified victims between January 2014 and September 2017 were citizens of Paraguay. Other identified victims were citizens of South Korea, Colombia, Brazil, Peru, and Sweden.

Source: Public Ministry.

Type of trafficking experienced by victims of Paraguay citizenship, 2014 – September 2017

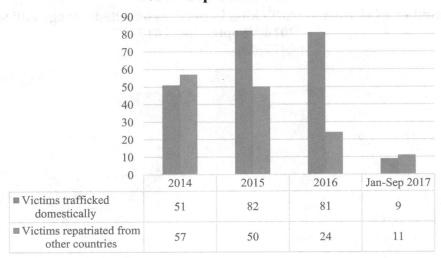

	2014	2015	2016	Jan-Sep 2017
■ Victims trafficked domestically	51	82	81	9
■ Victims repatriated from other countries	57	50	24	11

Source: Public Ministry.

Countries from which victims of trafficking in persons were repatriated, 2014 – September 2017

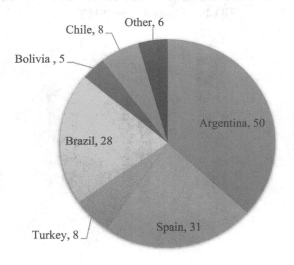

Source: Public Ministry.

The current legislation on trafficking in persons in Peru covers all forms of trafficking indicated in the UN Trafficking in Persons Protocol.

Victims

Number of number of users, victims, and witnesses, assisted at a national level for the crime of trafficking in persons in the Program of Protection and Assistance to Victims and Witnesses, 2014 – September 2017

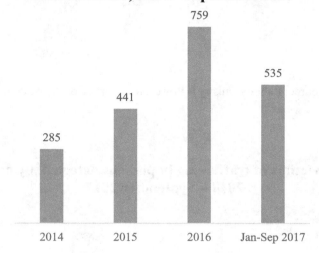

Source: Public Ministry – Prosecutor's Office of the Nation.

Number of victims of trafficking in persons served by the Program of Protection and Assistance to Victims and Witnesses, 2014 – September 2017

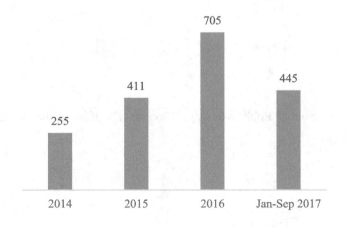

Source: Public Ministry – Prosecutor's Office of the Nation.

Number of witnesses of trafficking in persons served by the Program of Protection and Assistance to Victims and Witnesses, 2014 – September 2017

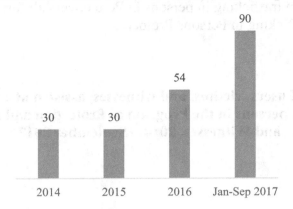

Source: Public Ministry – Prosecutor's Office of the Nation.

Number of victims of trafficking in persons detected, by age and sex, 2014 – September 2017

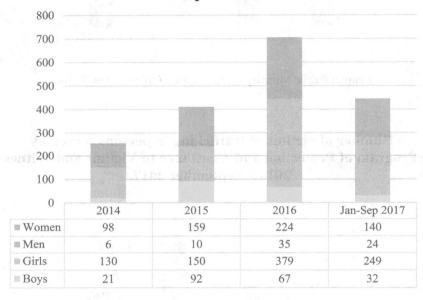

	2014	2015	2016	Jan-Sep 2017
■ Women	98	159	224	140
■ Men	6	10	35	24
■ Girls	130	150	379	249
■ Boys	21	92	67	32

Source: Source: Public Ministry – Prosecutor's Office of the Nation.

Number of victims of trafficking in persons detected, by form of exploitation, 2014 – September 2017

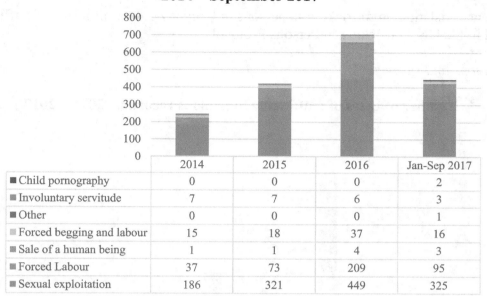

	2014	2015	2016	Jan-Sep 2017
■ Child pornography	0	0	0	2
■ Involuntary servitude	7	7	6	3
■ Other	0	0	0	1
■ Forced begging and labour	15	18	37	16
■ Sale of a human being	1	1	4	3
■ Forced Labour	37	73	209	95
■ Sexual exploitation	186	321	449	325

Source: Source: Public Ministry – Prosecutor's Office of the Nation.

Citizenships of persons identified as victims of trafficking in persons by state authorities, 2014 – September 2017

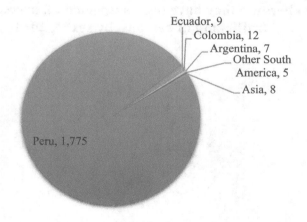

Source: Source: Public Ministry – Prosecutor's Office of the Nation.

The majority of victims who were citizens of Peru were trafficked domestically. In 2017, one victim was repatriated from another South American country.

Source: Public Ministry – Prosecutor's Office of the Nation.

–Uruguay–

The current legislation on trafficking in persons in Uruguay covers all forms of trafficking indicated in the UN Trafficking in Persons Protocol.

Investigations and suspects

Number of cases of trafficking in persons recorded, 2014 – 2017

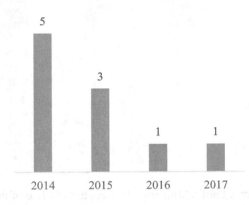

Source: Sistema de Gestión en Seguridad Pública – SGSP –
e Información de las Jefaturas de Policias a nivel nacional.

Number of persons brought into formal contact with the police and/or criminal justice system because they have been suspected of, arrested for or cautioned for trafficking in persons, by sex**, 2014 – 2017

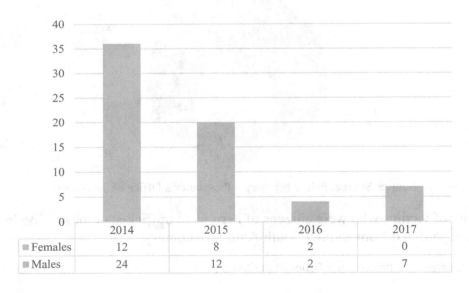

	2014	2015	2016	2017
Females	12	8	2	0
Males	24	12	2	7

Source: Sistema de Gestión en Seguridad Pública – SGSP –
e Información de las Jefaturas de Policias a nivel nacional.

**Note: Formal contact with the police and/or criminal justice system may
include persons suspected, arrested, or cautioned at the national level.

Number of persons prosecuted for trafficking in persons, by sex, 2014 – 2017

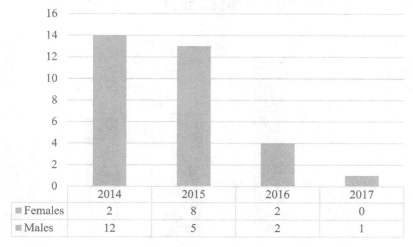

	2014	2015	2016	2017
■ Females	2	8	2	0
■ Males	12	5	2	1

Source: Sistema de Gestión en Seguridad Pública – SGSP –
e Información de las Jefaturas de Policias a nivel nacional.

Number of persons convicted of trafficking in persons, by sex, 2014 –2017

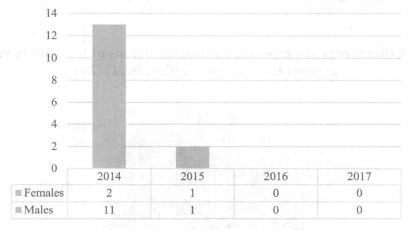

	2014	2015	2016	2017
■ Females	2	1	0	0
■ Males	11	1	0	0

Source: Sistema de Gestión en Seguridad Pública – SGSP –
e Información de las Jefaturas de Policias a nivel nacional.

During the reporting period between 2014 and 2017, the majority of convicted persons were Uruguayan citizens, with a smaller number of persons from the Dominican Republic and the Republic of Korea.

Source: Sistema de Gestión en Seguridad Pública – SGSP – e Información de las Jefaturas de Policias a nivel nacional.

Victims

All detected victims of trafficking in persons were women, reaching a peak of 138 in 2014, and 95, 91, and 73, in 2015, 2016, and 2017, respectively.

Source: Servicio de Atención a mujeres victimas de trata con fines explotación sexual – INMUJERES/MIDES.

Number of victims of trafficking in persons detected, by form of exploitation, 2014 – 2017

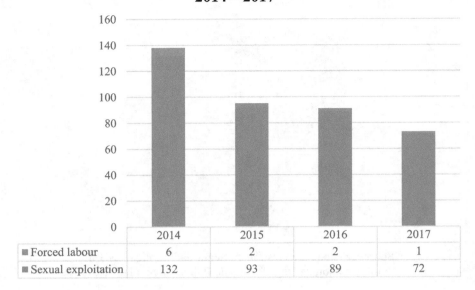

	2014	2015	2016	2017
■ Forced labour	6	2	2	1
■ Sexual exploitation	132	93	89	72

Source: Servicio de Atención a mujeres victimas de trata con fines explotación sexual – INMUJERES/MIDES

Citizenships of persons identified as victims of trafficking in persons by state authorities, 2014 – 2017

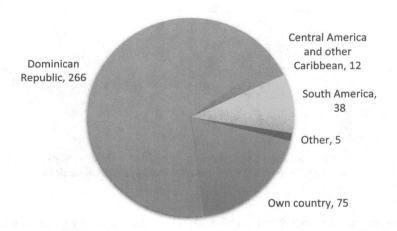

Source: Servicio de Atención a mujeres victimas de trata con fines explotación sexual – INMUJERES/MIDES

−Venezuela (Bolivarian Republic of)−

The current legislation on trafficking in persons in Venezuela covers trafficking of girls and women as well as international trafficking of males. Other forms of trafficking can be prosecuted by using other articles of the criminal code.

Investigations and suspects

Number of cases of trafficking in persons recorded, 2014 – September 2017

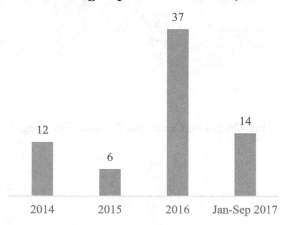

Source: National Office against Organized Crime and Terrorist Financing, Public Prosecutor's Office.

Number of persons brought into formal contact with the police and/or criminal justice system because they have been suspected of, arrested for or cautioned for trafficking in persons, by sex**, 2014 – September 2017

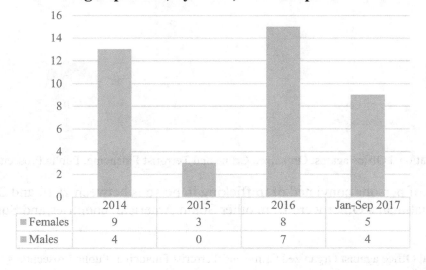

	2014	2015	2016	Jan-Sep 2017
■ Females	9	3	8	5
■ Males	4	0	7	4

Source: National Office against Organized Crime and Terrorist Financing, Public Prosecutor's Office.

**Note: Formal contact with the police and/or criminal justice system may include persons suspected, arrested, or cautioned at the national level.

Number of persons prosecuted for trafficking in persons, by sex, 2014 – September 2017

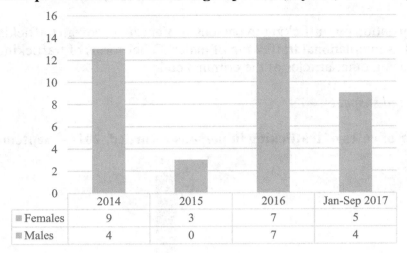

	2014	2015	2016	Jan-Sep 2017
▪ Females	9	3	7	5
▪ Males	4	0	7	4

Source: National Office against Organized Crime and Terrorist Financing, Public Prosecutor's Office.

Number of persons convicted of trafficking in persons, by sex, 2014 – 2016

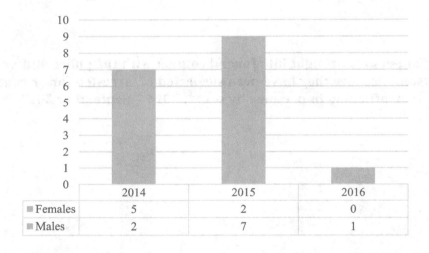

	2014	2015	2016
▪ Females	5	2	0
▪ Males	2	7	1

Source: National Office against Organized Crime and Terrorist Financing, Public Prosecutor's Office.

The majority of persons convicted of trafficking in persons between 2014 and 2016 were Venezuelan nationals. Other were from other South American countries and Sub-Saharan Africa.

Source: National Office against Organized Crime and Terrorist Financing, Public Prosecutor's Office.

Victims

**Number of victims of trafficking in persons detected, by age and sex,
2014 – September 2017**

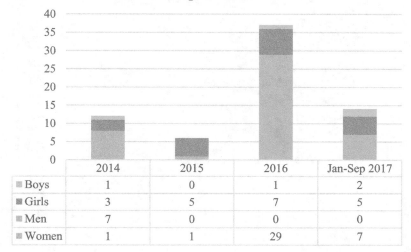

	2014	2015	2016	Jan-Sep 2017
▪ Boys	1	0	1	2
▪ Girls	3	5	7	5
▪ Men	7	0	0	0
▪ Women	1	1	29	7

Source: National Office against Organized Crime and Terrorist Financing, Public Prosecutor's Office.

**Number of victims of trafficking in persons detected, by form of exploitation,
2014 – September 2017**

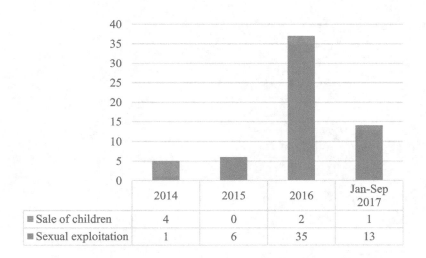

	2014	2015	2016	Jan-Sep 2017
▪ Sale of children	4	0	2	1
▪ Sexual exploitation	1	6	35	13

Source: National Office against Organized Crime and Terrorist Financing, Public Prosecutor's Office.

The majority of victims in the indicated period were citizens of Venezuela who were trafficked domestically. All other victims were citizens of Sub-Saharan African countries.

Source: National Office against Organized Crime and Terrorist Financing, Public Prosecutor's Office.

SUB-SAHARAN AFRICA

–Angola–

The current legislation on trafficking in persons in Angola covers all forms of trafficking indicated in the UN Trafficking in Persons Protocol.

Investigations and Suspects

In 2014, 5 cases of trafficking were sentenced for criminal prosecution. There were 25 suspected cases of trafficking of minors and nine suspected cases of trafficking for sexual exploitation and domestic servitude.

Source: ACP-EU Migration Action (2016). Angola Relatório de Estudo Base: Revisão dos regulamentos existentes e desenvolvimento de um conjunto de recomendações para a redacção da nova política nacional.

Victims

The Angolan government identified and rescued 17 potential victims of trafficking, with Instituto Nacional da Criança assisting 15 children that were victims of sexual and labour trafficking.

Source: ACP-EU Migration Action (2016). Angola Relatório de Estudo Base: Revisão dos regulamentos existentes e desenvolvimento de um conjunto de recomendações para a redacção da nova política nacional.

−Benin−

The specific offence on trafficking in persons in Benin covers trafficking of minors. Other articles of the criminal code are used to prosecute trafficking of adults.

Investigations and Suspects

In 2017, 105 persons were prosecuted for trafficking in persons and 30 persons were convicted.

Source: l'Office Central de Protection des Mineurs (OCPM), les Centres de Promotion Sociale (CPS) and les Organisations Non Gouvernementales (ONG).

Victims

In 2017, 536 victims of trafficking were recorded. Victims were all children, 361 girls and 174 boys.

Source: l'Office Central de Protection des Mineurs (OCPM), les Centres de Promotion Sociale (CPS) and les Organisations Non Gouvernementales (ONG).

The current legislation on trafficking in persons in Botswana covers all forms of trafficking indicated in the UN Trafficking in Persons Protocol. The Anti-Human Trafficking Act, No. 32 was introduced in 2014. Additionally, Article 114 of the Children's Act, No.8 of 2009, also addresses child abduction and child trafficking.

Investigations and suspects

Since the introduction of national trafficking in persons legislation in Botswana in late 2014, the Directorate of Public Prosecutions has recorded several investigations. In 2015, five investigations and seven prosecutions were completed. In the subsequent year, 12 cases were investigated and dually prosecuted. As of December 2017, 11 cases were before the courts and two were finalised with one recorded conviction.

Source: Directorate of Public Prosecutions, Ministry of Defence, Justice and Security, *Trafficking in Persons in the SADC Region: A Statistical Report (2017)*.

As of December 2017, a total of 25 suspected traffickers had been apprehended in Botswana. Of these, 60% were males from Botswana and Malawi. The rest were from countries in Sub-Saharan Africa and the Caribbean.

Source: Directorate of Public Prosecutions, Ministry of Defence, Justice and Security, *Trafficking in Persons in the SADC Region: A Statistical Report (2017)*.

Victims

Between 2015 and 2016, a total of 30 persons were identified as victims of trafficking in Botswana. Of these victims, 19 were adult males. Of child victims, the majority were female. The majority of both male and female victims were citizens of Malawi. All victims originated from Sub-Saharan African countries.

Source: Directorate of Public Prosecutions, Ministry of Defence, Justice and Security, *Trafficking in Persons in the SADC Region: A Statistical Report (2017)*.

Number of victims of trafficking in persons detected, by form of exploitation, 2014 – September 2017

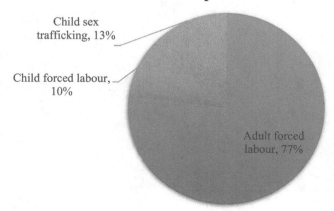

Source: Directorate of Public Prosecutions, Ministry of Defence, Justice and Security, *Trafficking in Persons in the SADC Region: A Statistical Report (2017)*.

–Burkina Faso–

The current legislation on trafficking in persons in Burkina Faso covers all forms of trafficking indicated in the UN Trafficking in Persons Protocol.

Victims

In 2015, a total of 550 children (199 girls, 351 boys) were identified as being victims of trafficking.

Source : Ministere de l'action sociale et de la solidarite nationale.

Child victims of trafficking in person, by sex, 2011 – 2014

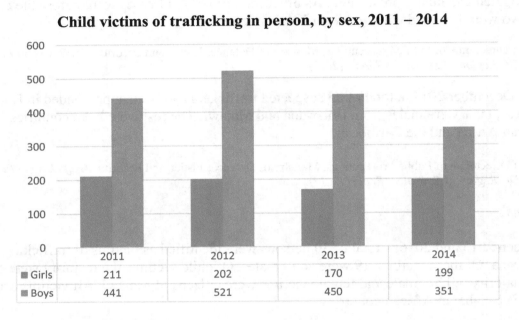

	2011	2012	2013	2014
■ Girls	211	202	170	199
■ Boys	441	521	450	351

Source : Ministere de l'action sociale et de la solidarite nationale.

–Cameroon–

The current legislation on trafficking in persons in Cameroon covers all forms of trafficking indicated in the UN Trafficking in Persons Protocol.

Investigations and Suspects

According to the police, in 2016, 34 men and 23 women were identified as trafficking offenders. Courts registered 23 cases of child trafficking. 11 cases were pending before trial, with five persons were convicted, two acquitted, and five at the level of preliminary enquiry in 2015.

Source: Ministère de la Justice.

Victims

A total of 67 victims were identified in 2016. Four were men, 47 were women, and 16 were minors.

Source: Ministère de la Justice.

–Central African Republic–

The current legislation on trafficking in persons in the Central African Republic covers all forms of trafficking indicated in the UN Trafficking in Persons Protocol.

Victims

In 2015, 39 children (28 boys, 11 girls) were identified as being newly recruited by armed groups in the Central African Republic. Of these, 21 were recruited by the Lord's Resistance Army (LRA), and 13 by ex-Séléka factions such as the Union for Peace in the Central African Republic (UPC).

From January 2014 to December 2015, a total of 5,541 children were separated from armed groups by the country task force. Of these, 4,274 were boys and 1,267 were girls.

Source: UN Security Council.

−Côte d'Ivoire−

The current legislation on trafficking in persons in Côte d'Ivoire was recently introduced in 2016 to cover trafficking in both adults and children for the purposes of sexual exploitation and forced labour.

Investigations and suspects

Number of cases of trafficking in persons recorded, 2014 – September 2017

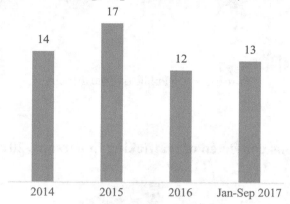

Source: Service Public of Côte d'Ivoire.

Number of persons brought into formal contact with the police and/or criminal justice system because they have been suspected of trafficking in persons, by sex, 2014 – September 2017

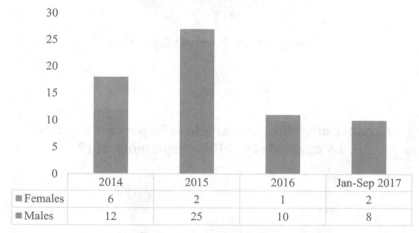

Source: Service Public of Côte d'Ivoire.

The same number of persons suspected of trafficking in persons were also prosecuted for the crime in the corresponding years.

Source: Service Public of Côte d'Ivoire

Number of persons convicted of trafficking in persons, by sex, 2014 – September 2017

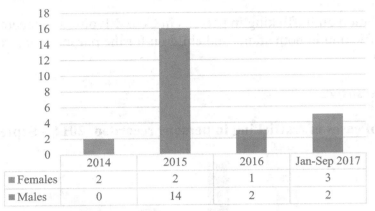

	2014	2015	2016	Jan-Sep 2017
■ Females	2	2	1	3
■ Males	0	14	2	2

Source: Service Public of Côte d'Ivoire.

Citizenships of persons convicted of trafficking in persons, 2014 - September 2017

Source: Service Public of Côte d'Ivoire.

Victims

Number of victims of trafficking in persons detected, by age and sex, 2014 – September 2017

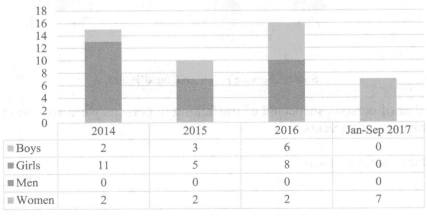

	2014	2015	2016	Jan-Sep 2017
■ Boys	2	3	6	0
■ Girls	11	5	8	0
■ Men	0	0	0	0
■ Women	2	2	2	7

Source: Service Public of Côte d'Ivoire.

Number of victims of trafficking in persons detected, by form of exploitation, 2014 – September 2017

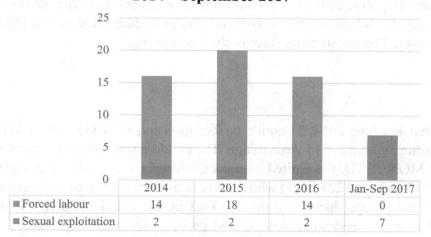

	2014	2015	2016	Jan-Sep 2017
■ Forced labour	14	18	14	0
■ Sexual exploitation	2	2	2	7

Source: Service Public of Côte d'Ivoire.

The detected victims during the period between the beginning of 2014 and September 2017 were all from surrounding African countries except for seven reported victims in 2017 who were nationals of China. All 16 domestic victims of trafficking in persons were domestically trafficked within the borders of Côte d'Ivoire.

Source: Service Public of Côte d'Ivoire.

–Democratic Republic of the Congo–

The Democratic Republic of the Congo does not have a specific offence of trafficking in persons. The sexual violence statute may be used to prosecute some trafficking for sexual exploitation cases. The constitution forbids child soldiering.

Victims

Between March and June 2014, 21 children (four girls and 17 boys) were recruited into armed groups, including eight under 15 years of age. The children were used as porters, cooks, escorts, and fighters. MONUSCO, the United Nations Children's Fund, and other partners identified 233 children (12 girls and 221 boys) who had escaped, surrendered or had been separated from armed forces and groups during the period. That included 131 children between 13 and 17 years of age formerly associated with armed groups, who were separated from the Armed Forces of the Democratic Republic of the Congo (FARDC) triage centres in Kitona (Bas-Congo), Kamina (Katanga), and Kotakoli (Equateur) between 1 and 10 April.

Between June and September, MONUSCO documented 128 cases of children (four girls and 124 boys) who had escaped or were separated from armed groups. Of these, five were Ugandan and one was Rwandan. MONUSCO continued to receive information from reliable sources indicating the recruitment and use of children by armed groups, including Mayi-Mayi Nyatura and FDLR-Forces combattantes Abacunguzi in Rutshuru territory, Allied Democratic Forces (ADF) in Beni territory, Cheka in Walikale territory, Mayi-Mayi Mulumba in Fizi territory, Mayi-Mayi Nakishale in Uvira territory, and Raia Mutomboki in Masisi territory.

During the first months of 2015, MONUSCO documented 298 cases of children (18 girls and 280 boys), including one Rwandan, who had escaped or were separated from armed groups. 69 were separated from the Forces démocratiques pour la libération du Rwanda-Forces combattantes Abacunguzi, 43 from Mayi-Mayi Raia Mutomboki, and 30 from Mayi-Mayi Nyatura. Furthermore, five children formerly associated with armed groups who had been detained by FARDC, were released.

Source: MONUSCO – UN Organization Stabilization Mission in the Democratic Republic of the Congo.

The Convention on the Rights of the Child expressed concerns over a significant number of girls which remain victims of sexual exploitation and forced labour in the hands of armed groups.

During the reporting period between 10 March and the 30 June 2017, MONUSCO documented 527 cases of grave violations of child rights. At least 269 children were separated or escaped from armed groups, including 14 girls. The main armed groups that recruited and used children were Kamuina Nsapu, Raia Mutomboki, Nyatura, Front for Patriotic Resistance in Ituri (FRPI), and Union des patriotes pour la libération du Congo (UPLC).

In the Kasaï provinces, militia groups, including Kamuina Nsapu, systematically recruited and used children in combat against FARDC. MONUSCO documented 28 new cases of child recruitment by Kamuina Nsapu militia, including eight girls, over the course of the reporting period.

Source: UN Convention on the Rights of the Child (2017). Concluding observations on the report submitted by the Democratic Republic of the Congo under article 12 (1) of the Optional Protocol to the Convention on the Rights of the Child on the sale of children, child prostitution and child pornography.

Large numbers of children continue to be recruited and used in armed conflict by non-state armed groups, such as the Forces démocratiques de libération du Rwanda, Raia Mutomboki and Nyatura, among others.

Source: UN Convention on the Rights of the Child (2017). Concluding observations on the combined third to fifth periodic reports of the Democratic Republic of the Congo.

The majority of trafficking is internal, and, while much of it is perpetrated by armed groups and rogue elements of government forces outside official control in the country's unstable eastern provinces, incidents of trafficking occurred throughout all 11 provinces.

Men and women working in unlicensed Congolese artisanal mines, many of whom began mining as children, are reported to be subjected to forced labour, including debt bondage, by mining bosses, other miners, family members, government officials, armed groups, and government forces. Many miners are, in effect, in bonded labour. Often, they are forced to continue working to pay off constantly accumulating debts for cash advances, tools, food, and other provisions at undisclosed interest rates. Intergenerational debt continues to exist as some miners inherit the debt of deceased family members.

Some members of Batwa, or pygmy groups, are subjected to conditions of forced labour, most commonly in agriculture, but also in mining and domestic service in remote areas of the DRC. Some Congolese women are forcibly prostituted in brothels or informal camps, including in markets, bars, and bistros in mining areas, by loosely organized networks, gangs, and brothel operators.

Children are engaged in forced and exploitative labour in small-scale agriculture, informal mining, and other informal sectors throughout the country. Children are subjected to forced and exploitative labour in the illegal mining of diamonds, copper, gold, cobalt, ore, and tin, as well as the smuggling of minerals.

Children ages 5-17 are usually forced to work in the production of cassiterite, wolframite, and coltan, while those ages 10-16 are forced to work in the production of gold.

Source: International Labour Organisation (2015). Draft Report on Forced Labour and Human Trafficking in the Southern African Development Community.

−Djibouti−

The current legislation on trafficking in persons in Djibouti was adopted in 2016 and covers all forms of trafficking indicated in the UN Trafficking in Persons Protocol.

Investigations and suspects

In Djibouti, no cases of trafficking in persons have been ever recorded.

Source: The Tribunal of First Instance.

–Ghana–

The current legislation on trafficking in persons in Ghana covers all forms of trafficking indicated in the UN Trafficking in Persons Protocol.

Victims

On 15 December 2015, the Department of Social Development under the Ministry of Gender, Children, and Social Protection (MOGCSP), in collaboration with representatives of the International Organization of Migration (IOM), the Anti Human Trafficking Unit of the Police Service, the South Africa Embassy, and the Human Trafficking Secretariat also under MOGCSP, recorded 21 Ghanaian minors trafficked to Pretoria, South Africa to play football. The trafficked children were between the ages of 9 and 16. All of the children came from different villages in Sefwi in the western part of the country.

Source: Ministry of Gender, Children and Social Protection (2016).

In 2015, following a rescue operation carried out by INTERPOL and GPS in the cocoa and mining sectors, a total of 50 minors were brought to the police station for an initial assessment. Following IOM and the social welfare office's screening, 27 minors were determined to be victims of trafficking or exploited/vulnerable cases. There were seven girls and 20 boys, between eight and 19 years old. 24 were Ghanaian nationals and three were Burkinabe living with family members in Ghana.

In 2015, 40 children (nine girls and 25 boys, aged seven to 21) benefitted from BTCTE sponsorship. In addition, three children were sponsored by private donors through the United States Association for International Migration (USAIM). From the end of 2015, BTCTE has generously committed to support the 20 children rescued on Lake Volta this year. As of 2016, IOM currently has 63 survivors under its care.

Source: IOM (2015). Ghana Annual Report.

In 2016, the IOM provided reintegration assistance, which consisted of vocational training, education, microbusiness loans, and provision of food packages. A total of 81 trafficked children benefited from one or more of these.

Migrant assistance: The Operations Department also assists stranded and vulnerable migrants and victims of trafficking through facilitating their dignified return home. The department assisted a total of 104 migrants through such interventions in 2016.

The number of victims of trafficking assisted with AVRR services in 2016 was:
five (four women and one man) from Kuwait (3), Kenya (1) and Niger (1).

Source: IOM (2016). Ghana Annual Report.

The current legislation on trafficking in persons in Guinea was introduced in October 2016 which is broadly in line with the UN Trafficking in Persons Protocol definition. Previously, the legislation only criminalized child trafficking.

Investigations and suspects

Number of cases of trafficking in persons and related offences recorded, 2014 – 2017

Source: National Committee against Trafficking in Persons and Similar Practices (CNLTPPA), Office for the Protection of Gender, Children and Morals (OPROGEM).

Number of persons brought into formal contact with the police and/or criminal justice system because they have been suspected of, arrested for or cautioned for trafficking in persons and related offences, by sex**, 2014 – 2017

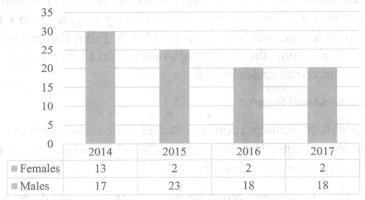

	2014	2015	2016	2017
■ Females	13	2	2	2
■ Males	17	23	18	18

Source: CNLTPPA.

**Note: Formal contact with the police and/or criminal justice system may include persons suspected, arrested, or cautioned at the national level.

Number of persons prosecuted for trafficking in persons and related offences, by sex, 2014 – 2017

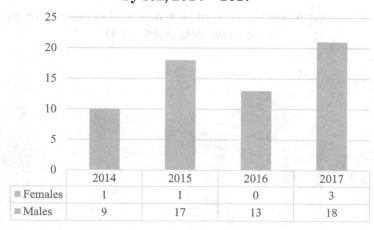

	2014	2015	2016	2017
■ Females	1	1	0	3
■ Males	9	17	13	18

Source: CNLTPPA.

Number of persons convicted of trafficking in persons and related offences, by sex, 2014 – 2017

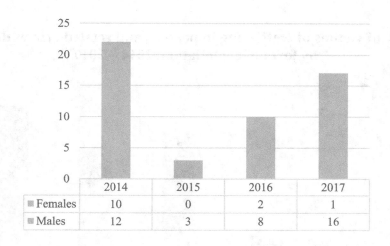

	2014	2015	2016	2017
■ Females	10	0	2	1
■ Males	12	3	8	16

Source: CNLTPPA.

The majority of persons convicted between 2014 and 2017 were citizens of Guinea and six were foreigners.

Source: CNLTPPA.

Number of victims of trafficking in persons and related crimes detected, by age and sex, 2014 – 2017

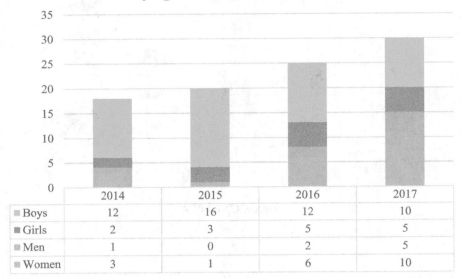

	2014	2015	2016	2017
Boys	12	16	12	10
Girls	2	3	5	5
Men	1	0	2	5
Women	3	1	6	10

Source: CNLTPPA, OPROGEM.

Number of victims of trafficking in persons and related crimes detected, by form of exploitation, 2014 – 2017

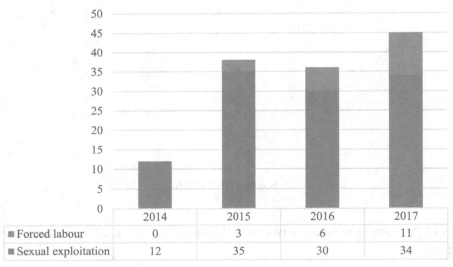

	2014	2015	2016	2017
Forced labour	0	3	6	11
Sexual exploitation	12	35	30	34

Source: CNLTPPA, OPROGEM.

In 2016, 78 citizens of Guinea were trafficked domestically. In 2017, 79 victims of Guinea were trafficked domestically and 120 were trafficked internationally.

Source: CNLTPPA.

Countries from which identified victims were repatriated, 2014 – 2017

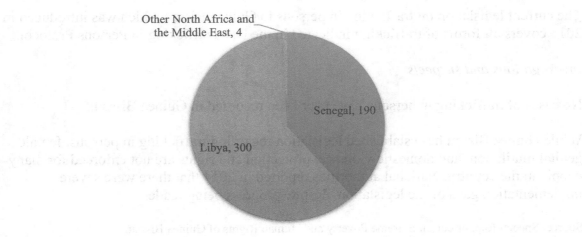

Other North Africa and the Middle East, 4

Senegal, 190

Libya, 300

Source: CNLTPPA.

−Guinea Bissau−

The current legislation on trafficking in persons in Guinea Bissau which was introduced in 2011 covers all forms of trafficking indicated in the UN Trafficking in Persons Protocol.

Investigations and suspects

No cases of trafficking in persons have ever been recorded in Guinea Bissau.

While Guinea Bissau has established legislation regarding trafficking in persons, female genital mutilation, and domestic violence, protection and rights are not enforced for many people in the country. National authorities reported in 2014 that there were severe implementation gaps of the legislation, despite progress being made.

Source: Special Rapporteur on Extreme Poverty and Human Rights of Guinea Bissau.

The practice of forced marriage is common in Guinea Bissau, especially in the Gabú and Bafatá regions. Forced marriage often results from poor families selling their daughters in exchange for money, land, or cattle. National authorities expressed concern that many of these forced marriages involve trafficking in persons.

Source: Special Rapporteur on Extreme Poverty and Human Rights of Guinea Bissau.

Poverty is also a significant problem in Guinea Bissau, which makes children vulnerable to violence, exploitation and abuse, trafficking, child labour, child marriage and commercial sexual exploitation.

Source: UN General Assembly.

Victims

On average, between 7 and 10 per cent of girls are forced into marriage before they reach age 15 while 29 per cent are married before reaching age 18. Evidence suggests that poverty exacerbates this issue, with 37 per cent of women from very poor households married before the age of 18.

Source: UN General Assembly.

According to a survey taken by the Ministry of Economics, Planning and Regional Integration, more than half (51%) of children between the ages of 5 and 14 are involved in child labour. This form of exploitation is more prevalent in rural areas (62% in rural areas, 37% in urban areas). Exploitation of children for forced labour occurs more frequently among children between the ages of 5 and 11 (56%) than children between the ages of 15 and 17 (44%). In addition, girls are more vulnerable to labour exploitation (53%).

Source: Ministry of Economics, Planning and Regional Integration.

–Kenya–

The current legislation on trafficking in persons in Kenya covers all forms of trafficking indicated in the UN Trafficking in Persons Protocol.

Investigations and suspects

Number of cases of trafficking in persons recorded, 2015 – September 2017

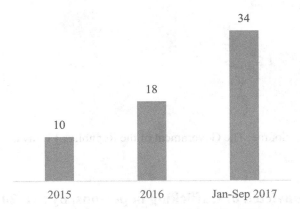

Source: The Government of the Republic of Kenya.

Number of persons brought into formal contact with the police and/or criminal justice system because they have been suspected of trafficking in persons, by sex, 2014 – September 2017

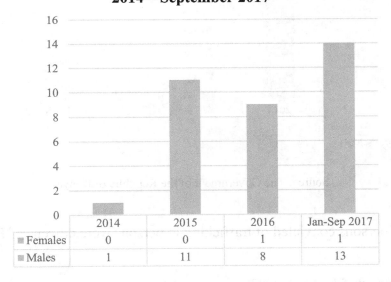

	2014	2015	2016	Jan-Sep 2017
Females	0	0	1	1
Males	1	11	8	13

Source: The Government of the Republic of Kenya.

Number of persons prosecuted for trafficking in persons, by sex, 2014 – September 2017

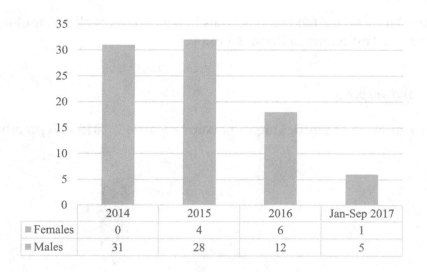

	2014	2015	2016	Jan-Sep 2017
■ Females	0	4	6	1
■ Males	31	28	12	5

Source: The Government of the Republic of Kenya.

Number of persons convicted of trafficking in persons, by sex, 2014 – September 2017

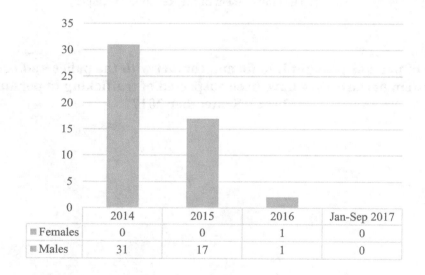

	2014	2015	2016	Jan-Sep 2017
■ Females	0	0	1	0
■ Males	31	17	1	0

Source: The Government of the Republic of Kenya.

The majority of persons convicted of trafficking in persons were citizens of Ethiopia and Somalia.

Source: The Government of the Republic of Kenya.

Victims

**Number of adult victims of trafficking in persons detected, by age and sex,
2014 – September 2017**

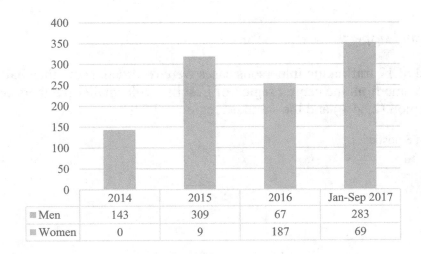

	2014	2015	2016	Jan-Sep 2017
▪ Men	143	309	67	283
▪ Women	0	9	187	69

Source: The Government of the Republic of Kenya.

**Number of victims of trafficking in persons detected, by form of exploitation,
2016 – September 2017**

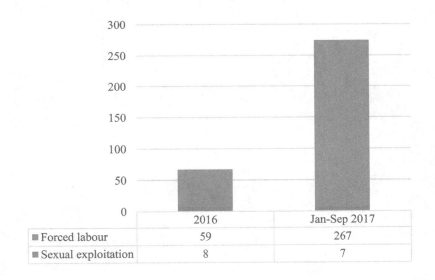

	2016	Jan-Sep 2017
▪ Forced labour	59	267
▪ Sexual exploitation	8	7

Source: The Government of the Republic of Kenya.

Detected victims of trafficking in persons between January 2014 and September 2017 were citizens of Ethiopia, Somalia, Kenya, Uganda, and Burundi.

Source: The Government of the Republic of Kenya.

−Lesotho−

The current legislation on trafficking in persons in Lesotho covers all forms of trafficking indicated in the UN Trafficking in Persons Protocol.

Investigations and suspects

In 2015, a total of 17 trafficking in persons cases were recorded. More than half of these cases (52.9%) came from the central region of Lesotho with smaller numbers coming from the northern region (29.4%) and the southern region (17.7%).

Source: Bureau of Statistics.

Victims

In 2014, the government identified 11 victims of trafficking in persons and referred five for services.

Source: International Labour Organisation (ILO).

–Liberia–

The current legislation on trafficking in persons in Liberia covers all forms of trafficking indicated in the UN Trafficking in Persons Protocol.

Investigation and Suspects

According to the Liberia National Police, there were two cases of human trafficking in January 2017 and one in February of the same year.

Source: Liberia National Police (2017).

In 2015, The UN Committee on the Elimination of Violence against Women welcomed the launch of a national action plan to combat trafficking in 2014 and the establishment of a national anti-trafficking task force. The Committee notes that Liberia remains a source and destination country for trafficking.

Source: UN Convention on the Elimination of All Forms of Discrimination against Women.

Victims

According to the UN Committee on the Elimination of Violence against Women, the government was investigating a case involving 14 Liberian girls who were trafficked to Lebanon in 2015.

Source: UN Convention on the Elimination of All Forms of Discrimination against Women.

–Madagascar–

The current legislation on trafficking in persons in Madagascar covers all forms of trafficking indicated in the UN Trafficking in Persons Protocol but does not follow the definition of exploitation in the Protocol. The Anti-Trafficking Law No. 38 was introduced in 2007 and amended in 2014

Investigations and suspects

Number of suspected traffickers detected, 2014 – 2017

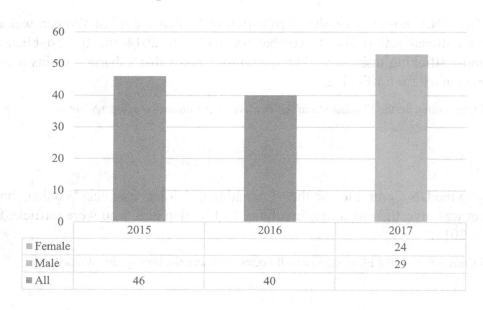

	2015	2016	2017
■ Female			24
■ Male			29
■ All	46	40	

Source: Ministry of Justice, Ministry of Population and Social Affairs,
Trafficking in Persons in the SADC Region: A Statistical Report (2017).

Between 2015 and 2017, identified traffickers were citizens of Southern African and Asian countries.

Source: Ministry of Justice, *Trafficking in Persons in the SADC Region: A Statistical Report (2017).*

In the same period, Madagascar recorded a total of 23 convictions: six each year in 2015 and 2017 and 11 in 2016. However, the majority of cases brought before the court system resulted in acquittals. Notably, out of 144 cases brought in 2015, 138 ended in acquittals and only six in convictions.

Source: Ministry of Justice, *Trafficking in Persons in the SADC Region: A Statistical Report (2017).*

Victims

Number of victims of trafficking in persons detected, 2014 – September 2017

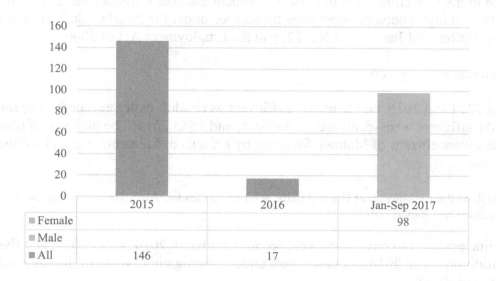

	2015	2016	Jan-Sep 2017
◼ Female			98
◼ Male			
◼ All	146	17	

Source: Ministry of Justice, Ministry of Population and Social Affairs,
Trafficking in Persons in the SADC Region: A Statistical Report (2017).

Government sources reported that between 2015 and 2016, victims were trafficked to the Middle East for the purposes of exploitation in the domestic sector and for sexual and labour exploitation.

Source: Bureau National de Lutte contre la Traite des Etres Humains (BNLTEH), Ministry of Justice, Ministry of Population and Social Affairs, *Trafficking in Persons in the SADC Region: A Statistical Report (2017).*

−Malawi−

The current legislation on trafficking in persons in Malawi covers all forms of trafficking indicated in the UN Trafficking in Persons Protocol and was introduced in 2015. Prior to this period, trafficking in persons cases were prosecuted under the Penal Code 7.01, The Child Care, Protection, and Justice Act No. 22, and the Employment Act of 2000.

Investigations and suspects

Between 2014 and 2016, all identified traffickers were adult males except for one minor. In 2014, 10 traffickers were identified, 15 in 2015, and 16 in 2016. The majority of identified traffickers were citizens of Malawi, followed by citizens of Mozambique, and a minority of Tanzanians.

Source: Malawi Police, Ministry of Home Affairs, Ministry of Gender, *Trafficking in Persons in the SADC Region: A Statistical Report (2017).*

In the same period, 14 convictions were recorded: three in 2014, six in 2015, and five in 2016. Additionally in 2016, six cases were under investigation. Many of the cases involved trafficking of children.

Source: Malawi Police, Ministry of Home Affairs, Ministry of Gender, *Trafficking in Persons in the SADC Region: A Statistical Report (2017).*

Victims

Number of victims of trafficking in persons detected, by sex, 2014 – 2016

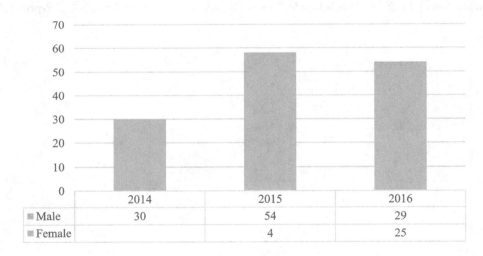

	2014	2015	2016
Male	30	54	29
Female		4	25

Source: Malawi Police, Ministry of Home Affairs, Ministry of Gender, *Trafficking in Persons in the SADC Region: A Statistical Report (2017).*

Number of victims of trafficking in persons detected, by sex and age, 2014 – 2016

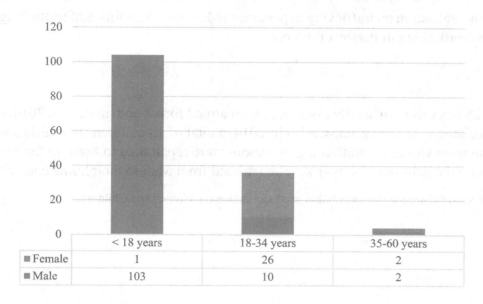

	< 18 years	18-34 years	35-60 years
■ Female	1	26	2
■ Male	103	10	2

Source: Malawi Police, Ministry of Home Affairs, Ministry of Gender,
Trafficking in Persons in the SADC Region: A Statistical Report (2017).

Number of victims of trafficking in persons detected, by form of exploitation, 2014 – September 2017

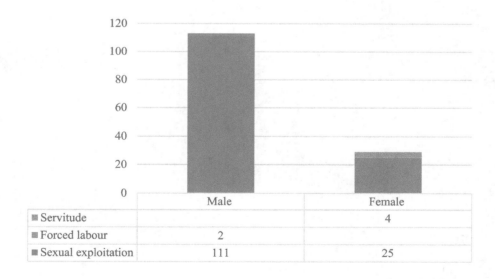

	Male	Female
■ Servitude		4
■ Forced labour	2	
■ Sexual exploitation	111	25

Source: Malawi Police, Ministry of Home Affairs, Ministry of Gender,
Trafficking in Persons in the SADC Region: A Statistical Report (2017).

–Mali–

The current legislation on trafficking in persons in Mali covers all forms of trafficking indicated in the UN Trafficking in Persons Protocol.

Victims

In 2013, 28 boys were officially associated with armed forces and groups. In 2014, eight boys were associated with such groups. Also in 2014, a total of 13 children (four girls and nine boys) who were victims of trafficking in persons were repatriated to Mali. In the same year, 29 children (six girls and 23 boys) were repatriated from Mali to their home countries.

Source: National Centre for Documentation and Information on Women and Children.

−Mauritius−

The current legislation on trafficking in persons in Mauritius covers all forms of trafficking indicated in the UN Trafficking in Persons Protocol.

Investigations and suspects

Number of cases of trafficking in persons recorded**, 2014 – August 2017

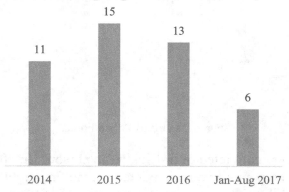

Source: Mauritius Police Force.

**The data presented represents the cases of trafficking in persons established under the Combatting of Trafficking in Persons Act of 2009 and the Child Protection Act of 1994.

Number of persons brought into formal contact with the police and/or criminal justice system because they have been suspected of, arrested for or cautioned for trafficking in persons, by sex**, 2014 – August 2017

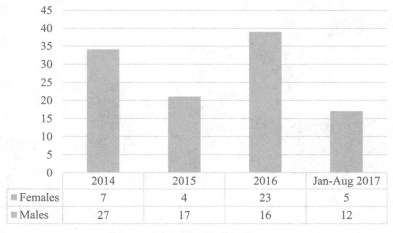

	2014	2015	2016	Jan-Aug 2017
■ Females	7	4	23	5
■ Males	27	17	16	12

Source: Mauritius Police Force.

**Note: Formal contact with the police and/or criminal justice system may include persons suspected, arrested, or cautioned at the national level.

Number of persons prosecuted for trafficking in persons, by sex, 2014 – August 2017

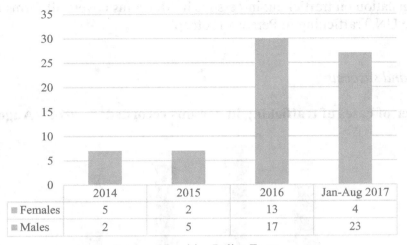

	2014	2015	2016	Jan-Aug 2017
■ Females	5	2	13	4
■ Males	2	5	17	23

Source: Mauritius Police Force.

In 2014, seven persons were convicted of trafficking in persons. In 2015, one person was convicted, while in 2016 no persons were convicted. In the first eight months of 2017, two persons were convicted. All persons convicted were citizens of Mauritius.

Source: Mauritius Police Force.

Victims

Number of victims of trafficking in persons detected, by age and sex, 2014 – August 2017

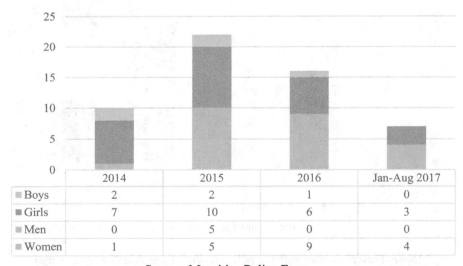

	2014	2015	2016	Jan-Aug 2017
■ Boys	2	2	1	0
■ Girls	7	10	6	3
■ Men	0	5	0	0
■ Women	1	5	9	4

Source: Mauritius Police Force.

Number of victims of trafficking in persons detected, by form of exploitation, 2014 – August 2017

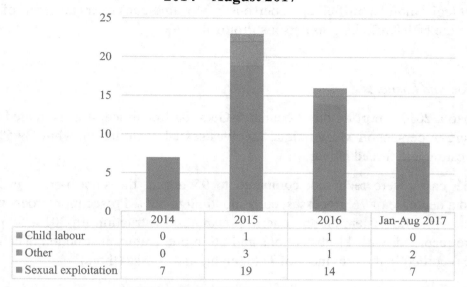

	2014	2015	2016	Jan-Aug 2017
■ Child labour	0	1	1	0
■ Other	0	3	1	2
■ Sexual exploitation	7	19	14	7

Source: Mauritius Police Force.

–Mozambique–

The current legislation on trafficking in persons in Mozambique covers all forms of trafficking indicated in the UN Trafficking in Persons Protocol.

Investigation and Suspects

According to a 2017 report by the Procurador-Geral da República, it is estimated that 10.5% of trafficking in persons in Mozambique involves sexual exploitation, while 89.5% concerns organ harvesting and forced labour.

In 2016, 19 cases were recorded, compared to 95 during the same period in 2015. This represented a decrease of 76 processes, corresponding to 80%. Prosecution orders were issued in 17 cases, with one abstention and one in preparatory instruction. In 2015, 58 prosecution orders were recorded, with 11 abstentions and 26 in preparatory instruction. The majority of cases were recorded in the provinces of Tete (eight) and Niassa (three).

Cases of trafficking in people with albinism was reduced from 51 in 2015 to 15 in 2016, with the aid of programmes that guarantee protection, social, and legal assistance.

Source: PGR Procuradoria Geral Da Republica (2017).

Victims

Six of the human trafficking victims identified in 2017 were citizens from Mozambique and from other southern African countries. For the other victims identified, citizenship was unreported.

Source: PGR Procuradoria Geral Da Republica (2017).

–Namibia–

The current legislation on trafficking in persons in Namibia covers all forms of trafficking indicated in the UN Trafficking in Persons Protocol.

Investigation and Suspects

According to the International Organisation for Migration in 2015, actual data on the extent of human trafficking and smuggling in Namibia are difficult to obtain. However, the Ministry of Health and Social Services identified 17 cases of reported human trafficking offences. Of these, seven were recorded in the Omaheke region, eight in the Kunene region, and two in the Khomas region.

Source: International Organisation for Migration.

Victims

In 2016, the Human Rights Committee expressed concern that women and children were trafficked within the country for the purpose of forced labour and sexual exploitation, including forced prostitution.

Source: UN International Covenant on Civil and Political Rights.

–Niger–

The current legislation on trafficking in persons in Niger covers all forms of trafficking indicated in the UN Trafficking in Persons Protocol.

Investigations and suspects

Number of cases of trafficking in persons recorded, 2014 – 2016

Source: Ministry of Justice

Number of persons prosecuted for trafficking in persons, by sex, 2014 – 2016

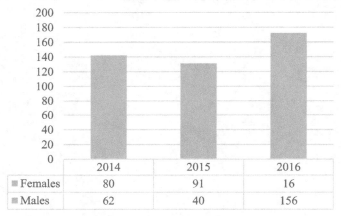

	2014	2015	2016
Females	80	91	16
Males	62	40	156

Source: Ministry of Justice.

Number of persons convicted of trafficking in persons, by sex, 2014 – 2016

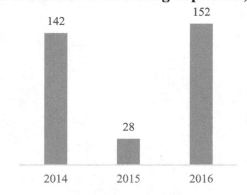

Source: Ministry of Justice.

In 2014, of the 142 persons convicted of trafficked in persons, 62 were males and 80 were females. In 2016, of the 152 persons convicted, 150 were males and two were females. The majority of persons convicted of trafficking in persons between 2014 and 2016 were citizens of Niger or other West African countries.

Source: Ministry of Justice.

Victims

Number of victims of trafficking in persons detected, by age and sex, 2014 – 2016

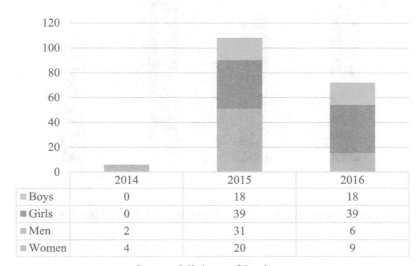

	2014	2015	2016
Boys	0	18	18
Girls	0	39	39
Men	2	31	6
Women	4	20	9

Source: Ministry of Justice.

The majority of victims of trafficking in persons were citizens of Niger or other West African countries. Primarily, victims were trafficked internationally to other countries in Africa with a small number trafficked to Europe.

Source: Ministry of Justice.

−Nigeria−

The current legislation on trafficking in persons in Nigeria covers all forms of trafficking indicated in the UN Trafficking in Persons Protocol.

Investigations and suspects

Number of cases of trafficking in persons recorded, 2014 – August 2017

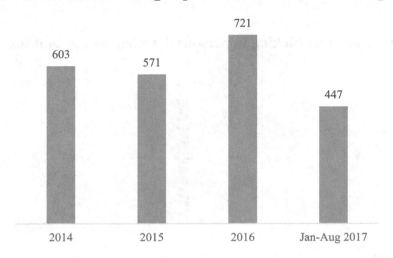

Source: National Agency for the Prohibition of Trafficking in Persons.

Number of persons brought into formal contact with the police and/or criminal justice system because they have been suspected of or arrested for traffickin in persons, by sex, 2014 – August 2017

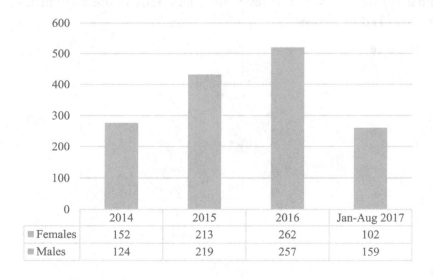

	2014	2015	2016	Jan-Aug 2017
Females	152	213	262	102
Males	124	219	257	159

Source: National Agency for the Prohibition of Trafficking in Persons.

Number of persons prosecuted for trafficking in persons, 2014 – August 2017

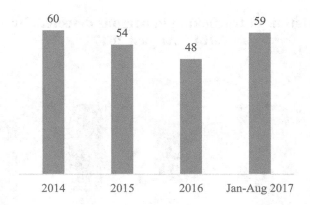

Source: National Agency for the Prohibition of Trafficking in Persons.

Additional information

In 2016, 28 males and 20 females were prosecuted for trafficking in persons. In 2017, 31 males and 28 females were prosecuted.

Source: National Agency for the Prohibition of Trafficking in Persons.

Number of persons convicted of trafficking in persons, by sex, 2014 – August 2017

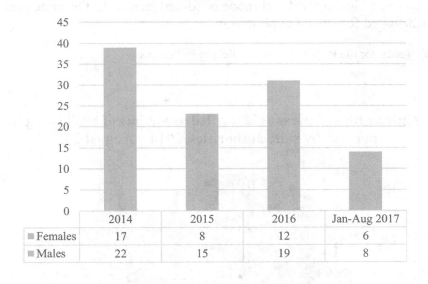

	2014	2015	2016	Jan-Aug 2017
Females	17	8	12	6
Males	22	15	19	8

Source: National Agency for the Prohibition of Trafficking in Persons.

National authorities reported that all persons convicted in the indicated period for trafficking in persons were nationals of Nigeria.

Source: National Agency for the Prohibition of Trafficking in Persons.

**Number of victims of trafficking in persons detected, by age and sex,
2014 – August 2017**

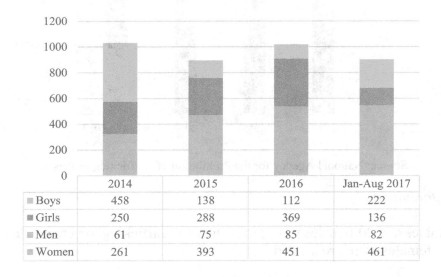

	2014	2015	2016	Jan-Aug 2017
▪ Boys	458	138	112	222
▪ Girls	250	288	369	136
▪ Men	61	75	85	82
▪ Women	261	393	451	461

Source: National Agency for the Prohibition of Trafficking in Persons.

During the reporting period, the majority of detected victims were trafficked for the purposes of forced labour and sexual exploitation. Between January 2014 and August 2017, a total of 1,318 persons were trafficked for the purpose of forced labour. In the same period, 1,299 persons were trafficked for sexual exploitation.

Source: National Agency for the Prohibition of Trafficking in Persons.

**Citizenships of persons identified as victims of trafficking in
persons by state authorities, 2014 – August 2017**

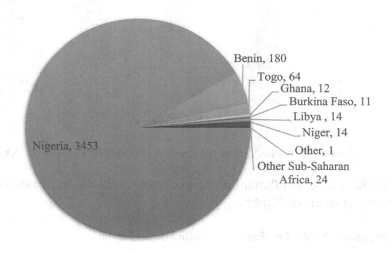

Source: National Agency for the Prohibition of Trafficking in Persons.

Countries from which identified victims were repatriated, 2014 - August 2017

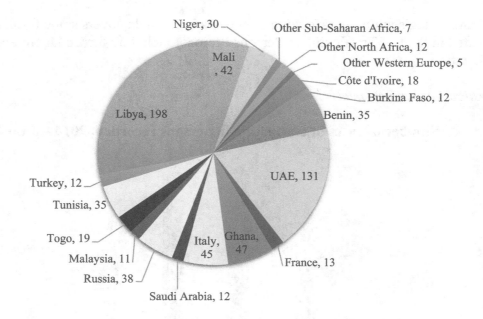

Source: National Agency for the Prohibition of Trafficking in Persons.

Additional information

Officials reported that in 2014, 815 citizens of Nigeria were trafficked domestically within the borders of Nigeria while 126 were repatriated from other countries.

Source: National Agency for the Prohibition of Trafficking in Persons.

−Rwanda−

The current legislation on trafficking in persons in Rwanda covers some forms of trafficking indicated in the UN Trafficking in Persons Protocol including forced labour and sexual exploitation.

Investigations and suspects

Number of cases of trafficking in persons recorded, 2014 − June 2017

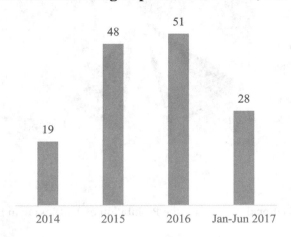

Source: National Public Prosecution Office.

Number of persons brought into formal contact with the police and/or criminal justice system because they have been suspected of trafficking in persons, by sex, 2014 − October 2017

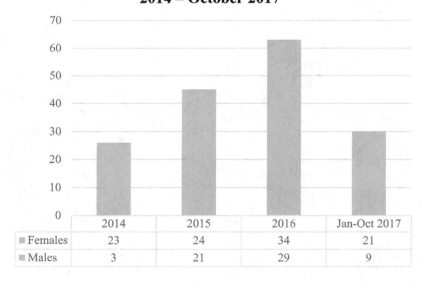

	2014	2015	2016	Jan-Oct 2017
Females	23	24	34	21
Males	3	21	29	9

Source: Rwanda National Police Criminal Records Office.

Number of persons prosecuted for trafficking in persons, by sex, 2014 – June 2017

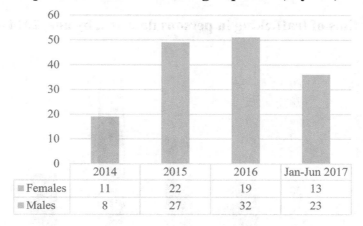

	2014	2015	2016	Jan-Jun 2017
Females	11	22	19	13
Males	8	27	32	23

Source: National Public Prosecution Authority Office.

Number of persons convicted of trafficking in persons, by sex, 2015 – June 2017

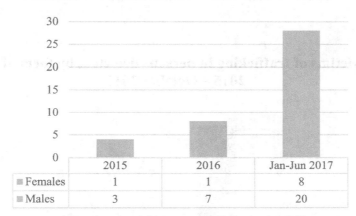

	2015	2016	Jan-Jun 2017
Females	1	1	8
Males	3	7	20

Source: National Public Prosecution Authority Office.

Citizenships of persons convicted of trafficking in persons, 2015 - June 2017

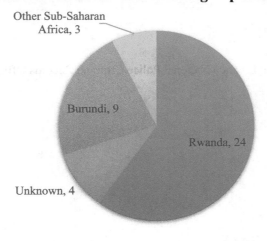

Source: National Public Prosecution Authority Office.

Victims

Number of victims of trafficking in persons detected, by age, 2014 – October 2017

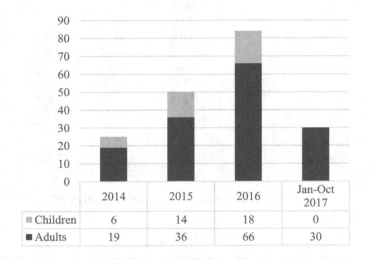

	2014	2015	2016	Jan-Oct 2017
■ Children	6	14	18	0
■ Adults	19	36	66	30

Source: Rwanda National Police Criminal Records Office.

Number of victims of trafficking in persons detected, by form of exploitation, 2015 – October 2017

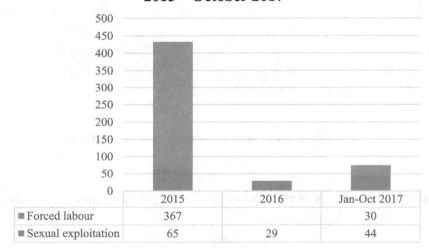

	2015	2016	Jan-Oct 2017
■ Forced labour	367		30
■ Sexual exploitation	65	29	44

Source: Rwanda National Police Criminal Records Office.

Citizenships of persons identified as victims of trafficking in persons by state authorities, 2015 – October 2017

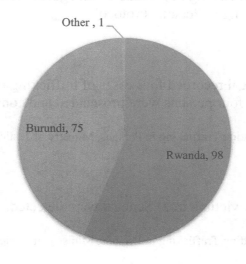

Other , 1

Burundi, 75

Rwanda, 98

Source: Rwanda National Police Criminal Records Office.

In 2016, national authorities reported that 11 citizens of Rwanda were trafficked domestically, while 51 identified victims were trafficked internationally. Between January and October 2017, three identified victims were trafficked domestically and 33 were repatriated from other countries.

Source: Rwanda National Police Criminal Records Office.

Countries from which identified victims were repatriated, 2016 - October 2017

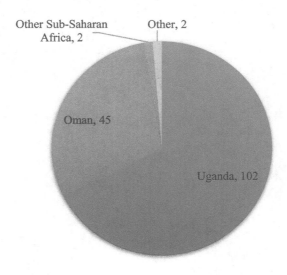

Other Sub-Saharan Africa, 2

Other, 2

Oman, 45

Uganda, 102

Source: Rwanda National Police Criminal Records Office.

The current legislation on trafficking in persons in Senegal covers all forms of trafficking indicated in the UN Trafficking in Persons Protocol.

Investigations and suspects

National authorities in Senegal recorded four cases of trafficking in persons in 2014 and three in 2015. During this period, four persons were prosecuted and convicted of the crime.

Source: National Unit for Combatting Trafficking in Persons, Ministry of Justice.

Victims

Between 2014 and 2015, six victims from Senegal were detected.

Source: National Unit for Combatting Trafficking in Persons, Ministry of Justice.

−The Republic of Sierra Leone−

The current legislation in The Republic of Sierra Leone, the Anti Trafficking Act of 2005, covers all forms of trafficking indicated in the UN Trafficking in Persons Protocol.

Investigations and suspects

Number of cases of trafficking in persons recorded, 2014 −2017

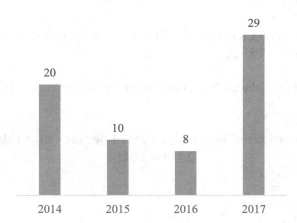

Source: Transnational Organized Crime Unit, Rogbana

In 2014, 2015, and 2017, respectively, one, two, and seven persons were prosecuted for trafficking in persons with no recorded convictions.

Source: Transnational Organized Crime Unit, Rogbana

Victims

In 2014, 2015, and 2017, respectively, one, five, and 10 child victims were detected. Additionally, in 2015 and 2017, respectively, one and 10 adult victims were detected. All were trafficked for forced labour according to the authorities of Sierra Leone. Many of the victims were citizens of Sierra Leone. Some victims were repatriated from Ghana and Guinea, and nine victims were repatriated from Kuwait.

Source: Transnational Organized Crime Unit, Rogbana

The current legislation on trafficking in persons in South Africa covers all forms of trafficking indicated in the UN Trafficking in Persons Protocol.

Investigations and suspects

In both 2014 and 2015, seventeen offences of trafficking in persons were recorded by national authorities in South Africa.

Source: Provincial Report and the National Prosecuting Authority National Statistics.

Number of persons investigated for trafficking in persons and related offences, by sex, 2014 – 2015

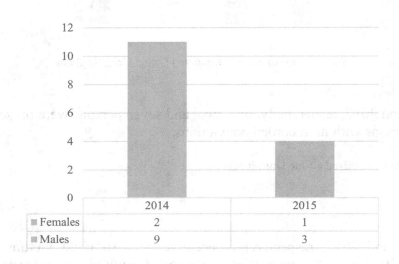

	2014	2015
■ Females	2	1
■ Males	9	3

Source: Provincial Report and the National Prosecuting Authority National Statistics.

Eleven persons were prosecuted for trafficking in persons in 2014 and nine in 2015. Of those persons prosecuted, seven were convicted in 2014 and three were convicted in 2015.

Source: The National Prosecuting Authority.

The majority of persons convicted between 2014 and 2015 were citizens of South Africa and other Sub-Saharan African countries.

Source: Directorate for Priority Crime Investigation.

Victims

In 2014, national authorities in South Africa detected 55 total victims of trafficking in persons. The detected victims were trafficked for the purposes of sexual exploitation, forced labour, removal of organs, and forced marriage.

Source: Department of Social Development, Priority Crime Management Centre Statistics.

Citizenships of persons identified as victims of trafficking in persons by state authorities, 2014 – 2015

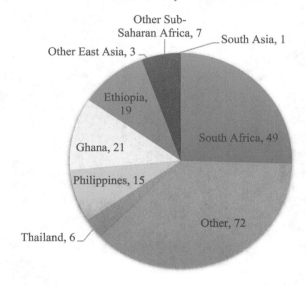

Source: The Department of Home Affairs.

Between 2014 and 2015, the majority of citizens of South Africa were trafficked domestically.

Source: Priority Crime Management Centre.

–The United Republic of Tanzania–

The current legislation on trafficking in persons in The United Republic of Tanzania covers all forms of trafficking indicated in the UN Trafficking in Persons Protocol.

Investigations and Suspects

According to police statistics for the year 2015, 45 cases of human trafficking were recorded between January and December. This was an increase from the year of 2014, when 21 cases were recorded.

Source: Tanzania Police Force.

–Uganda–

The current legislation on trafficking in persons in Uganda covers all forms of trafficking indicated in the UN Trafficking in Persons Protocol.

Investigations and Suspects

In 2015, the government investigated 108 trafficking cases, reporting 15 prosecutions and three convictions.

Source: The Republic of Uganda Judiciary.

Victims

The Ministry of Internal Affairs investigated 21 cases of human trafficking and provided welfare support to 12 victims between 2016 and 2017.

Source: Ministry of Internal Affairs.

–Zambia–

The current legislation on trafficking in persons in Zambia covers all forms of trafficking indicated in the UN Trafficking in Persons Protocol.

Investigations and suspects

In 2015, national authorities recorded 13 suspected cases of trafficking in persons, mainly in the western province of Zambia.

Source: 2015 National Gender Based Violence Crime Statistics by Province (Zambia Police Service - Victim Support Unit).

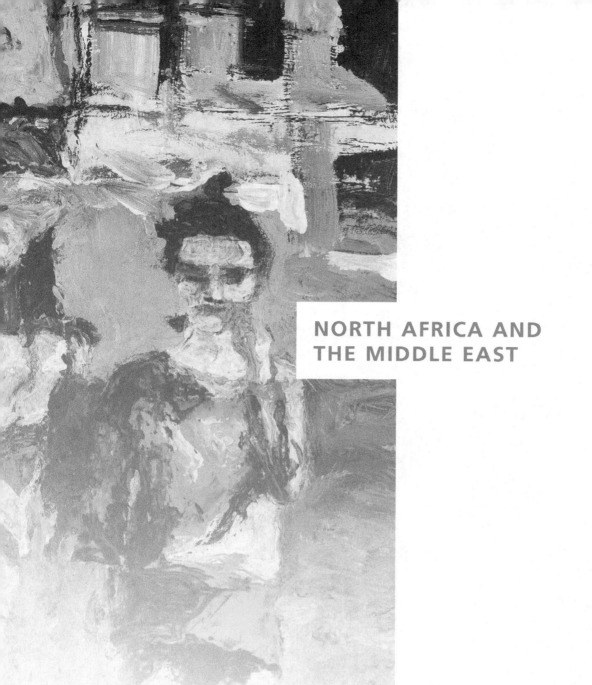

NORTH AFRICA AND THE MIDDLE EAST

The current legislation on trafficking in persons in Algeria was introduced in November 2009 and covers all forms of trafficking indicated in the UN Trafficking in Persons Protocol.

Investigations and suspects

The Ministry of Justice reported seven offenses of trafficking in persons from the beginning of 2014 until the end of 2017. Between 2016 and 2017, a total of 20 people were brought into formal contact with the police and/or criminal justice system because they had been suspected of, arrested for, or cautioned for trafficking in persons.* While a total of 40 people were prosecuted for trafficking in persons, no person was convicted of the crime between 2015 and 2017. In 2014, one person was convicted of trafficking in persons.

Source: The Ministry of Justice and the National Gendarmerie.

*Note: Formal contact with the police and/or criminal justice system may include persons suspected, arrested, or cautioned at the national level.

Victims

Number of victims of trafficking in persons detected, by age and sex, 2014 – September 2017

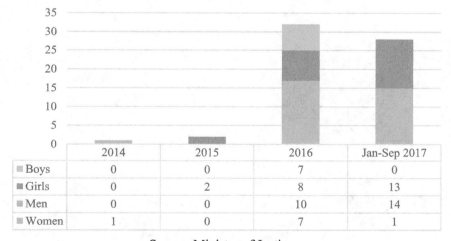

	2014	2015	2016	Jan-Sep 2017
Boys	0	0	7	0
Girls	0	2	8	13
Men	0	0	10	14
Women	1	0	7	1

Source: Ministry of Justice.

Between 2014 and 2017, three victims for the purpose of sexual exploitation were detected, all female. In 2017, 14 adult men and 13 girls were trafficked for forced work. In 2016, a significant number of victims were detected who were trafficked for the purpose of forced begging. A total of 32 victims were detected, consisting of 10 adult men, seven adult women, seven girls, and eight boys.

Source: Ministry of Justice.

Citizenships of persons identified as victims of trafficking in persons by state authorities, 2014 – August 2017

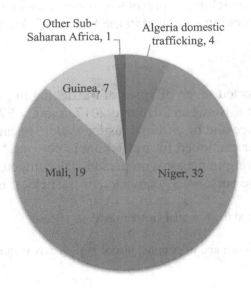

Source: Ministry of Justice.

−Bahrain−

The current legislation on trafficking in persons in Bahrain covers all forms of trafficking indicated in the UN Trafficking in Persons Protocol.

Investigations and suspects

Number of cases of trafficking in persons recorded, 2010 – August 2015

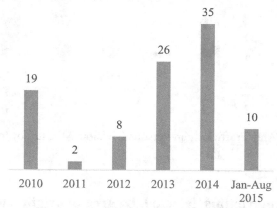

Source: Anti-Trafficking in Persons Division, Ministry of Interior.

In 2010, four males and four females were convicted of trafficking in persons. No persons were convicted in 2011, while in 2012, four males and two females were convicted. In 2013, eight males and six females were convicted. In 2014, 12 males and three females were convicted. No persons were convicted between January and August 2015. All convicted persons were citizens of Bahrain, countries in the Middle East, Asia, and Eastern Europe.

Source: Anti-Trafficking in Persons Division, Ministry of Interior.

Victims

Number of victims of trafficking in persons detected, by age and sex, 2010 – August 2015

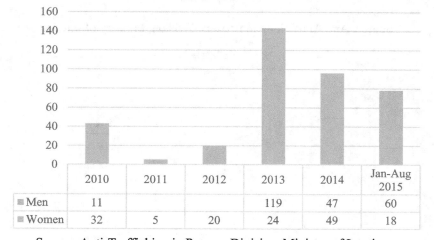

	2010	2011	2012	2013	2014	Jan-Aug 2015
Men	11			119	47	60
Women	32	5	20	24	49	18

Source: Anti-Trafficking in Persons Division, Ministry of Interior.

Number of victims of trafficking in persons detected, by form of exploitation, 2010 – August 2015

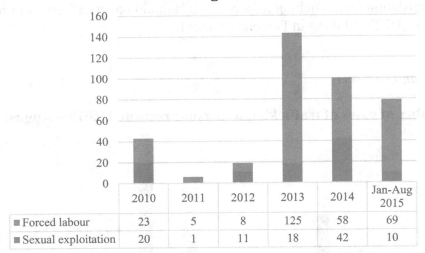

	2010	2011	2012	2013	2014	Jan-Aug 2015
■ Forced labour	23	5	8	125	58	69
■ Sexual exploitation	20	1	11	18	42	10

Source: Anti-Trafficking in Persons Division, Ministry of Interior.

Victims of trafficking victims detected, by area of origin, 2012 – August 2015

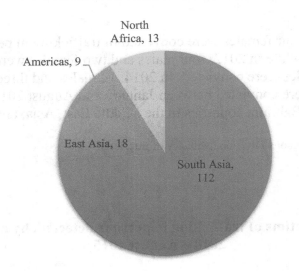

Source: Anti-Trafficking in Persons Division, Ministry of Interior.

– Egypt –

The current legislation on trafficking in persons in Egypt was introduced in 2010 and covers all forms of trafficking indicated in the UN Trafficking in Persons Protocol.

Investigations and suspects

Number of cases of trafficking in persons recorded, 2014 – July 2017

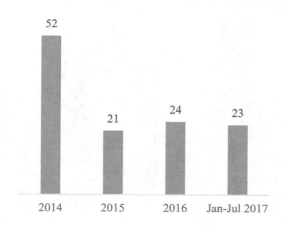

Source: The National Coordinating Committee for Combating and Preventing Illegal Migration and Trafficking in Persons

Number of persons brought into formal contact with the police and/or criminal justice system because they have been suspected of, arrested for or cautioned for trafficking in persons, by sex**, 2014 –2017

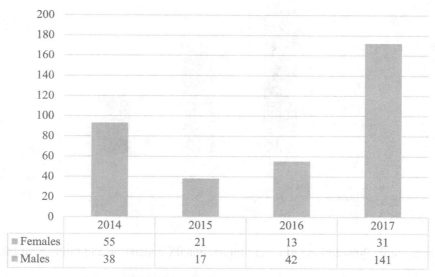

	2014	2015	2016	2017
Females	55	21	13	31
Males	38	17	42	141

Source: The National Coordinating Committee for Combating and Preventing Illegal Migration and Trafficking in Persons

**Note: Formal contact with the police and/or criminal justice system may include persons suspected, arrested, or cautioned at the national level.

In 2014, 21 males were convicted of trafficking in persons, while six females were convicted.

Source: Public Prosecution Office and International Cooperation and Human Rights Office.

Victims

Number of victims of trafficking in persons detected, by age and sex, 2014 - 2017

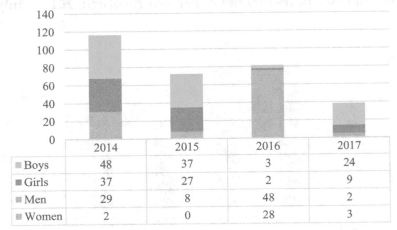

	2014	2015	2016	2017
Boys	48	37	3	24
Girls	37	27	2	9
Men	29	8	48	2
Women	2	0	28	3

Source: Public Prosecution Office and International Cooperation and Ministry of Interior.

Number of victims of trafficking detected, by form of exploitation when reported, 2014 – 2017

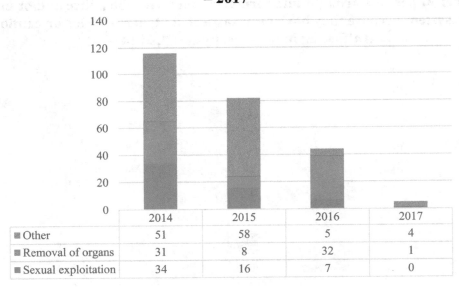

	2014	2015	2016	2017
Other	51	58	5	4
Removal of organs	31	8	32	1
Sexual exploitation	34	16	7	0

Source: Public Prosecution Office and International Cooperation and Ministry of Interior.

All persons identified as victims by state authorities in 2014 and 2015 were Egyptian nationals. All victims were domestically trafficked within Egypt.

Source: Public Prosecution Office and International Cooperation and Ministry of Interior.

The current legislation on trafficking in persons in Israel covers all forms of trafficking indicated in the UN Trafficking in Persons Protocol.

Investigations and suspects

In 2014, 2015, and 2016 respectively, 17, 10, and nine cases of trafficking in persons were recorded. In the same years, a total of 29 persons were brought into formal contact with the police and/or criminal justice system because they were suspected of, arrested for or cautioned for trafficking in persons. The majority of these persons were males.

Source: Israel Police.

In 2014, six persons were prosecuted for trafficking in persons. In 2015, five were prosecuted, while in 2016, two persons were prosecuted. In 2014 and 2016, six persons were convicted of trafficking in persons in both years. In 2015, three persons were convicted. The majority of these persons were males and Israeli citizens.

Source: Israel State Attorney's Office.

Victims

Number of victims of trafficking in persons detected, by age and sex, 2014 – 2016

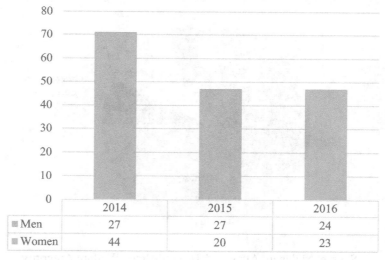

	2014	2015	2016
■ Men	27	27	24
■ Women	44	20	23

Source: Israel Police, Ma'agan, Atlas, and Tesfa Shelters.

Additional information

In 2014, eight children were residing with women in shelters who were identified as victims of trafficking, however were not necessarily recognized as victims of trafficking.

Source: Israel Police, Ma'agan, Atlas, and Tesfa Shelters.

Number of victims of trafficking in persons detected, by form of exploitation, 2014 – 2016

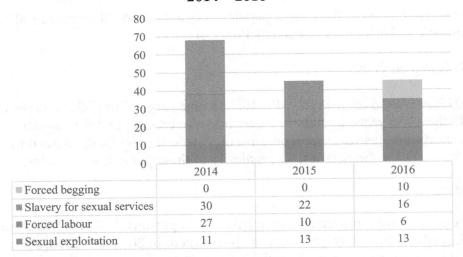

	2014	2015	2016
■ Forced begging	0	0	10
■ Slavery for sexual services	30	22	16
■ Forced labour	27	10	6
■ Sexual exploitation	11	13	13

Source: Ma'agan, Atlas, and Tesfa Shelters.

Citizenships of persons identified as victims of trafficking in persons by state authorities, 2014 – 2016

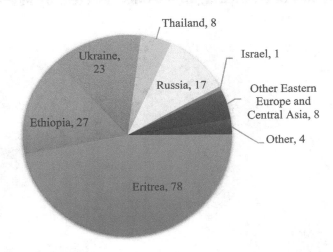

Source: Ma'agan, Atlas, and Tesfa Shelters, Welfare Authority.

One citizen of Israel was repatriated from North America in 2016.

Source: Ma'agan, Atlas, and Tesfa Shelters, Welfare Authority, and the Courts Authority.

The current legislation on trafficking in persons in Jordan covers all forms of trafficking indicated in the UN Trafficking in Persons Protocol.

Investigations and suspects

Number of cases of trafficking in persons recorded, 2014 – 2017

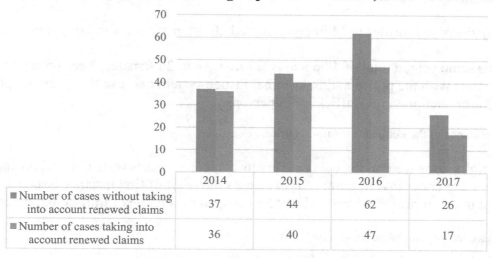

	2014	2015	2016	2017
▪ Number of cases without taking into account renewed claims	37	44	62	26
▪ Number of cases taking into account renewed claims	36	40	47	17

Source: Official information from Jordan authorities.

Victims

Number of victims of trafficking in persons registered in criminal courts, by age and sex, 2014 – 2017

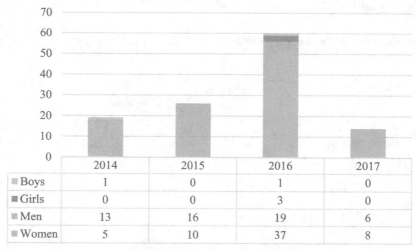

	2014	2015	2016	2017
▪ Boys	1	0	1	0
▪ Girls	0	0	3	0
▪ Men	13	16	19	6
▪ Women	5	10	37	8

Source: Official information from Jordan authorities.

−Kingdom of Morocco−

The current legislation on trafficking in persons in Morocco was introduced in August 2016 and covers all forms of trafficking indicated in the UN Trafficking in Persons Protocol. Before 2016, forced labour involving children and forced prostitution were used to prosecute trafficking related cases.

Investigations and suspects

In 2017, national authorities in Morocco reported 20 offences of trafficking in persons.

During the same year, a total of 47 persons, 27 males and 20 females, were brought into formal contact with the police and/or criminal justice system because they were suspected of, arrested for or cautioned for trafficking in persons.

Source: Presidency of the Public Prosecutor's Office.

In 2017, eight cases were in the court of first instance, four cases were decided on appeal, four cases were under investigation, for two cases the court of first instance issued a judgement under appeal. Two cases the court dropped the charge of trafficking in persons.

Source: Presidency of the Public Prosecutor's Office.

Victims

National authorities detected 27 victims in 2017. Of these, 9 were male children, 8 were female children, and 10 were adult females. All victims were trafficked within the domestic borders of the country.

During the same year, 22 were trafficked for the purpose of sexual exploitation, and five were trafficked for forced labour.

Source: Presidency of the Public Prosecutor's Office.

−Kuwait−

The current legislation in Kuwait, "Law no. 9 of 2013 on Combatting Trafficking in Persons and Smuggling of Migrants", covers all forms of trafficking indicated in the UN Trafficking in Persons Protocol.

Investigations and suspects

Number of cases of trafficking in persons recorded, 2015 – 2017

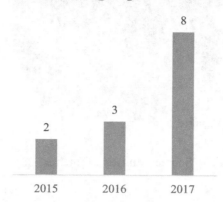

Source: Ministry of Interior.

Number of persons prosecuted for trafficking in persons, 2015 –2017

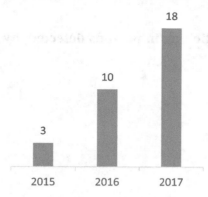

Source: Ministry of Interior.

Number of persons convicted of trafficking in persons, 2015 – 2017

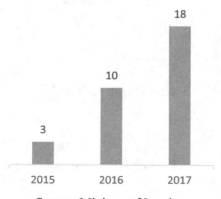

Source: Ministry of Interior.

Citizenships of persons convicted of trafficking in persons, 2014 –2017

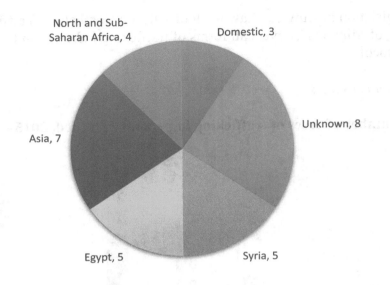

Source: Ministry of Interior.

Victims

Number of victims of trafficking in persons detected, by age and sex, 2015 - 2017

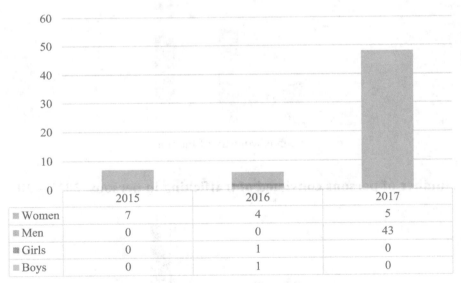

	2015	2016	2017
▪ Women	7	4	5
▪ Men	0	0	43
▪ Girls	0	1	0
▪ Boys	0	1	0

Source: Ministry of Interior.

Number of victims of trafficking detected, by form of exploitation, 2015 – 2017

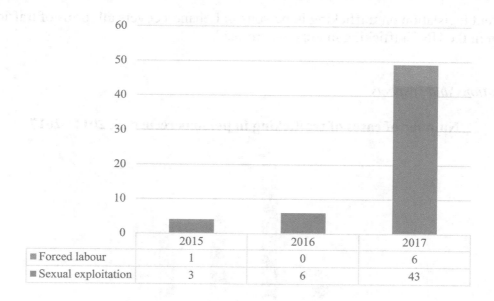

	2015	2016	2017
▪ Forced labour	1	0	6
▪ Sexual exploitation	3	6	43

Source: Ministry of Interior.

Citizenships of persons identified as victims of trafficking in persons by state authorities, 2015 –2017

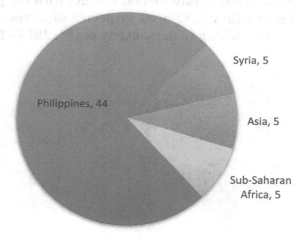

Source: Ministry of Interior.

The current legislation on trafficking in persons in Lebanon covers all forms of trafficking indicated in the UN Trafficking in Persons Protocol.

Investigations and suspects

Number of cases of trafficking in persons recorded, 2014 –2017

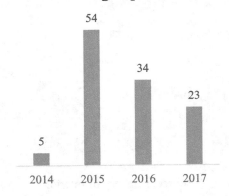

Source: Directorate General of Internal Security Forces.

Number of persons brought into formal contact with the police and/or criminal justice system because they have been suspected of, arrested for or cautioned for trafficking in persons, by sex**, 2014 –2017

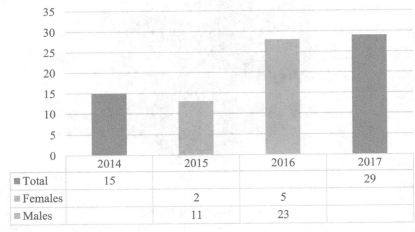

	2014	2015	2016	2017
▪ Total	15			29
▪ Females		2	5	
▪ Males		11	23	

Source: Directorate General of Internal Security Forces

**Note: Formal contact with the police and/or criminal justice system may include persons suspected, arrested, or cautioned at the national level.

Number of persons prosecuted for trafficking in persons, by sex, 2015 –2017

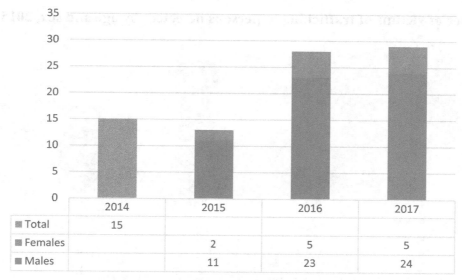

	2014	2015	2016	2017
■ Total	15			
■ Females		2	5	5
■ Males		11	23	24

Source: Directorate General of Internal Security Forces.

Citizenships of persons investigated for trafficking in persons, 2014 –2017

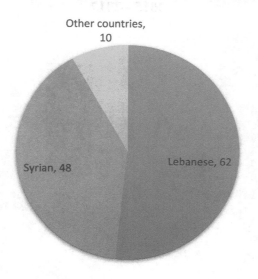

Source: Directorate General of Internal Security Forces.

Victims

Number of victims of trafficking in persons detected, by age and sex, 2015 –2017

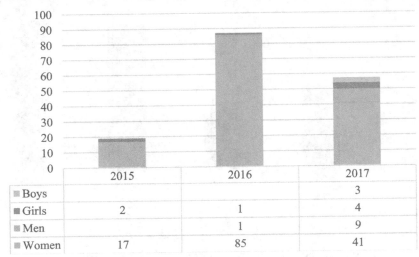

	2015	2016	2017
◼ Boys			3
◼ Girls	2	1	4
◼ Men		1	9
◼ Women	17	85	41

Source: Directorate General of Internal Security Forces.

Number of victims of trafficking in persons detected, by form of exploitation, 2015 –2017

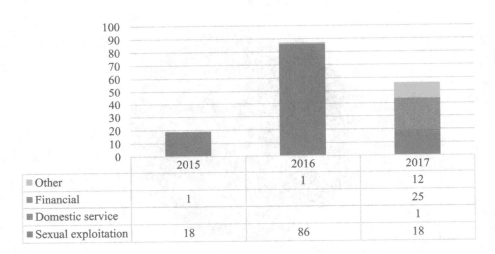

	2015	2016	2017
◼ Other		1	12
◼ Financial	1		25
◼ Domestic service			1
◼ Sexual exploitation	18	86	18

Source: Directorate General of Internal Security Forces.

Citizenships of persons identified as victims of trafficking in persons by state authorities, 2014 – 2017

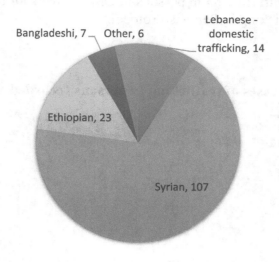

Bangladeshi, 7

Other, 6

Lebanese - domestic trafficking, 14

Ethiopian, 23

Syrian, 107

Source: Directorate General of Internal Security Forces.

The current legislation on trafficking in persons in Oman covers all forms of trafficking indicated in the UN Trafficking in Persons Protocol.

Investigations and suspects

Number of cases of trafficking in persons recorded, 2014 –2017

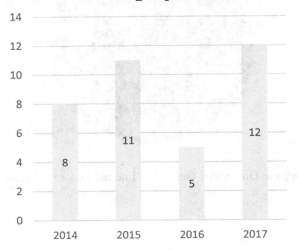

Source: Ministry of Foreign Affairs.

Number of persons brought into formal contact with the police and/or criminal justice system because they have been suspected of, arrested for or cautioned for trafficking in persons, by sex**, 2014 –2017

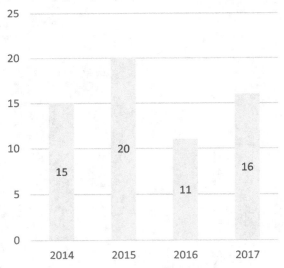

Source: Ministry of Foreign Affairs.

Number of persons prosecuted for trafficking in persons, by sex, 2014 –2017

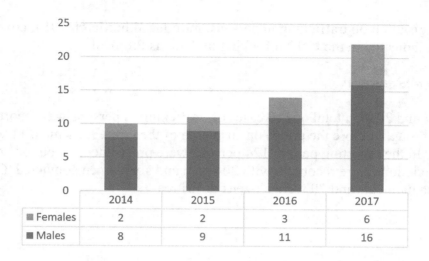

	2014	2015	2016	2017
■ Females	2	2	3	6
■ Males	8	9	11	16

Source: Ministry of Foreign Affairs.

Between 2014 and 2016, 10 people were convicted for trafficking in persons, two citizens of Oman and eight citizens from South Asian countries.

Victims

Number of victims of trafficking in persons detected, by age and sex, 2015 –2017

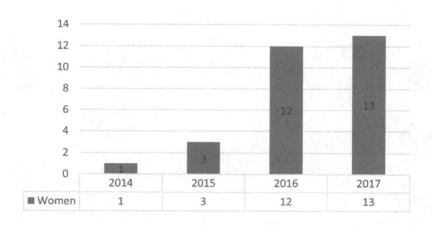

	2014	2015	2016	2017
■ Women	1	3	12	13

Source: Ministry of Foreign Affairs.

Between 2014 and 2016, 19 victims were trafficked for sexual exploitation and nine forced to work as dancer. Most victims were citizens from South Asia (23) and five from South East Asia.

Source: Ministry of Foreign Affairs.

–Sudan–

The current legislation on trafficking in persons, introduced in March 2014, covers all forms of trafficking, indicated in the UN Trafficking in Persons Protocol.

Investigations and suspects

Between 2017 and 2018, a total of 110 cases of trafficking in persons was reported. 244 persons were brought before the police on suspicion of the crime (231 men, 11 women, and two children). In the reporting period, 124 persons were prosecuted, all but one offender male. 210 convictions were recorded, with 204 men and six women convicted. Of these, 106 were Sudanese nationals and 70 were citizens of Eritrea.

Source: Office of Public Prosecution.

Victims

During the reporting period between 2017 and 2018, a total of 421 victims was reported. The government reported that the following number of victims were transferred to secure homes and provided psychological and medical assistance: 256 men, 128 women, 20 girls, and 17 boys. Of these, 195 were citizens of Eritrea.

Source: Office of Public Prosecution.

−Syrian Arab Republic−

The current legislation in the Syrian Arab Republic, Legislative Decree 3 of 2010, covers all forms of trafficking indicated in the UN Trafficking in Persons Protocol.

Investigations and suspects

Number of persons brought into formal contact with the police and/or criminal justice system because they have been suspected of, arrested for or cautioned for trafficking in persons, by sex**, 2014 – 2017

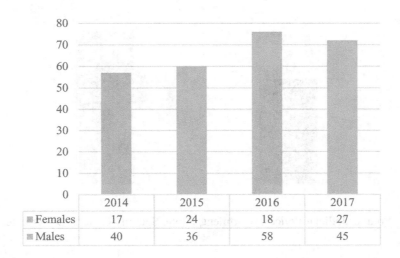

	2014	2015	2016	2017
▪ Females	17	24	18	27
▪ Males	40	36	58	45

Source: Records of the Directorate for Combating Trafficking in Persons.

**Note: Formal contact with the police and/or criminal justice system may include persons suspected, arrested, or cautioned at the national level.

Number of persons prosecuted for trafficking in persons, by sex, 2014 –2017

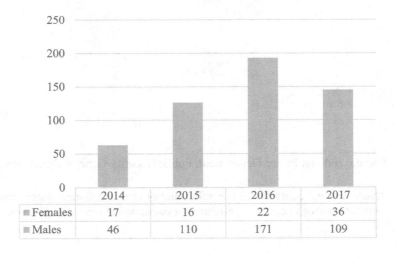

	2014	2015	2016	2017
▪ Females	17	16	22	36
▪ Males	46	110	171	109

Source: Records of the Directorate for Combating Trafficking in Persons.

The current legislation on trafficking in persons in Tunisia covers all forms of trafficking indicated in the UN Trafficking in Persons Protocol. Prior to 2016, there was no specific law criminalizing trafficking in persons in Tunisia.

Investigations and suspects

Number of cases of trafficking in persons recorded, 2016 – September 2017

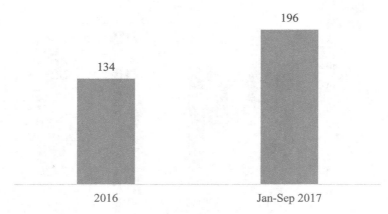

Source: Judicial Police Department, Public Security General Directorate.

Number of persons brought into formal contact with the police and/or criminal justice system because they have been suspected of, arrested for or cautioned for trafficking in persons, by sex**, 2016 – September 2017

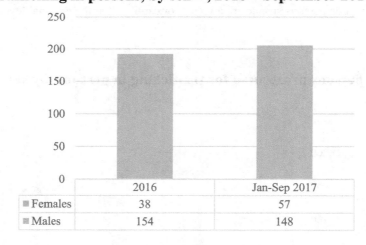

	2016	Jan-Sep 2017
Females	38	57
Males	154	148

Source: Judicial Police Department, Public Security General Directorate.

**Note: Formal contact with the police and/or criminal justice system may include persons suspected, arrested, or cautioned at the national level.

Citizenships of persons convicted of trafficking in persons, 2016 – September 2017

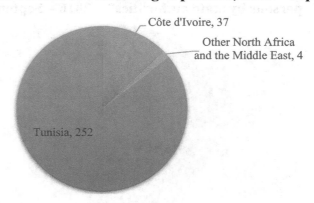

Source: Judicial Police Department, Public Security General Directorate.

Victims

**Number of victims of trafficking in persons detected, by age and sex,
2016 – September 2017**

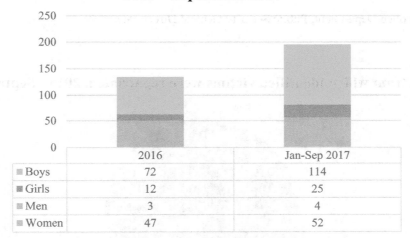

	2016	Jan-Sep 2017
■ Boys	72	114
■ Girls	12	25
■ Men	3	4
■ Women	47	52

Source: Judicial Police Department, Public Security General Directorate.

**Number of victims of trafficking in persons detected, by form of exploitation,
2016 – September 2017**

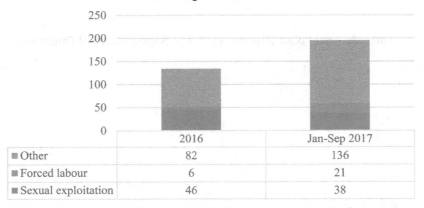

	2016	Jan-Sep 2017
■ Other	82	136
■ Forced labour	6	21
■ Sexual exploitation	46	38

Source: Judicial Police Department, Public Security General Directorate.

Citizenships of persons identified as victims of trafficking in persons by state authorities**, 2016 – September 2017

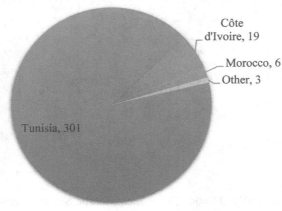

Source: Judicial Police Department, Public Security General Directorate.

In 2016, 84 Tunisian citizens were trafficked domestically, while 46 were repatriated from other countries. In the first nine months of 2017, 139 Tunisian citizens were trafficked domestically and 38 were repatriated from other countries.

Source: Judicial Police Department, Public Security General Directorate.

Countries from which identified victims were repatriated, 2016 - September 2017

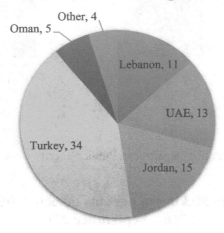

Source: Judicial Police Department, Public Security General Directorate.

−United Arab Emirates−

The current legislation on trafficking in persons in the United Arab Emirates covers all forms of trafficking indicated in the UN Trafficking in Persons Protocol.

Investigations and suspects

Number of cases of trafficking in persons recorded, 2014 –2017

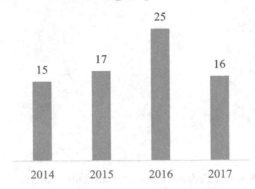

Source: Federal and local prosecution offices.

Number of persons brought into formal contact with the police and/or criminal justice system because they have been suspected of, arrested for or cautioned for trafficking in persons, by sex**, 2014 –2017

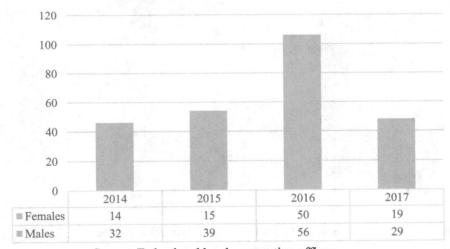

	2014	2015	2016	2017
Females	14	15	50	19
Males	32	39	56	29

Source: Federal and local prosecution offices.

**Note: Formal contact with the police and/or criminal justice system may include persons suspected, arrested, or cautioned at the national level.

Number of persons prosecuted for trafficking in persons, by sex, 2014 –2017

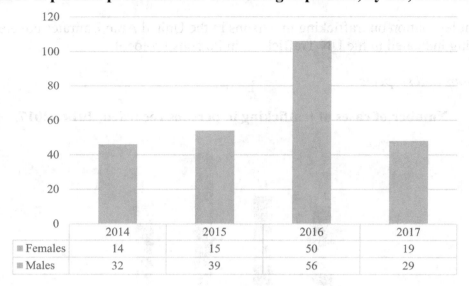

	2014	2015	2016	2017
▪ Females	14	15	50	19
▪ Males	32	39	56	29

Source: Federal and local prosecution offices.

Number of persons convicted of trafficking in persons, by sex, 2014 – September 2017

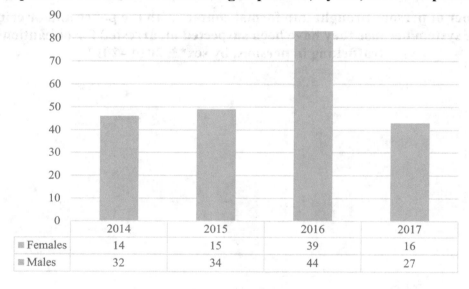

	2014	2015	2016	2017
▪ Females	14	15	39	16
▪ Males	32	34	44	27

Source: Federal and local prosecution offices.

During the reporting period, 208 persons convicted of trafficking in persons were citizens of Asian countries and 13 were citizens of African countries.

Source: Federal and local prosecution offices.